MESSAGES AND MEANINGS:
AN INTRODUCTION TO SEMIOTICS

by Marcel Danesi
University of Toronto

Volume 2 in the Series:
Media, Communication, & Culture Studies
Series Editor:
Marcel Danesi, *University of Toronto*

Canadian Scholars' Press Inc.   Toronto   1993

Messages and Meanings: An Introduction to Semiotics

First published in 1994 by
Canadian Scholars' Press Inc.
180 Bloor St. W., Ste. 402
Toronto, Ontario
M5S 2V6

Canadian Cataloguing in Publication Data

Main entry under title:
Messages and Meanings: An Introduction to Semiotics
ISBN 1-55130-027-3

1. Semiotics. 2. Signs and symbols. I. Title. II. Series.

P99.D36   1993   302.2   C93-095414-9

Printed and bound in Canada

Table of Contents

PART II: *Making the Human World*

Introduction

The world of human beings is a world of messages and meanings. We continually receive and make messages in order literally to *make* sense of *who* we are, of *where* we are in the cosmos, and of *why* we are here. If there is one trait that distinguishes the human species from all others it is precisely this capacity and urgent propensity to look for and *make* meaning of life.

This book is intended as a course on how we make messages and on how these are intrinsically intertwined with the need for meaning. It is directed both towards a general audience and students taking introductory courses in semiotics, communications, media or culture studies. It is based on my lecture notes and on my classroom teaching experiences connected with a first-year course in semiotics and communication theory I have been giving at Victoria College of the University of Toronto since the mid eighties. I have written this book so that a broad audience can appreciate and understand, in a clear and general way, the fascinating and vital work going on in this area of inquiry, most of which is often too technical or even abstruse for general consumption. For this reason, both the presentational style and contents of the book are designed specifically for beginning students, and interested readers generally, who want, or need, an overview of semiotic theory and practice. Prior technical knowledge is not necessary. I have made every attempt possible to build upon what the reader, in my view, already knows intuitively about messages and meanings. Nevertheless, the writing is not so diluted as to make the book a kind of popular "all you wanted to know about semiotics, but were afraid to ask" trade book. Some effort to understand the contents of each chapter on the part of the reader will be required. Some of the more technical parts might require some re-reading.

Since the focus of the book is practical, the usual critical apparatus of references to the technical literature is kept to a minimum. However, each chapter ends with a *Suggestions for Further Reading* section for the reader wishing to pursue the subject matter discussed therein more fully. This book can also be used as a complementary or supplementary text to similar or cognate courses and programs of study (e.g. psychology, mythology, literary studies, culture studies, communication theory, etc.). A convenient glossary of technical terms is included at the end of the book.

The plan of the text is as follows. There are three parts, each consisting of five chapters. The first part, *Making Messages and Meanings*, introduces the basic notions, concepts and personages that make up the discipline of semiotics. The opening chapter defines semiotics and provides a brief overview of the field. The second chapter then describes and illustrates the basic signifying processes that humans utilize to make their messages and meanings. The remaining three chapters in this part zero in on the main forms and features of sign-making. They look respectively at how we use our body, visual perception and language semiotically. The second part, *Making the Human World*, shifts the focus to the world of culture, to the communal sense-making characteristics that enfold its universe. The themes dealt with, in five separate and consecutive chapters, are metaphor, myth, clothing, food and space. These chapters are meant to illustrate how cultures work from the specific vantage point of semiotic theory and practice. Finally, part three, *The Medium Makes the Message*, extends the semiotic purview to encompass the study of communication and media *per se*. The topics dealt with in this part in order are television, advertising, postmodernism, animal communication and, to conclude, the current views put forward by sociobiologists and artificial intelligence researchers on human consciousness.

I must warn the reader that the topics chosen for the book, and the contents of each chapter, reflect my own approach to semiotics. The presence of the author in the text is inevitable. My own teaching and writing styles cannot help but be influenced by what I think. I am incapable of couching my discourse exclusively in the "passive voice." But whether the reader agrees or disagrees with any of my semiotic analyses, it is my sincere hope that the book will stimulate a critical perspective about meaning- and message-making that he or she might not have had previously. In my view, that and that alone will have made the writing of this book worth the while.

I wish to thank the editorial staff at Canadian Scholars' Press for all their advice, support and expert help. I am especially grateful to Pam Hamilton, without whom this book would have never come to fruition. I am also indebted to the Press for allowing me to share my particular approach to semiotics with a larger public. I thank Victoria College for having allowed me the privilege of teaching and co-ordinating its Program in Semiotics. In this regard, I would like especially to mention Dr. Eva Kushner, the President, Dr. Alexandra Johnston, the previous Principal, and Dr. William Callahan, the present Principal. I am also thankful to Lynn Welsh and Julie Berger for the constant help and support I have had from them in running the Program over the years. Another debt of gratitude goes to the many students I have taught over the years for their encouragement, insights, and enthusiasm. My students are the motivating force behind this book. Finally, I simply must thank my family, Lucy, Danila, Chris, and Pumpkin (our cat) for all the patience and tolerance they have had with me over my incessant pontifications about semiotics. More importantly, I ask their forgiveness for the grumpiness and neglect of family duties that writing a book entails.

Marcel Danesi
Victoria College, 1993

Part 1

Making Messages and Meanings

WHAT IS SEMIOTICS?

Preliminary Remarks

Consider the color red. Does it mean anything? A semiotician would hardly view an answer to this question as trivial. The *meaning* of this color depends, semiotically, on *where* or in *what* substance it is located and on *who* sees it. If it appears as a traffic light signal, it means "stop" to a motorist or pedestrian at a city block or intersection. If someone wears a red armband during a political rally, that person is sending out the message that he or she espouses a particular kind of political ideology, often labeled as "left-wing" or "radical." Red also commonly stands for "blood" in medical logos, for "danger" in road flags, for an emotional state in verbal expressions *(He was so embarrassed, he turned red),* and the list could go on and on. Moreover, a semiotician would stress that no one knows what the "word-sign" *red* really means at a basic level of representation. It is really no more than a convenient "label" speakers of English agree to use to arbitrarily designate a band or portion of frequency on the light spectrum as it manifests itself in the world of nature. That same portion could have been easily "segmented" or labeled with more words; or, on the other hand, it could have been conceived as part of a larger light-frequency fragment.

Welcome to the world of *semiotics*! It is a type of scientific inquiry that studies virtually anything we do and use to *represent* the world around us and to *make* messages about it. To the semiotician, human beings are *makers*. *Homo sapiens* is, from the perspective of semiotics, to be studied as *Homo faber* (the maker). The example of the color (and the word) *red*, which a semiotician would call a *sign*, typifies the kinds of questions he or she would ask. The semiotician refers to the meaningful location of this specific light-frequency property as *context*, to its meaning in specific contexts as *signification*, to the ways in which it generates a meaning as *code-based*, and to the ways in which a message is understood as *interpretation*. The example of *red* also shows *how* semioticians carry out their work. To unravel the meaning of any message, a semiotician would ask a series of specific questions: *Who* created the message? *What* medium (verbal, nonverbal, etc.) was employed? *For whom* was it intended? *In what* context was it transmitted? *To what* code does it belong? *How many* meanings are possible under the circumstances in which it was transmitted?

This chapter examines what semiotics is and does in a general way. It defines semiotics, meaning, signification, semiosis, codes, context and a few other basic concepts. Few of us realize that semiotics is one of the oldest "sciences" known to civilization. And few of us are consciously aware of the fact that we live in a world of our own semiotic making, a world built from the substance of signs. To the semiotician, topics such as wrestling and detergent brand names, which might at first appear to be trivial, reveal as much about human cognitive activity and human actions as does the study of speech or problem-solving. Semiotics teaches us how to read or interpret the meaning inherent in any human-made message or artifact. It is the "science of messages and meanings" and of the signs and codes we use to produce and understand them.

Defining Semiotics and Signs

In this stress-riddled world, everyone is aware of how much the mind can influence the body. But it is not commonly known that the science of semiotics grew out of attempts by the first physicians of the Western world to understand how this mind/body interaction operates within specific cultural domains. Indeed, in its oldest usage, the term *semiotics* was applied to the study of the observable patterns of physiological symptoms induced by particular diseases and of how people experienced them. The first doctors apparently realized that there was an intrinsic bond between how we feel and how we think; and that the expression of our thoughts is anchored in this mind/body relation.

The etymology of the term *semiotics* is traceable to the Greek word *sema*—"marks, signs" (singular *semeion*). It is commonly defined as the science or "doctrine" (in the sense of systematic study) of signs. A *sign* is anything—a word, a gesture, an object, etc.—that stands for something or someone. Therefore, anything in the world is eligible to become a sign. The color *red* becomes a sign the instant it is used to stand for the traffic command "stop," for "political radicalness," for "a verbal expression designating embarrassment" and so on. The nature and use of signs will be dealt with in more detail in the second chapter. For the time being, note that signs literally *represent* the world of beings, objects, ideas, and events: i.e. they "present them again" within the confines of mental space. They allow us, figuratively speaking, to carry the world around with us in our heads. Note as well that the "substances" used to make signs vary widely. A sign can be, for instance, an object such as an armband or a word such as *red*. Signs constitute the elements of such common *codes* as hand gestures, facial expressions, language, music, paintings, religious ceremonies, architectural styles, car designs, body image, sports events, clothing—in a nutshell, anything that has been *made* by humans. Signs can be thought of as the "materials" we need and employ to create our artifacts, from words to social institutions. Human beings are indeed makers: they constantly make with their hands and with their minds. In fact, humans never stop making, at home, at work, during leisure hours. There is something in our nature that seems to constantly drive us to make artifacts—physical and mental.

Semiotics versus Semiology

As mentioned above, in its oldest usage the term *semiotics* (or more accurately, *semeiotics*) referred to the observable pattern of physiological symptoms induced by specific diseases. Hippocrates (460?-377? B.C.)—the founder of medical science—viewed the ways in which a disease was reported by patients as the basis upon which to carry out an appropriate diagnosis and upon which to formulate a suitable prognosis. The term *semiotics* has become the general one used for the systematic study of signs. In his *Course in General Linguistics* of 1916, compiled by his students after his death from the notes they took during his course, the Swiss linguist Ferdinand De Saussure (1857-1913) used the term *semiology*, instead, to refer to the systematic study of signs. Saussure coined this term in obvious analogy to other terms ending in *-logy* (from Greek *logos*—"word"). Saussure's term bears witness to his apparent belief in the supremacy of language as a semiotic code. Here's what he had to say about language:

> Language is a system of signs that expresses ideas, and is
> therefore comparable to a system of writing, the alphabet
> of deaf-mutes, symbolic rites, polite formulas, military
> signals, etc. But it is the most important of all these
> systems. (Saussure 1916/1966: 16)

Nowadays, the term *semiotics* is preferred, given its greater generality. It is the term that will be used throughout this text. Semiotic method includes both the *synchronic* and the *diachronic* study of signs. The former refers to the study of signs at a given point in time, normally the present, and the latter to the study of how signs change, in form and meaning, over time. As a case in point, consider the word-sign *person*. Synchronically, it can be defined as a noun signifying any human being. But a diachronic analysis reveals a different and very interesting story. Incidentally, the study of how word-signs change in meaning over time is known as *etymology*. In ancient Greece, the word *persona* signified a "mask" worn by an actor on stage. Subsequently, it came to have the meaning of "the character of the mask-wearer." This meaning still exists in the theater term *dramatis personae* "cast of characters" (literally "the persons of the drama"). Eventually, the word came to have its present meaning. It is interesting to note that the connection between "personhood" and the theater is still very much alive in our cultural thinking. This is why we say that people "play roles in life," "interact," "act out their feelings," "put on a proper face [mask]" and so on.

An interesting definition of *semiotics* is provided by Umberto Eco in his 1976 book, *A Theory of Semiotics*. Eco, incidentally, is the author of the best-selling novel *The Name of the Rose*, which has recently stimulated a lot of interest in semiotics among the public at large. He defines semiotics as "the discipline studying everything which can be used in order to lie," because if "something cannot be used to tell a lie, conversely it cannot be used to tell the truth; it cannot, in fact, be used to tell at all" (Eco 1976: 7). This is, despite its apparent facetiousness, a rather insightful statement. It implies that we have the capacity to represent the world in any way we want through signs, even in misleading and deceitful ways. This capacity for subterfuge and artifice is a powerful one indeed. We can get people to act erroneously and at their peril by our intentional misuse of signs: we can cause a tragedy on the road by intentionally wiring the traffic lights to flash green on all sides at once; we can incite people to kill others by telling them deceitful lies; and so on. Eco's remark is a notable one indeed.

The definition that has become the most widely adopted one is the one articulated by the American logician and mathematician Charles Sanders Peirce (1839-1914), who along with Saussure is considered to be the founder of the modern study of signs. He defined semiotics as the "doctrine" of signs, the latter being anything that "stands to somebody for something in some respect or capacity" (Peirce 1958/2: 228).

At first, Peirce's definition of *sign* might seem to be too vague and somewhat confusing. But consider again the example of the color *red*. Is it a sign according to Peirce's definition? Yes, because it is *something*, in this case a physical property of light, which *stands to somebody* (a motorist, a pedestrian, a political demonstrator, etc.), *for something in some respect or capacity* ("stop," "political radicalness," etc.). So, while Peirce's definition might appear initially to be nebulous, it is actually a rather clear and concise one.

The systematic study of signs is to be differentiated from what has come to be known as *communication science*. Although the two share much of the same conceptual and methodological territory, communication theorists generally focus more on the study of message-making as a process, whereas semioticians center their attention more on *what* a message means and on *how* it creates meaning. Semiotics, thus, is directed to the study of the different varieties of signs, to the codes into which these signs are organized, and to the culture within which these codes operate. Semiotics studies *signification* first and *communication* second. *Semiotics* is also to be differentiated from *semantics*, the science which studies how linguistic *texts* (words, sentences, etc.) are used to represent the world. The field of semiotics proper has become a truly enormous one. It now includes, among other things, the study of how animals communicate *(zoosemiotics)*, of nonverbal communication *(kinesics* and *proxemics)*, of aesthetics, of rhetoric, of visual communication, of myths and narratives—in sum, of anything that allows us to make meaning and sense of the world.

The meaning of the term "scientific study" for semioticians is not the traditional one. In Western culture the term *science* has always been synonymous with the "objective" knowledge of "facts" of the natural world, gained and verified by exact observation, experiment, and ordered thinking. The starting point for scientific objectivism is Ancient Greece, when, ever since Aristotle, Western culture has come to embrace the idea that the physical universe is a great machine operating according to natural laws. Aristotle laid the foundations for the experimental investigation of matter by claiming that these laws were determinable objectively by human reason. By the time of the Renaissance, when the methods of Western scientific inquiry started to produce truly staggering discoveries about the world and its inhabitants, the question arose logically as to whether or not the mind could also be studied "scientifically."

For the semiotician, on the other hand, we can only study what we ourselves have made, including mathematics and physics. The axioms, propositions, and theorems of Euclidean geometry, for instance, are not present in the universe in the precise ways that we have specified them. Rather, they constitute a cognitive strategy for organizing and rationalizing our visual perceptions of space. Semiotics studies the *artifacts* that our mind has produced, for, in their form and contents, these put on display how the mind goes about its work.

Meaning and Signification

It is important to make a clear-cut distinction, from the very outset, between *meaning* and *signification.* The former is used here in its broad dictionary definition of "anything that is intended." This definition constitutes an obvious logical circularity that cannot be avoided. In their 1923 work, titled appropriately *The Meaning of Meaning*, Ogden and Richards gave 23 meanings of the word *meaning*, showing how problematic a term it is. They also made a key distinction between *meaning* on the one side, and *sense* and *reference* on the other. *Sense* alludes literally to the physical nature of meaning. A sign must be received and perceived by our "biological sensors," so to speak, before it can have any "meaning" in the first place. At this basic level, meaning is anchored in a biologically-based reaction to the stimuli present in the world. *Reference*, on the other hand, is the process by which our sense reactions are projected back onto the world through the use of signs.

Signification is a much more specific term. It denotes, as its name implies, the thoughts that a sign evokes. The concepts associated with *signification* are: *interpretation, denotation, connotation, paradigm, syntagm* and *structure.*

First and foremost, it is obvious that the use of a sign entails an *interpretation* of what it stands for. This involves, in Peircean terms, knowing that something is in fact being used to stand for something else. Peirce designated the "something" used as the *representamen*, rather than *sign*, and the "something else" as the *object,* rather than *referent.* He knew that problems in associating the *sign/representamen* to the *object/referent* were always bound to arise because the range of interpretation would always vary from individual to individual. Peirce referred to this aspect of the sign as the *interpretant's* processing (or decoding) of the sign. For Peirce, it is this "triangular relation" that coheres into the signification process:

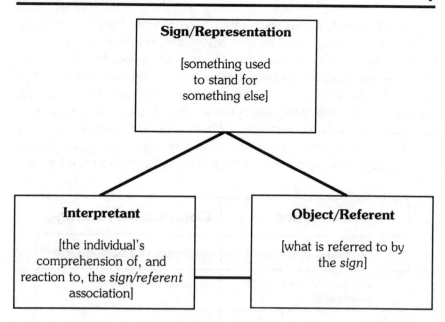

Consider again the example of the color *red*. It can be used to constitute a *representamen* because it is an actual physical phenomenon. As such, it can be employed to refer to "political radicalness," the *object*, when worn as an armband at a political rally. But, according to who does the interpreting, it will be understood in various ways: if one knows that the armband wearer is a prankster, he or she will interpret the sign differently than someone who does not know the wearer; if one is himself or herself a political radical, he or she will interpret the wearing of the armband differently from a political conservative; and so on. But this does not mean that interpretation is a boundless or infinite process The meaning range of a sign is constrained by a series of factors, including conventional agreements as to what a *representamen* can refer to, the nature of the *code* to which it belongs, the nature of the *referent* (concrete objects are less subject to interpretation variation than abstract concepts), and so on. Without such "inbuilt constraints" signification and communication would be practically impossible. It should be noted in passing that a special case in interpretation emerges when the *representamen* stands for itself, rather than for something else. Such cases of "self-reference"—e.g. the sign *word* stands for a "word"—often cause problems in interpretation. They are responsible for many of the logical paradoxes that philosophers talk about: e.g. what does the statement "This is not a sentence" mean? Can it mean anything?

The sign's primary meaning is called its *denotation*. This is the meaning or referential connection established between *representamen* and *object*. But this meaning core can be extended freely to other domains of reference. This extensive process is known as *connotation*. Consider the word-sign *house*. Its denotation can be paraphrased as "any structure for human habitation." The denotative uses of this sign can be seen in utterances such as "I bought a new *house* yesterday," "*House* prices are continually going up in this city," "We repainted our *house* the other day," and so on. But, by connotative extension, the same sign can be used to mean such things as:

Utterance	Connotative Meaning
1. "The *house* in session"	*legislative assembly, quorum*
2. "The *house* roared with laughter"	*audience in a theater*
3. "They sleep at one of the *houses* at Harvard University.	*dormitory*

Note, however, that the basic elements of the sign's denotative meaning must be present in its extended uses for signification and communication to be successful. So, in the above sentences the denotative elements "structure," "human," and "habitation" are necessarily implicit: a legislative assembly, a theater audience, and a dormitory do indeed imply "structures" of special kinds that "humans" can be said to "inhabit." Any connotative utilization of the word *house* is constrained by this "semantic structure;" i.e. the word-sign *house* can be applied to refer to anything that involves or implicates humans coming together for some specific reason. Even in an utterance such as "MIT *houses* some of the greatest ideas in computer science" it can be easily seen that this semantic structure is implicitly present, for, after all, it is human beings who are the generators of ideas in structures such as universities.

Connotation allows humans to make new meanings with a limited set of signs within certain boundaries *ad infinitum*. There is another use of the term *connotation* that is worthy of mention here. We can use, for example, a change in tone of voice to convey different meanings with the word *yes*. If we say it with a normal tone of voice it is a sign of affirmation. If, however, we raise our voice as in a question, then it can relay doubt or incredulity as the case may be. This change of meaning is also connotative. In such instances, connotation involves a personal dimension (feelings, perspective, etc.).

The distinction between denotation and connotation has always been the general guiding principle in lexicography—the making of dictionaries. The idea has been to unravel first the prime denotative components which make up the reference system of individual lexical items. The history of the making of dictionaries, therefore, is the history of how humans make meaning in human language. The word is considered to be a "symbolic bridge" between referents and the system of verbal signs which allows us to codify and communicate our perceptions of reality. The denotative primes that lexicographers search for can be compared to the axioms of geometry or to the atoms of nature: i.e. each word is perceived to have a molecular structure composed of "atoms" of meaning. All other meaning potentialities for the word, including its connotations, are relegated to its "combination" with the semantic molecules of other words in the syntactic and discourse contexts in which it can be used. Another way of referring to denotation in the recent semantic literature is to call it *core meaning* and to connotation as *encyclopedic knowledge*.

Once a sign has been invented, it then enters into two fundamental relations with the other signs within a specific *code* (language, gesture, etc.). It must, first, have some feature in its *representamen* that allows our perceptual system to differentiate it from all other signs. In the case of minimal word pairs such as *pin/bin*, *fun/run*, etc., for instance, it is the difference in the initial sound that keeps the word-signs distinct. This differentiation relation is known as *paradigmatic* structure. Signification cannot occur without paradigmatic relations between signs. In traditional approaches to the study of languages, the concept of paradigmatic structure, or *opposition*, has been used to show how, for example, verbs are conjugated. The forms *am*, *are*, *is* of the verb *to be* are related paradigmatically because they signal different subjects:

Word-sign = verb form	**Paradigmatic aspect**
(I) am	*first person singular form*
(you, we, they) are	*second person singular and plural form/first person plural form/third person plural form*
(he, she, it) is	*third person singular form*

As the sign enters into a paradigmatic (differential) relation with other signs in a code, it simultaneously forms combinatory patterns with them. These are known as *syntagmatic* relations. The color red is distinguishable only because there are other colors (no matter how we demarcate and label them) with which it combines to form the light spectrum. Word-signs such as the verb forms *am*, *are*, *is* are joined up with other forms—e.g. *am* is preceded by *I* as subject—to make phrases and sentences. Incidentally, the study of verbal syntagmatic structure is called more precisely *syntax*.

An analogy to high school analytical geometry can perhaps be helpful in understanding paradigm and syntagm in signification. The so-called "Cartesian plane" is demarcated by the use of two axes crossing at right angles, the *x*- and *y*- axes. The point p1 (2, 3), for instance, is defined by its location with respect to these two axes: it is found two equally-calibrated units to the right of the *y*-axis and three equally-calibrated units up from the *x*-axis; whereas the point p2 (-2, -3) is defined as a point located two equally-calibrated units to the left of the *y*-axis and three equally-calibrated units down from the *x*-axis:

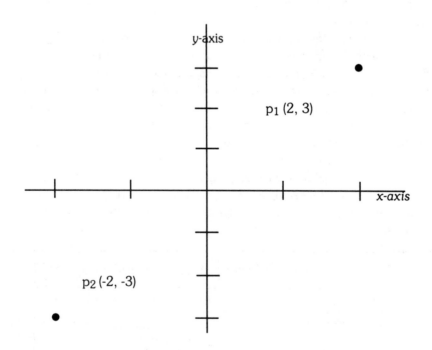

In this two-axial system the points p1 and p2 are defined in relation to each other in terms of the two axes. Indeed, they can be said to *exist* by virtue of the fact that the two axes are there. If we remove the axes, we also remove the framework for relating the points. As a consequence, the two points can be seen to "disappear." Now, think of the Cartesian plane as a "code" (an equally-calibrated plane), and the points p1 and p2 as two "signs" within the code. Then, their location with respect to the two axes is the relation that keeps them "paradigmatically" distinct. At the same time, these points can be seen to be "syntagmatically" related, since by joining them up they form the "structure" known as the *line* p1-p2:

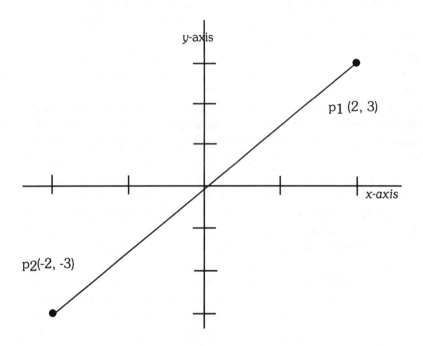

Finally, it should be noted that signs and their relations have *structure*, a discernible (repeatable and predictable) shape, pattern or form that allows them to "fit" into a code. It is obvious that the elements {*a, b, c, d, e*...} have a shape or form that assigns them to the code known as "the Roman alphabet." On the other hand, the elements {1, 2, 3, 4, 5...} reveal a structural form that assigns them to a different code, "the integers." Think of signs as pieces of a jigsaw puzzle. These have visual features on their "faces" that keep them distinct from each other, as well as differently-shaped "edges" that allow us to join them together in specific ways to complete the overall jigsaw picture. The word *structure* refers to the fact that signs relate to each other in specific and easily recognizable ways, in ways that are analogous to the pieces of a jigsaw puzzle.

Messages

The primary function of signs is to help us *represent* the world around us: i.e. to literally recall the things we have perceived and noted through the cognitive activity that a sign (a word, a gesture, a drawing, etc.) sets in motion. Signs can be extended by connotation to cover a broad range of reality and human actions. So, at a rudimentary level of cognition, signs are "referent preservers:" i.e. they allow us to resee, rehear, refeel, etc. something or someone by the triadic association they have with the thing or being (*representamen—object—interpretant*).

A secondary function of signs is that they allow us to *communicate* our thoughts to others. The act of communication is achieved by the creation of *messages*. These are the *texts* (verbal and nonverbal) that transmit signs from one person to another. The study of communication falls just outside the perimeter of semiotics proper; but it is not tangential to it. Indeed, communication can be defined as "bilateral semiosis," the two-person making of meaning. Messages, therefore, are subject to the requirements of communication events or systems. The main features of these are: *medium*, *channel*, *sender*, *receiver*, *noise*, *redundancy* and *feedback*.

The *medium* is the physical or technical means by which a message is transmitted, i.e. by which it is converted into a *signal*. A verbal message, for instance, involves the human voice as its medium if it is articulated with the vocal organs, or the markings on a piece of paper if it is written. This message can also be converted technologically into radio or television signals. The "natural" media we use for communication include the voice (speech), the face (expressions) and the body (gesture, posture, etc.). The "artifactual" media we commonly employ to convey messages include books, paintings, sculptures, photographs, letters, architecture, etc. Finally, the "mechanical" media we routinely use to make and send messages include telephones, radios, television sets, computers, videos, etc. The *channel* is the term used to refer to the physical characteristics of the medium: e.g. vocally-produced sound waves can be transmitted through the channel of the immediate physical environment or through technologically-produced channels (e.g. radio and television waves).

Any act of message transmission occurs between a *sender* and a *receiver*. To the semiotician, both are participants and contributors to the making of the meaning inherent in the message. The *sender* is said to *encode* the meaning—literally to use the code (e.g. language) to construct the message text—and the *receiver* to *decode* the meaning—literally to use the same code to understand the meaning.

The term *noise* refers to the fact that a message can be impacted upon by some interfering element in the channel or medium (physical or psychological) to distort it or partially efface it. In mechanical channels (e.g. radio systems), *noise* can be detected as electronic static. In verbal communication, *noise* can vary from the interruption of a message by some exterior sound to the speaker's lapses of memory. *Redundancy* is a feature of the code that helps to counteract *noise*. The predictability of words in many sentences ("Roses are red, violets are…"), the repetition of elements (sounds, words, etc.) to relay the same thing, both all "redundant" features which, nevertheless, are there to increase the likelihood that a message will get decoded. The opposite of redundancy is *entropy*—the lack of predictability in the message-making process. Finally, *feedback* is the term used to refer to the fact that *senders* in a communication system can monitor their message texts after they have been transmitted to assay and determine their effect on the receiver. *Feedback* information includes detecting reactions (facial expressions, bodily movements, etc.) in the receiver that indicate the effect of the message on him or her. Feedback helps the sender adjust his or her message text to make it more effective.

It should be noted that despite all attempts to make human communication as effective, unambiguous and unequivocal an event as possible through protracted learning and education, it seems that human message-making is always subject to the vagaries and contingencies inherent in the act of interpretation, in the nature of media and channels, in the receiver's "state of mind," and so on. There is no such thing as a "precise" and "exactly" communicated message.

Semiosis

Semiosis is the term commonly used to refer to the innate capacity of human beings to produce and understand signs of all kinds, from those belonging to simple physiological signaling systems to those which reveal a highly complex symbolic structure. The renowned semiotician Thomas Sebeok, of Indiana University, defines *semiosis* discerningly as "the capacity for containing, replicating and extracting messages, and of extracting their significance" (Sebeok 1985: 452). Semiosis starts out as a process that transforms the world of physical, perceptual-organismic reality into one of mental, reflective reality. I will refer to the former state of mind as the "factual" world, and to the latter as the "artifactual" world. The term "factual" is used to encompass both the biological world we share with all organisms, and the species-specific world of the human imagination—literally the ability to "make pictures" in the mind and to "remake" them in any way that we like. This is the world that we inherit by virtue of the fact that we have a body and a brain. It undergirds *common* sense-making in the species. The artifactual world, on the other hand, is anchored in symbolic thought. This world is not inherited biologically by subsequent generations. It must be transmitted to them in some culturally-specific context and form. It is imperative, when talking about semiosis, not to confuse *common* sense with *communal* sense, i.e. with the habitual opinions and perspectives of the tribe.

Sensorial structures in the human organism generate common sense: i.e. the universal, or *common*, capacity in all humans to model the external world in terms of the categories of sensory experience. *Communal* sense emerges as a kind of "meaning agreement" made by members of a specific group. Common, or factual, sense is the ability to register commonly-shared patterns of perception. It is a form of semiosis that derives from bodily experience. Communal or artifactual sense, on the other hand, is a form of semiosis that is established by convention and social agreement within a group or tribe.

To see the difference between factual and artifactual semiosis, let us take as an example the notion of "sex." In the factual part of the mind, humans the world over can literally "sense" and "model" imagistically and affectively the essence of "maleness" and "femaleness": i.e. humans, like other animals, can sense and feel differences in sex. These are due to the biological system reacting to the signals, urges and responses in the environment that are "presented" to the inner world of the organism. In humans, these are then "re-presented" as signs. It is only when these intuitive "modelings" of maleness and femaleness are transformed further that "artifactual" models of maleness and femaleness—"masculinity" and "femininity" respectively—are forged and institutionalized culturally. So too affective "bonding" is a perceived state; love, kindness, etc. are its culturally-conceptualized derivatives. To feel affective bonding as a taste sensation, for instance, is the basis for language such as *love is sweet*, and for institutionalized behavior such as the use and giving of sweets at love-acknowledging rituals (St. Valentine's Day, weddings, etc.). The factual world is a universal, biologically-based world of feeling, the artifactual one a relativistic culture-specific one. Semiosis is the process that transforms the factual world into an artifactual one.

It is to be noted that not all semioticians think in precisely this way. Like any "human science" semiotics is subject to differences and variations in theory and method. Since ancient times, approaches to the study of semiosis have been influenced by two opposite perspectives—rationalism vs. empiricism. Even though its origins can be traced to Plato, the former has come, in the modern era, to be associated with the writings of René Descartes (1596-1650) who was influential in entrenching the view that the mind exists independently of physiological and social experiences. On the other hand, empiricists, who also trace their roots to Ancient Greece, have always viewed semiosis as a consequence of sensorial contact with the environment. In essence, the rationalist holds that mentality is an *a priori*, innate capacity, while the empiricist argues for an *a posteriori*, environmentally-conditioned genesis of it. Methodologically, the rationalist position involves adopting a deductive approach to the study of mind and signification, while the empiricist perspective implies embracing an inductive one.

This time-worn debate is raging on even in these sophisticated times. In my view, access to the workings of the semiosic capacity entails a methodology that goes well beyond traditional rationalist and empiricist paradigms in themselves, yet enlists them both in a complementary and reciprocal fashion.

Learning Signs

The study of how signs and signifying behavior in general are learned falls outside the purview of semiotics proper. The acquisition of signifying behavior is more properly studied as a *psychosemiotic* phenomenon. Here, it is sufficient to mention that two basic processes are involved in its acquisition. I will refer to them as *osmosis* and *mimesis*.

Osmosis refers to the fact that signs are acquired in relation to physical stimuli and contact with others. During childhood the human being's modes of interaction with the environment are centered upon a constantly-developing consciousness of Self. The child is typically concerned with learning about how the Self fits into the scheme of things. At puberty, the child's consciousness becomes progressively more sensitive to the presence of others. Social cognition soon begins to dominate his or her thinking and actions.

Osmosis is the term chemists use to describe the process by which a substance takes on the characteristics of the environment in which it finds itself. Water, for instance, will take on the shape of the container into which it is poured. In organisms, osmosis can be analogously defined as the largely unconscious tendency to assimilate or absorb features of the environment and of other organisms within it. The human organism is biologically disposed to acquire, and be shaped by, feeling and sensory structures, and the signs used to represent them. The philosopher Susanne Langer (1948) convincingly argued that, at this most primary level of mind, we apprehend the world through "feeling;" i.e. we "feel" that the world has a structure. She called this the "presentational" form of cognition and semiosis. The reaction to, and semiosic representation of, these feeling structures can be mimetic or osmotic—i.e. consciously or unconsciously imitative of them. Osmosis extends to the assimilation of behavior apprehended in relation to social stimuli felt to be meaningful. The bodily postures, facial expressions, modes of dress and discourse features that characterize semiosis in general can be said to result from this tendency. *Mimesis* can be defined simply as conscious osmosis. It is the inclination of human beings to consciously imitate certain features of the environment in order to acquire them. Mimesis, too, extends to social situations. We always imitate behaviors that are perceived to be desirable or socially advantageous.

In the interest of historical accuracy, it should be pointed out that the study of how osmotic and mimetic tendencies form a semiosic continuum among the body, the mind and culture has a long tradition. In this century, for instance, early psychological research on metaphor by the Wurzburg psychologists foreshadowed many of the ideas being discussed today. And one should not forget the pioneering attempt by Ogden and Richards (1923) to argue for an intrinsic relation among literal, affective, and social meaning in their fascinating treatise mentioned above. Nor should one overlook the work of the *Gestalt* psychologists in the forties and fifties who frequently investigated cross-cultural factors in the verbalization of sensorial experiences. And in 1957, Osgood, Suci and Tannenbaum devised a technique, known as the "Semantic Differential," for plotting meaning in terms of associative scales.

The work of the Swiss psychologist Jean Piaget (1896-1980) in this century on the development of mental functions in terms of how they are formed exemplifies how the mind-body-culture vinculum governs the ontogenesis of rationality. The three stages of development that Piaget posited—sensory-motor, concrete operations, formal-logical thinking—have become widely accepted as the primary biological milestones on the route to cognitive development. Piaget has shown, in a phrase, that humans progress from a sensory and concrete stage of mind to a reflective and abstract one. Around the age of two, children, according to Piaget's observations, start to develop symbolic abilities derived from mental images. As these become more dynamic, they prepare the child for more abstract thinking. Knowledge in the child emerges in terms of a direct relation to events in the immediate environment. Self-knowledge arises later.

Critical reactions against Piaget's theory have stemmed from perceiving in it a certain determinism and an overemphasis on cognitive processes at the expense of affect and emotion. And it is in having combined the affective and social dimensions with cognitive growth that, in my view, the work of both the Russian psychologist L. S. Vygotsky (1896-1934) and the contemporary American psychologist Jerome Bruner supplements and balances out Piagetian psychology. Vygotsky proposed developmental stages that go from external (physical and social) actions toward internal cognitive constructions and interior speech ("thinking in words"), via the mind's ability to construct images of external reality. His definition of speech as a "microcosm of consciousness" is particularly reflective of this. Language is a kind of "symbolic modeling device." At birth children can perceive and think of the world easily in nonverbal ways. As the child grows older, he or she starts to use language to take on progressively larger portions of thought. This is why the child speaks to himself or herself during play. The child is thinking, not communicating. Around puberty the verbal code overlaps almost completely with cognition and, therefore, becomes virtually indistinguishable from it. As adults we literally "let our language do our thinking for us," so difficult is it to think without words. Bruner suggests that the construction of the intellect starts with an "enactive" stage, passes through an "iconic" stage, and finally reaches a "symbolic" stage. Action, imagination and abstract thought are the chrono-logically-related stages through which each child passes on the way to mature thinking: i.e. the child first employs non-verbal symbols (action, play, drawing, painting, music, etc.), then imaginative constructs (narratives, fables, drama-tizations, etc.), and finally oral expression and creative writing on the way to the development of abstract thought.

It should also be mentioned here, since it is germane to the theme of this section, that one of the more significant findings to emerge in the early 1980s from the field of neuroscience has been the likelihood that the right hemi-sphere of the brain is a crucial "point-of-departure" for processing novel stimuli: i.e. for handling input for which there are no preexistent cognitive codes or programs available. Its greater connectivity with other centers in the complex pathways of the brain makes it a better "distributor" of new information. The left hemisphere, on the other hand, has a more sequentially-organized structure and, thus, finds it more difficult to assimilate information for which no previous categories exist. If this is indeed the case, then it suggests that the brain is prepared to interpret new information primarily in terms of its physical and contextual characteristics.

Codes

The *texts* that humans constantly make—speeches, common discourses, poems, myths, novels, television programs, paintings, scientific theories, musical compositions, etc.—are "windows" that open out onto the landscape of consciousness and cognition. Our messages and texts become meaningful, or signifying, because they are constructed with the semiotic substances of *codes*. These are the systems that contain specific kinds of signs and the relations that inhere among them. Language, dress, gesture, etc. are examples of codes. The signs in the language code, for instance, are sounds, words, tones, etc.; the relations include the opposition of sounds (*pin* vs. *bin*), the combination of sounds into syllables (*plan* but not *pfan*), the combination of words into sentences *(That woman is a semiotician* but not *That a semiotician is woman*), and so on. The signs in the dress code are the items of clothing that we wear; the relations include the ways in which we combine the items of clothing for various occasions, how we use clothing to indicate profession, and so on. Codes are directive and highly influential of behavior. The social codes involved in greeting, fashion, manners, rankings, etc. are all effective shapers of how we think of others and of ourselves.

As an example, consider the connotations involved in the "social code of the automobile." Outside of this social code, the automobile can be defined simply as a human artifact whose primary objective is to extend the human organism's locomotive capacity (walking, running, etc.) in mechanical ways. But, as a social code, it designates much more. As a test of your knowledge of this code, think of the social connotations involved in driving a *Mercedes Benz* versus a *Volvo*. If I were to ask you what type of person drives each one, you would immediately be able to provide me with a "socially meaningful" answer. Perhaps you would say that lawyers, executives and other highly-paid professionals drive a Mercedes, while professors, clerks and the like drive Volvos. The reason for this is that the car's social connotations (and therefore its price, design, etc.) are *coded*. This same type of coding extends to all areas of social interaction: the types and brand names of food, cigarettes, beer, etc. we consume give off coded messages of who we are, or, at least, aspire to be in our society.

Essentially, then, codes constitute human-made systems of intermediation between individuals and reality. A *culture* can be defined, therefore, as a kind of "macro-code," consisting of the numerous codes which a group of individuals habitually use to interpret reality. Codes are largely developed by a community and are, consequently, largely impersonal with respect to the ways in which they generate meaning.

Context

Signs have no meaning unless they are located and conceptualized within some specific *context*. In its most rudimentary sense, a *context* is the environment, physical and social, in which signification occurs.

Consider, as an example, a crumpled up and discarded cigarette package. If it is encountered on a sidewalk on a city street somewhere it would be interpreted unequivocally as a piece of "garbage" or "rubbish." But if that same item of trash is encased in a picture frame and then hung on a wall in an art gallery, its assigned meaning would change rather dramatically. Visitors to the gallery would tend to interpret it quite differently as, say, a "sign" or "symbol" of a "throw-away society." What has happened here is that the package's *context* of occurrence—its location on a sidewalk or in a picture frame displayed in an art gallery—determines its signification. The location in an art gallery implies the activation of a mental code pertaining to such places: anything on display within a gallery requires the observer to extract some meaning from it. Our experience of a sign or a message clearly depends on our knowledge of such codes and the varying contexts in which these occur or to which they are applied. In this sense, codes and their contexts are shaped and often fixed by communal sense-making or *convention*, literally a "coming together," a signifying process established by general social agreement or contract.

Let us return one last time in this chapter to the color *red*. It is obvious that its meaning depends on contextual factors. It is instructive to note that the context involves, above all else, a cultural dimension. The various meanings *red* has in our culture may or may not coincide with those ascribed to the same color, or its equivalent(s), in other cultures. A few examples to illustrate this point will suffice. To many North American aboriginal peoples, the color *red* has always signified success and triumph. The Ancient Egyptians painted their bodies red to enhance their beauty, a practice which many anthropologists see as the origin of cosmetics. To the Pawnees of North America, painting one's body red symbolizes life, i.e. the symbolic embodiment of life probably associated with the perceived color of blood.

While the specifics of color signification and symbolism may vary from culture to culture what emerges as universal is the tendency to use color as a sign, as a meaning-making substance of the mind. Phylogenetically, this probably implies that the gradations of light frequency picked up by the human eye in nature came to take on great significance among our early ancestors. After all, the different "colors" of plants, animals, and objects (natural and artifactual) have always permitted humans to perceive the world, conceptualize it, classify it and "understand" it in their own signifying terms. So, while the specific contexts and connotations of colors vary widely throughout cultures, the tendency to use them for signification is universally common. The objective of anthropology is to document such variation; that of semiotics is to seek out its nature in the substance of signs.

Concluding Remarks

This chapter has attempted to describe what semiotics is and does. The perspective adopted here, and throughout the remainder of this text, is that semiosis interconnects the body, the mind and culture. In antiquity the science of semiotics coincided with the origins of medicine. As a science of *signs*, including bodily symptoms, it grew out of attempts by the first medical doctors to understand how the interaction between the body and the mind operated within specific cultural domains. In Italy, the term *semeiotica* continues, in fact, to be used in medical science to refer to the study of symptoms.

So, from the dawn of civilization to the present age, it has always been recognized—at least implicitly—that there is an intrinsic connection between the body, the mind and culture, and that the process that links these three dimensions of human existence is semiosis. The *raison d'être* of semiotics is, arguably, to investigate whether or not reality can exist independently of the signifying codes that human beings create to represent and think about it. The view adopted throughout this book is that the world of sensorial survival-based experience, which I have designated the "factual" world, is transformed into a human-made, or "artifactual," one through semiosis. In the factual domain, clothes, for instance, enhance our survival; through semiosic transformation, clothes become dress codes, or artifacts, that send out all kinds of messages (elegance, rank, mood, etc.). Such is the nature of the human condition.

In closing this opening chapter, it should be mentioned that as we approach the end of the twentieth century, there has been a significant increase in the worldwide study of semiotics *as a science*, rather than as a technique for students and scholars of literature, philosophy, and the visual arts—traditionally the primary "users" of semiotics. The scientific approach makes it possible for semiotics to ally itself with the biological and cognitive sciences in a co-operative effort to study how humans generate and understand meaning structures. The world of objects and experience has no meaning in the sense that it wants to "say something" about itself. Only humans feel a need to say something *about* the world. We insist on meaning.

Indeed we can't help but interpret the world in meaningful ways. Semiotics helps us understand why and how we do it.

SUGGESTIONS FOR FURTHER READING

The works listed at the end of each chapter include both those mentioned in the chapter and others that elaborate upon its themes.

It should be noted that there are several English-language journals devoted to semiotics. As I write, these include *Semiotica*, edited by Thomas A. Sebeok and published by Mouton de Gruyter of Berlin; the *American Journal of Semiotics*, edited by Dean MacCannell and published by the Semiotic Society of America; *Recherches Sémiotiques/Semiotic Inquiry*, published by the Canadian Semiotic Association; and *Signifying Behavior*, edited by Marcel Danesi and published by Canadian Scholars' Press Inc. Moreover, the idea that the human arts and sciences are interconnected to a fundamental core of sign-based capacities was chosen by the Sebeoks—Thomas and Jane Umiker— to initiate in 1986 a series of yearly anthologies of studies called *semiotic webs* and published in Berlin by Mouton de Gruyter. The webs feature articles on the interlacing and interfacing of semiotic research with other disciplines, providing a kind of database for those working in the fields of semiotics and communication studies that includes information on semioticians, semiotic organizations, research projects and the like.

Barthes, R. (1968). *Elements of Semiology*. London: Cape.

Berger, A. A. (1984). *Signs in Contemporary Culture: An Introduction to Semiotics*. Salem: Sheffield.

Bruner, J. (1990). *Acts of Meaning*. Cambridge, Mass.: Harvard University Press.

Eco, U. (1976). *A Theory of Semiotics*. Bloomington: Indiana University Press.

Fiske, J. (1982). *Introduction to Communication Studies*. London: Routledge.

Hawkes, T. (1977). *Structuralism and Semiotics*. Berkeley: University of California Press.

Langer, S. (1948). *Philosophy in a New Key*. Cambridge, Mass.: Harvard University Press.

Leach, E. (1976). *Culture and Communication*. Cambridge: Cambridge University Press.

MacCannell, D. and MacCannell, J. F. (1982). *The Time of the Sign: A Semiotic*

Interpretation of Modern Culture. Bloomington: Indiana University Press.

McLuhan, M. (1964). *Understanding Media.* London: Routledge and Kegan Paul.

Morris, C. W. (1938). *Foundations of the Theory of Signs.* Chicago: University of Chicago Press.

Nöth, W. (1990). *Handbook of Semiotics.* Bloomington: Indiana University Press.

Ogden, C. K. and Richards, I. A. (1923). *The Meaning of Meaning.* London: Routledge and Kegan Paul.

Osgood, C. E., Suci, G. J. and Tannenbaum, P. H. (1957). *The Measurement of Meaning.* Urbana: University of Illinois Press.

Peirce, C. S. (1958). *Collected Papers.* Cambridge, Mass.: Harvard University Press.

Piaget J. (1969). *The Child's Conception of the World.* Totowa, N.J.: Littlefield, Adams & Co.

Piaget, J. and Inhelder, J. (1969). *The Psychology of the Child.* New York: Basic Books.

Saussure, F. de (1916/1966). *Course in General Linguistics.* Paris: Payot.

Sebeok, T. A. (1976). *Contributions to the Doctrine of Signs.* Lanham: University Press of America.

Sebeok, T. A. (1976). *Contributions to the Doctrine of Signs.* Lanham: University Press of America.

Sebeok, T. A. (1979). *The Sign and Its Masters.* Austin: University of Texas Press.

Sebeok, T. A. (1981). *The Play of Musement.* Bloomington: Indiana University Press.

Sebeok, T. A. (1985). Pandora's Box: How and Why to Communicate 10,000 Years into the Future. In: M. Blonsky (ed.), *On Signs*, pp. 448-466. Baltimore: Johns Hopkins University Press.

Sebeok, T. A. (1986). *I Think I Am a Verb: More Contributions to the Doctrine of Signs.* New York: Plenum.

Sebeok, T. A. (1991). *A Sign is Just a Sign.* Bloomington: Indiana University Press.

Solomon, J. (1988). *The Signs of Our Time.* Los Angeles: Jeremy P. Tarcher.

Vygotsky, L. S. (1961). *Thought and Language.* Cambridge, Mass.: MIT Press.

IT'S ALL IN THE SIGN!

Preliminary Remarks

Consider the notion of "health." We often say that this "bodily condition" is characterized by "signs." As it turns out, this colloquial depiction of health is quite an accurate one from the standpoint of semiotics. Indeed, the *definition* or *representation* of health, and the successful treatment of disease, are dependent to a large extent upon cultural perceptions and models of "health" and "disease." Specifically, it can be said that health constitutes a culturally-specific code whose meaning is delimited by the particular signs within the code used to represent bodily processes. As in the case of any semiotic code (e.g. food, clothing, etc.), the semantic relations among its signs are maintained by a paradigmatic opposition—"healthy" vs. "non-healthy." The ways in which we talk about being healthy, the ways in which we visualize a healthy complexion, bodily state, etc. constitute the signs of the code which define health and its converse. This "health code" is, in other words, a cognitive strategy for organizing and rationalizing the flux of changes that the body is perceived to undergo.

The hypothesis upon which most of Western medicine has conventionally operated is, on the contrary, the one that claims that bodily health is a knowable phenomenon to all physicians in all cultures in exactly the same cognitive ways. However, the reliance on the traditional scientific arguments to support such an objectivist perspective has been weakened in this century by the intriguing theoretical debates in another science, physics. The great twentieth-century physicist Werner Heisenberg (e.g. 1949) was, in fact, the first scientist to debunk the notion that science was capable of discovering so-called "objective reality." His uncertainty, or indeterminacy, principle—for which he won the Nobel Prize in 1931—has come to have a profound influence on scientific thinking in the latter part of this century. In essence, Heisenberg showed that the idea of an objectively-knowable universe, independent of our culturally-shaped modes of observing, is just *that*—a human idea. Heisenberg argued that the construct of "objective reality" had to be replaced by the one of "observer-dependent reality."   His uncertainty principle, whose repercussions are being felt in all the sciences (including the medical ones), lends substantial credibility to the argument that conceptualizations of health and disease are dependent in large part upon the ways in which cultures represent them semiotically

This chapter will focus on how signs do their work of representing the world and, ultimately, of constituting the codes we use to think about it. Semiotically speaking, health is what we say it is. Specifically, I will look at Saussure's dissection of the sign into *signifier* and *signified*, at Peirce's fundamental typology of signs as *iconic*, *indexical*, and *symbolic*, at the nature of cultural representation, and at how signs allow us to manipulate the world.

Signifier and Signified

As mentioned in the previous chapter, Ferdinand de Saussure is consid-ered to be one of the founders of modern linguistics and semiotics. His definition of the sign has become a widely-accepted one and merits attention here.

For Saussure the sign had an arbitrary connection to reality. More technically, the relation between the sign and its object was not necessarily motivated by some physical feature. A sign, according to Saussure, was made up of two parts: a *signifier* and a *signified*. The *signifier* is the physical part of the sign, the actual substance of which it is composed (sound-waves, alphabet characters, etc.); the *signified* is the mental concept to which it refers. The *signifier* is similar to Peirce's *representamen* and the *signified* to his *object*. Since Saussure believed that signifieds are common, by and large, to all members of the same culture who share the codes to which they appertain, he claimed that there was no need for what Peirce called an *interpretant* dimension to signification.   For Saussure, the interaction between *signifier* and *signified* resulted in conventionally-determined proc-esses of *signification*, independent of the sign-user's viewpoint. Thus, for instance, the mental concept "tree" can be represented by a visual signifier, like a drawing, or a verbal signifier, like the word *tree*. Saussure claimed that the arbitrariness of the connection was proven by the fact that any signifier— e.g. *tree* in English, *arbre* in French, etc.—could be used to refer to the signified "tree." There is no intrinsic motivation for either word-sign, *tree* or *arbre*, to represent the mental concept in question. For Saussure, onomatopoeic words—words that imitate the sounds made by their referents (*chirp, drip, boom, zap*, etc.)—were the exception not the rule in language. Moreover, the highly variable nature of onomatopoeia across languages showed that even this phenomenon was subject to arbitrary cultural perceptions. For instance, the sounds made by a rooster are represented by the signifier *cock-a-doodle-do* in English, but by *chicchirichí* (pronounced "keekeereekee") in Italian; similarly, the barking of a dog is represented by *bow-wow* in English but by *ouaoua* (pronounced *wawa*) in French. Saussure suggested that such onomatopoeic creations were only approximate and more or less conventional imitations of perceived sounds.

Peirce's Basic Triad

As was discussed in the previous chapter, Charles Peirce related the connection between sign and referent to the vagaries of the human interpreter. This does not mean that Peirce viewed signification as necessarily open-ended; but rather that it was *potentially* infinite. For Peirce, we will always find some new meaning in some context for a sign, no matter how conventionalized the sign's utilization may have become. Peirce also provided us with a triadic typology of signs which has now become part of the standard technical lexicon of semiotic theory and practice. He differentiated among *icons, indexes (indices)* and *symbols* as the primary kinds of signs human beings use to represent the world. These were not, however, mutually exclusive. Signs can, for instance, be partially iconic and symbolic: e.g. the cross in Christian religions stands both for the actual shape of the "cross" on which Christ was crucified (iconic sign) and "Christianity" (symbolic sign).

Icon

An *icon* is a sign that resembles its referent in some way. In Saussurean terms, it is a sign in which the signifier is made to look or sound like the signified. Photographs, maps, Roman numerals such as I, II, and III, etc. are all iconic signs because they are meant to portray their signified in some isomorphic—visually mimetic—way. Onomatopoeic words such as "drip," "bang," "screech," etc. are signifiers made to be intentionally sound-imitative. Iconicity, or mimetically-motivated representation, can be found in many of our cultural artifacts and works of art. Beethoven's "Pastoral" symphony or Rossini's "William Tell Overture" contain various musical icons that are evocative of the sounds found in nature (bird calls, thunder, wind, etc.). Commercially-produced perfumes are artificial icons of animal smells indicating sexual arousal or interest.

For many semioticians, especially those of the Peircean school of thought, iconicity constitutes the primary mode of representation. The claim is that semiosis is at first tied to the operations of our sensory apparatus. It is only through repeated usage in cultural contexts that it eventually becomes free of sensory control. Iconicity, for many, lies at the core of how the human organism responds first and foremost to the world.

Iconic signs are what I have called in the previous chapter "factual" models of the world. And there exists evidence scattered all over the literature in the various human sciences to suggest that iconicity is indeed a fundamental semiosic tendency in the human organism. Recently, David McNeill (1992) has done extensive cross-cultural research on the tendency to use gesture concomitantly during narrative discourse. His work has shown rather dramatically how factual-iconic thinking has power over the ways we conceptualize. McNeill argues that there is a unity between language and gesture. He has painstakingly analyzed, over a ten-year period, how individuals engaged in narrative discourse—of different cultures, children as well as adults, some even neurologically impaired—invariably manifest the tendency to represent the mental images inherent in discourse in terms of gestural forms. McNeill shows, consequently, that gestures derive from a more fundamental, emotional, factual level that has a visible impact on the ways in which narrative discourse is expressed. So, for instance, if I were to talk of "large" things, then my hands would tend to show "largeness" by a cupping action that involves moving them outward in a kind of "swelling" motion. Vice versa, if the underlying focus of my message was "smallness," I would tend to use the opposite gesture. It seems, if McNeill is right, that we have a constant need to literally "draw" our thoughts with our hands.

The first inscriptions, cave drawings, and other kinds of pictographic signs of humanity were, no doubt, the end result of the use of the hands to represent the world iconically. Pictorial representation is the most abstract form of iconic expression. It is likely that the imitative hand movements used to portray shapes were transferred to a cave wall or to an object by means of some sharp cutting tool. These pictorial representations constitute humanity's first genuine works of art. The earliest of these goes back some 30,000 years. They took two main forms: the vivid carvings of animals which cover the roofs and walls of caves, such as those at Lascaux in France and Altamira in Spain; and the small sculptures and relief carvings of animals and female figures found in caves throughout Europe. As the hand movements used to make such works of art became more abbreviated, the figures made by *Homo sapiens* became more condensed and abstract. This led to the invention of *writing*. The earliest form of writing was vastly different from the alphabetic or syllabic writing systems that came to be based on vocal language:

The fascinating research of Schmandt-Besserat (1978, 1989, 1992) has, in fact, shown that the origins of alphabetic writing lie in a previous iconic medium of representation. Schmandt-Besserat has traced the earliest precursor of modern writing systems to the symbols found on clay tokens discovered in western Asia that belong to the Neolithic era. Made out of elemental shapes, these tokens were used as image-making objects. They were obviously employed to express something concretely in visual mimetic form.

Primordial iconicity has left its residues in the structure of language and in our propensity to use iconic forms of representation, especially the gestural which is a universal mode of representation that can satisfy all social needs. The child developmental literature, moreover, makes it saliently obvious that children invariably pass through an initial stage of iconicity before they develop language. Gestural communication in children seems to follow from the models of iconic representation that they pick up from their environment. These are used for practical purposes (e.g. pointing to something desired) and are probably reinforced by osmosis with adult gesture. It is intriguing to note that, although vocal language eventually becomes the dominant form of communication, the gestural modality does not vanish completely. It remains a functional subsystem of human language that can always be utilized as a more generic form of communication when an interaction is otherwise impossible. This happens typically when two interlocutors speak different languages. And, of course, in individuals with impaired vocal organs, gesture constitutes the only possible mode of communication.

The research on children's drawings (e.g. Krampen 1991, Cox 1992) shows that children literally codify their environment iconically at about the same time that they utter their first words. If a drawing instrument is put in the child's hand, that child will almost instinctively use it to draw—a "skill" that no one has imparted or transmitted to the child. This instinctual propensity to draw is manifest as well in doodling, which is a residual tendency of our childhood propensity to represent the world in images. All the available artifacts coming from the pre-civilized world bear witness to this "innate" capacity in the human being. The child must be exposed to language in order for him or her to acquire it; that same child does not, however, need to be exposed to visual art in order for him or her to draw. If given drawing materials around the age of two or three, young children happily scribble randomly on the drawing surface. As time passes, however, their scribbling becomes more and more controlled; geometrical shapes such as rude circles, crosses, and rectangles, at first accidentally produced, are repeated and gradually perfected. Although children, with parental prompting, may learn to label circles as "suns" or "faces," they do not set out to draw anything in the environment, but instead seem spontaneously to produce forms that become refined through practice into precise, repeatable shapes. The act of making shapes is pleasurable in itself and appears to be intrinsically satisfying; usually identification is provided, if at all, only after the child finishes drawing. Of course, shapes eventually suggest "things" to the child as the ability to use symbols develops, but in the beginning, pleasure and satisfaction occur without larger or more explicit associations of meaning. This form of activity in the presymbolic child is perhaps truly an example of "art for art's sake." Iconicity is clearly a fundamental force in symbol creation.

Iconicity is not limited to the visual channel. Audio-oral iconicity is a dominant force in semiosis as well. Children invariably emit sounds osmotically when they play to accompany their rhythmic movements, to imitate the sounds of their toys, and to generate emotional responses in other children. Speech itself evokes physiological responses because it literally issues forth from the body. The first words of children are, in fact, the result of osmosis intersecting with conceptual development. In a recent study of four infants from different language backgrounds, Boysson-Bardies and Vihman (1991) have shown that the first words stem from what I have called here osmotic and mimetic adaptation processes.

Index

An *index* is a sign with a direct existential connection to its referent. Smoke is an index of fire; a cough is an index of a cold; and so on. The most typical manifestation of indexicality is the pointing *index* finger. We use this form of semiosis to point out and locate things in the environment. As such, indexicality is tied to a more fundamental force of semiosis that semioticians call *deixis*, which is defined simply as the process of locating objects, beings, and events in the environment. Deixis can also involve the language code. Words such as *here*, *there*, *up*, *down*, etc. all imply spatial location. Indexicality and deixis seem to indicate an inherent feature of cognition that can only be described as an extension of visual sensory experience into the domain of abstract thought.

Deixis is more latent in language, a primarily symbolic code, than one would at first suspect. Consider, for instance, verbal constructions such as *think up*, *think over*, and *think out*:

Even though these verbs have abstract referents, they nonetheless evoke images of location and movement. The construction *think up* elicits a mental image of upward movement, thus portraying the abstract referent as an object being extracted physically from a kind of mental terrain; *think over* evokes the image of an internal eye scanning the mind; *think out* suggests the action of taking the referent out of the mind so that it can be held up, presumably, to the scrutiny of the eyes. This kind of latent deixis constitutes a semantic means by which languages locate and identify beings, objects, events, processes, and activities being talked about, or referred to, in relation to the spatiotemporal contexts created and sustained by the act of utterance and the participation in it, even when such contexts are purely imaginary. Thus, certain verbal forms like the personal pronouns *I*, *you*, etc. are indexes because they allow us to refer differentially to people in relation to their location. Similarly, all adverbs of place—*here*, *there*, *above*, *below*, etc.—are all verbal indexes that allow the language code to take over the function of the pointing finger in order to allow us to locate and identify beings, objects, and events in the surrounding environment.

Symbol

A *symbol* is a sign that has an arbitrary or conventional relation to some referent. Words, in general, are symbolic signs. But any signifier—objects, sounds, figures, etc.—can take on symbolic significance. A cross can stand symbolically for the concept "Christianity;" a "V" configuration made with the index and middle fingers can stand symbolically for the concept "peace;" and so on. Indeed, the symbolic mode of representation is one of the greatest achievements of the human mind. The iconic and indexical modes of representation are biologically more fundamental, since these emerge spontaneously without any training. But the symbolic mode operates totally within the artifactual-cultural order of representation and must be acquired in relation to this order.

The claim of some semioticians—and it is my own view as well—is that the symbolic mode of representation is a derivative of the more fundamental modes. For instance, we have seen above that verbal constructions such as *think up* and *think over* have deictic "residues" in their referential system. Indexical and iconic residues are, in fact, much more frequent in language than might at first seem. This will be discussed again in subsequent chapters. The fact that the child first learns to represent something more naturally by manipulating or drawing it and then naming it later is also suggestive evidence that the symbolic mode is dependent upon the iconic mode, or at least overlaps with it. This kind of incidental evidence is rather substantial. Actually, the debate on iconicity and symbolic thinking goes back to Plato, who separated the image *(eikon)* from the idea *(eidos)*. This set in motion the tendency to view symbolic representation and especially language as separate from mental imagery and iconicity and as more powerful shapers of cognition. Descartes reinforced this notion by claiming that nonverbal forms of thought proceeded without logic, and so could not be studied scientifically. The Cartesian view ignored, of course, the Renaissance tradition of *ingenium* , "ingenuity," and the fact that even Plato used myths and invented narratives. Descartes' own style of presentation, too, unfolded in the form a fable.

Consider how the iconic mode can be enlisted to solve such symbolic artifacts as logical puzzles. Here is a typical one:

> There are twenty socks in a drawer, scattered at random.
> Ten are red and the other ten are blue in color. Without
> looking inside the drawer, what is the least number of
> socks that you must remove in order to get a matching
> pair?

The tendency of many of us, so easily accustomed to symbolic abstract thinking, is to say that eleven socks must be removed from the drawer. The reasoning goes somewhat like this: "I'll keep removing socks up to the *breakpoint* of ten, when I know for certain that I will get a change in color and therefore a match." A shift to the iconic mode of thinking, which literally *performs* the act of removing socks (i.e. it represents it visually and experientially), reveals the real solution. The iconic mode of reasoning goes like this: "I will start by removing one sock. This will be of *one* of the two colors, say, red. Then, assuming the worst case scenario, I will then pull out a sock of *the other* color (blue). Now, the *next* sock I remove from the drawer will be of *one* or *the other* color. If it is red, it matches my first sock; if it is blue it matches my second sock. In either case, I will need to remove only *three* socks at random from the drawer in order to get a matching pair. The symbolic mode of thinking can then be enlisted to "generalize" the solution of this puzzle. The experiment works with 20, 30, 45, 689, 2300, and indeed with any number of socks, as a moment's reflection will reveal. So, in general symbolic terms it can be said that the 3 sock removals are independent of the number, n, of socks scattered at random in the drawer. The general solution goes like this: "given n socks in a drawer of which m are of one color and an equal number, *m*, are of another color, it will take three random removals from the drawer to get a matching pair."

The iconic, indexical, and symbolic categories posited by Peirce are clearly not separate or distinct. We normally enlist all three kinds of signs to represent the world simultaneously in various degrees. The following example of a "hybrid" sign is provided by Fiske (1982, p. 52):

In this sign, the triangle is a *symbol* meaning, arbitrarily, "warning." The cross in the center is a "mixture" of *icon* and *symbol*. It is iconic in that its form visually aims to represent a "crossroads." But since the cross figure could easily be interpreted to represent "church," or "hospital," it is symbolic insofar as we need to know that it has been chosen, by convention, to refer to the "crossroads" referent. Finally, the entire sign is an *index* because when it is placed near a crossroads it literally *indicates* that we are about to reach a crossroads physically and spatially.

To conclude this discussion on signs, an illustrative example of how semiosis works is in order. Let us say that you see, as a referent, a "ball" nearby. Now, imagine that you have a clump of clay in your hands. With this clump you can easily produce the three basic types of signs to refer to the ball. If you were to indicate the ball *indexically*, then you might shape the clay into a pointing finger aimed in the direction of the ball. If, instead, you were to represent it *iconically*, then you would probably shape it into a smooth round clump that would look like the ball. Finally, you could represent the ball symbolically any way you wanted to, by, for example, using strips of clay as alphabet letters to write out the word *ball*. In the first case of representation, the sign you made with the "clay signifier" had an existential (indicating) relation with its referent; in the second case, it had a similarity or likeness relation to it; and in the last case, it had a conventional relation to it. Note that in all three cases, the details of the signifying process will vary somewhat from person to person. This "variation" is due, as Peirce pointed out, to the interpretant's participation in the act of semiosis.

The following chart summarizes the three basic forms of meaning-making:

Sign Type	Signifying Process	Examples
index	by causal or existential connection with the referent (the referent can be figured out)	smoke symptoms, etc.
icon	by resemblance (the referent can be reseen, reheard, etc.)	drawings of all kinds (charts, diagrams, maps), photos, pictures, sculptures, etc.
symbol	*By convention (the relation to the referent must be learned)*	words, gestures

Cultural Representation

Peirce's triadic typology tells us how we make signs and, therefore, how semiosis in the human species unfolds. We are continually groping with how to understand the world. And we can easily create new signs to help us interpret the world around us. But, by and large, we literally let our culture "do the understanding" for us. We are born into an already-fixed system of signification based on representational codes that will largely determine how we will come to understand the world around us. Only if, hypothetically, all our knowledge (which is maintained in the form of codes and the media that allow us to transmit them) were somehow effaced from the face of the earth, would we need to go right back to our primordial tendencies to represent the world all over again, iconically and indexically. Think what would happen if, over night, all the books, videos, memories, and vital cultural codes like languages were obliterated from the face of the earth. What would we do? Would the next generation live together in the same cultural space? Would it have to start *tabula rasa* to reinvent the world as we now know it?

This discussion is meant to emphasize how crucial the role played by culture—the totally human-made world of artifacts—is in the formation of the human being. All artifacts are human "inventions." This includes laws and scientific theories. But this does not mean, as the German philosopher

Friedrich Nietzsche (1844-1900) despondently believed, that our artifacts are no more than tokens of artifice and, therefore, that nothing is real. After all, the "artifactual" theory of aerodynamics is used rather successfully to fly planes; theories about cell structure and function allow doctors to cure various diseases; and so on. The ability to invent and represent the world semiotically actually enhances our survivability. The signs that we make all the time derive ultimately from having "sensed" and "felt" the world in some specific way. Inside the mind, we continually make connections among our sense-derived forms. These connections can then be "tried out," so to speak on the world. If they "work" as "imagined," it is because they are ultimately made up of the substance of sensation. We go from *sentio ergo sum* ("I feel, therefore I am") to Descartes' state of *cogito ergo sum.* ("I think, therefore I am"). Our cogitations are "real" because they are derived ultimately from our biologically-determined survival modes of sensing and feeling.

Thinking rarely takes place without a repertory of signifying forms that evoke specific referents. The images that our mind generates all the time are organized and rendered "transportable" by our signs and codes. These are kept "in storage" by the memory system where they consolidate into our acquired models of space, time, emotions, etc. It is here that we use our imagination both to conjure up the past and to make predictions about the future. As the philosopher of science Jacob Bronowski (1977, p. 25) remarked, this is the feature of the human mind that makes it unique among all species:

> The images play out for us events which are not present to our senses, and thereby guard the past and create the future—a future that does not yet exist, and may never come to exist in that form. By contrast, the lack of symbolic ideas, or their rudimentary poverty, cuts off an animal from the past and the future alike, and imprisons it in the present. Of all the distinctions between man and animal, the characteristic gift which makes us human is the power to work with symbolic images.

It is to be noted that our memory system appears to be equipped to handle and coordinate our different semiosic capacities efficiently. The neuroscientific research on memory has, in fact, shown that there are two forms of storage in the brain, the spatial and the verbal, located in the right and left hemispheres respectively. The spatial form seems to be involved in storing iconic information, whereas the verbal one is a handler of symbolic information. The functions of the right hemisphere would seem to reflect general properties of the human mind, whereas the left hemisphere appears to be organized according to culture codes, especially language. There exists in the human brain, therefore, a memory storage system for multisensory images independent of cultural codes (and therefore of languages), and a culturally-constrained semantic system for verbal meanings and relations. Bilinguals, for example, would seem to have one imagery system as do monolinguals, but two distinct semantic ones.

When using artifactual-symbolic thinking, it is easy to forget that there is a semiosic connection linking the body to the mind and to culture. This is the view put forward by the philosopher Karl Popper (e.g. Popper and Eccles 1977). Popper classifies the world of the mind into three domains. "World 1" is the domain of physical objects and states, including human brains which can affect physical objects and processes by means of neuronal synapses—electrical-type impulses between brain cells—transmitting messages along nerve paths that cause muscles to contract or limbs to move. It is also the world of "things." World 1 can be inhabited both by human-built artifacts and by all organisms. "World 2" is the whole domain of subjective experiences. This is the level at which the concept of Self emerges, as the mind allows humans to differentiate themselves from the beings ("others"), objects, and events of the outside world. It is at this level that we perceive, think, plan, remember, dream, and imagine. "World 3" is the domain of knowledge in the objective sense, containing the externalized artifacts of the human mind. It is, in other words, the totally human-made world of culture.

Consciousness emerges and resurfaces each time that the mind "descends" into World 2. The act of making meaning is an act of consciousness. The mind cannot possibly descend into World 1. It can think about it, but it will never "know" it. There is evidence that animals have a form of consciousness (e.g. Griffin 1992) and an experiential domain similar to that of humans, which can be called "factual," in keeping in line with the terminology introduced in this book. This is the ability to know a sensation and to react to it in purposeful ways. The ethological evidence shows that animals can indeed react factually and purposefully to stimuli. The problem is trying to determine to what extent this form of consciousness becomes imaginative and inventive, transforming felt experience into a reflective symbolic type. Do animals have World 2 and World 3 experiences that would allow them to literally look for their "selves" in the substance of their thoughts? As the biologist Jacob von Uexküll (1909) cogently argued at the turn of this century, it is unlikely that we will ever be able to "know" how animals "know," given our different anatomical and neurological systems. Moreover, it is highly unlikely that we will ever be able to penetrate the workings of our own biological systems to discover how they form the physical substrate of consciousness. The search to find some evolutionary, or genetic, World 1 basis to consciousness using World 3 structures such as scientific theorizing, therefore, will invariably turn out to be a futile enterprise.

To show how cultural-symbolic (World 3) representation becomes a dominant one in cognition, consider the example of health with which I started off this chapter. The ways in which a culture represents health determines the medical treatment of disease. What is considered to be healthy in one culture may not coincide with views of "healthiness" in another. Health, like all the phenomena codified by scientists, cannot be defined ahistorically, aculturally or in purely absolutist terms. As a corollary, it is obvious that for any treatment of a disease to be meaningful (and consequently effective), it will have to be grounded in cultural reality.

This semiotic perspective does not deny the existence of events and states in the body that will lead to its malfunctioning. All organisms have an innate warning system that alerts them to dangerous changes in bodily states. But only in the case of the human organism are fluctuations in bodily functions codified semiotically and thus made available to reflective consciousness. Once a specific pattern of fluctuation has been selected and codified as "healthy," then its absence or its converse becomes an immediate sign of "disease." Problems in interpreting this indexical sign as indicative of a "disease state" emerge when an individual comes from a culture which has not codified the bodily fluctuations in question in similar ways.

An illustrative analogy is in order. The world of flora and fauna is classified semiotically by all cultures into a dichotomy of "edible" and "non-edible" categories. However, the inclusion of an item in one or the other category is a culture-specific decision. Rabbits, many kinds of flowers, and silkworms, for instance, would be classified by and large as "non-edible" by North American culture. However, Europeans regularly cook rabbit meat and various types of flowers, and Mexicans eat cooked silkworms with no adverse physical reactions whatsoever. But if such substances were to be presented to North Americans in a prepared culinary form, chances are, given the semiotic valence they have in their own culture, that they would suffer an adverse reaction if told what they were eating. This example shows, in an intuitively obvious way, how culture can influence our physical responses.

Perhaps the best way to approach the body/mind/culture nexus in the domain of health is to enlist the ideas of Giambattista Vico (1668-1744), the great eighteenth century Neapolitan philosopher whose 1725 book, *The New Science* (Bergin and Fisch 1984), offers some truly remarkable insights on how to understand this interaction. In his penetrating analysis of the human mind, Vico posits, in effect, the existence of two cognitive layers—a deep and a surface one. At the deep level our sense impressions are registered and organized into categories which schematize our physiological and affective responses to the stimuli and signals present in the environment in the form of images. This is the primordial function of the human imagination, and it is at this deep level that one can talk of "universals" (e.g. Verene 1981). It is only when these mental images of bodily experiences are codified, especially by language, that a surface form of cognition crystallizes. The particular characteristics of this form will, clearly, vary from person to person and from culture to culture. Surface-level signs (symbols) eventually become independent from their imagistic origins and generate highly abstract systems of thought that subsequently guide the mind's efforts to understand the world of reality. These efforts produce our institutions, scientific theories, and ultimately our cultures.

Vico's insights on the nature of mind suggest that there is an objective reality to which the human organism responds in universal ways. At this deep level, the mind transforms sensorial inputs into image schemas. But only those schemas codified semiotically (e.g. by language) become subsequently retrievable as units of recurring and meaningful pattern. Therefore, problems in understanding health conceptually can be seen to emerge at the culturally-shaped surface level of cognition. The semiotic categories that make up this level (e.g. the words used to describe a healthy state) eventually develop into culturally-specific models of health and disease.

The question now becomes: How do we come to conceptualize health in culturally-specific ways? Even a superficial consideration of this question will suggest that we do so through the template of the surface-level signs that cultures utilize to represent health and its converse. Thus, for instance, in some cultures a "healthy body" is considered to be one that is lean and muscular. Conversely, in others it might be conceptualized as being one that is plump and rotund. A "healthy lifestyle" might be seen by some cultures to inhere in rigorous physical activity, while in others it might be envisaged as inhering in a more leisurely and sedentary form of behavior.

But perhaps the "semiotic key" that allows us best to access the conceptualization of health in a culture is the language used to refer to "healthy" and "unhealthy" states. Consider, for example, the following common metaphorical portrayals of health by our own culture (Lakoff and Johnson 1980, p. 15 and p. 50):

(1)   Your at the *peak* of your health

(2)   My health is *down*.

(3)   You're in *top* shape.

(4)   My body is in perfect *working order*.

(5)   My body is *breaking down*.

(6)   My health is going *down the drain*.

(7)   His pain *went away*.

(8)   I'm going to *flush out* my cold.

The first three sentences represent health in terms of an orientation analogy: i.e. the state of being healthy is depicted as being oriented in an upwards direction, while the opposite state is portrayed as being oriented in a downwards direction. This is probably because in our culture, as Lakoff and Johnson (1980, p. 15) point out, serious "illness forces us to lie down physically." Sentences (4) and (5) compare health, and its converse, to a machine. And in the last three sentences health and its converse are envisaged as being entities within a person. This is why they can *go away*, they can be *flushed out*, and so on.

The study of formulas such as these reveals that they underlie the representation of most of our concepts. The cognitive power of metaphor will be discussed in chapter six. Suffice it to say here that metaphor reveals the ways in which we perceive, think, and act.

It is interesting to note that even before the current wave of fascination with metaphor, the writer Susan Sontag wrote a compelling book in 1978, *Illness as Metaphor*, that has become a classic study of how metaphor shapes our conceptualizations of disease. A decade later, after the advent of AIDS, Sontag (1989) followed this up with a sequel study on the metaphors we commonly use to portray this dreaded contemporary disease. The main point made by Sontag in these two books is that illness is not a metaphor, but that cultures invariably think of diseases in metaphorical ways. Using the example of cancer, Sontag (1979, p. 7) points out that in the not-too-distant past the very word *cancer* was said to have killed some patients who would not have necessarily succumbed to the malignancy from which they suffered: "As long as a particular disease is treated as an evil, invincible predator, not just a disease, most people with cancer will indeed be demoralized by learning what disease they have." Sontag's point that people suffer more from conceptualizing about their disease than from the disease itself is, indeed, a well-taken and instructive one.

It is also interesting to note that medical practitioners can easily come under the spell of health and body symbolism. The cultural shaping of health and disease concepts probably takes its origins from the fact that the functioning of the human body is of utmost importance to both the individual and society. Our body is as much symbol as organic substance. The semiotic transformation of the body can have serious consequences for the practice of medicine. Hudson (1972), to quote just one example, found that medical specialists trained in private British schools were more likely to achieve distinction and prominence by working on the head as opposed to the lower part of the body, on the surface as opposed to the inside of the body, and on the male as opposed to the female body. Hudson correctly suggested that the only way to interpret such behaviors was in cultural terms: i.e. parts of the body, evidently, possessed a symbolic significance which influenced the decisions taken by medical students: "students from an upper-middle-class background are more likely than those from a lower-middle-class background to find their way into specialties that are seen for symbolic reasons as desirable." Examples such as this highlight the intrinsic interconnection that exists between medical practice and the cultural context in which it takes place.

The body is an image of society. It conforms to the structure of the social order and vice versa. As the first physicians of the civilized world suspected, a successful health care strategy is, in large part, dependent upon it being synchronized with cultural codes and expectations.

Consider the research conducted by psychologists on the experience of pain. This area of inquiry has long been shaped by a strictly physical view: namely that pain "is a specific sensation subserved by a straight-through transmission system from skin to brain, and that intensity of pain is proportional to the extent of tissue damage" (Melzack, 1988, p. 288). But research has shown that pain thresholds are also influenced by non-physical factors, such as the unique past history of the individual and his or her cognitive experiences. This suggests that culturally-specific conceptual models of pain can affect the patient's response and threshold patterns. As a specific example, consider the experience of childbirth. As Melzack (1972, p. 223) observes, in North American culture "childbirth is widely regarded as a painful experience." However, anthropologists have documented "cultures in which the women show virtually no distress during childbirth." Melzack, a psychologist, goes on to provide what is, remarkably, a semiotic explanation of such a behavioral discrepancy (p. 223):

> Can this mean that all women in our culture are making up their pain? Not at all. It happens to be part of our culture to recognize childbirth as possibly endangering the life of the mother, and young girls learn to fear it in the course of growing up. Books on "natural childbirth" ("childbirth without fear") stress the extent to which fear

increases the amount of pain felt during labor and birth
and point out how difficult it is to dispel it.

The semiotic study of cultural representation is, obviously, a rather crucial one. After all, the physician becomes an effective healer only when he or she views the patient not as a collection of symptoms, disordered functions, damaged organs and disturbed emotions, but as a human being in his or her individual and cultural totality.

The Symbolic Manipulation of the World

The symbolic (World 3) order is a powerful one. The mental artifacts (codes, theories, etc.) that characterize this order can be projected back onto the factual-natural world to manipulate it.

Consider the following engineering dilemma. Let us suppose that a tunnel has to be dug to go right through the middle of a mountain. We cannot obviously measure the length that the tunnel should be directly. However, my World 3 mind provides me with an easy plan to do this by means of the Pythagorean theorem. So, I can choose a point **A** on one side of the mountain and another point **B** on the other, such that both points are visible from a point **C** to the right, with **C** chosen so that angle **ACB** is a right angle (90^0). Then, by aligning **A** with **A′** (the entrance to the mountain on one side) and **B** with **B′** (the entrance to the mountain on the other side) I can, in effect, measure the require length. It is, clearly, a straightforward task to measure **AC** and **BC**, since these lengths have been chosen to permit their measurability. Now, the Pythagorean tells us that $AB^2 = AC^2 + BC^2$. This allows me to determine the length **AB** easily because I know the lengths **AC** and **BC** and because I have learned to solve algebraic equations of this type in high school. Then, by subtracting the distance **AA′** and **BB′** from this length, I will have found out how long I will have to build my tunnel:

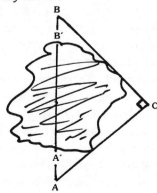

The reason why a symbolic language like the Pythagorean theorem works—i.e. allows us to manipulate reality—is because it traces its origin to experience and observation, in this case the observation of the relation among the three sides of figures shaped like right-angled triangles. The Pythagorean theorem is no more than a convenient shorthand for this discovery. The surface level of mind does indeed allow us to impose a conceptual framework on the events, beings, and objects in the world. One's world-view is built up from the acquisition of such codes in specific cultural contexts. But the fact that a specific culture predisposes its users to attend to certain specific perceptual events—e.g. right-angled triangular figures—does not imply that members of other cultures are incapable of perceiving the world in similar ways, nor that our symbolic artifacts "fabricate" reality. The world is "sensed" in the same way by all humans in the deep level of mind. The illusory "mind-world" built from the conceptual materials forged by symbols is a product of surface-level cognitive activity. It is important not to confuse these two levels.

Concluding Remarks

In this chapter, the focus has been on how signs are constructed and on how they allow us to represent the world. The iconic, indexical, and symbolic signs we use constantly and automatically are the elements that make up the mental frames, or conceptual filters, we use to understand the world. Such understanding unfolds, indeed, "within signs." Consciousness of the world rarely exists independently of semiosis.

It was also claimed in this chapter that abstract symbols are end-products rather than points-of-departure. The starting point is, of course, the level of bodily sensations captured by basic signifying processes (e.g. indexical and iconic semiosis). The progression from sensory to conceptual thought is achieved by the fact that signification forms a continuum that links the body, the mind, and culture. The brain's ability to manufacture signs is a basic survival strategy in all life forms. In humans the persistence of the iconic mode of thought suggests that concepts start out as mimetic or osmotic portrayals of the physical environment. These are at first tied to the operations of our sensory apparatus. It is only after they have become routinized through cultural diffusion that they become free of sensory control and take on an abstract quality. Iconicity lies at the core of how the human organism responds to the world.

The biologist Jakob von Uexküll (1909) argued that every organism has different inward and outward "lives." The key to understanding this duality is in the anatomical structure of the organism itself. Animals with widely divergent anatomies do not live in the same kind of world. There exists, therefore, no common world of objects shared by humans and animals equally. The work of von Uexküll has shown that an organism does not perceive an object in itself, but according to its own particular kind of preexistent mental modeling system that allows it to interpret the world of beings, objects, and events in a biologically-programmed way. This system is grounded in the organism's body, which routinely converts the external world of experience into an internal one of representation in terms of the particular features of the mental system with which a specific species is endowed. Signs are forged within the human organism as extensions of the body's response system. No matter how bizarre or unearthly the shape of creatures which might inhabit alien planets, we are likely to recognize them as animals nonetheless. The chief basis for this recognition is that they are bound to give off "signs of life." Without signs we would not be able to make the messages and the meanings that we constantly do.

The recent findings compiled by scientists of the mind are beginning to corroborate, when viewed synthetically and cumulatively, what Vico maintained over two and half centuries ago: namely, that there is a continuity between the body, the mind, and culture. It is indeed instructive to note once again that the analysis of the body's genetically-programmed system of symptoms in the ancient world laid the foundation for modern medical practices. A symptom is an indexical sign that indicates some malfunction or "interrupted" bodily process which, in the mind of the physician, points to, or "represents," a disease.

So, from the dawn of civilization to the present age, it has always been recognized in Western culture—at least implicitly—that there is an intrinsic connection between nature and culture. The *raison d'être* of philosophy is, arguably, to investigate whether or not reality can exist independently of the signifying codes that human beings create to represent and think about it. Is the physical universe a great machine operating according to natural laws that may be discovered by human reason? Or, on the other hand, is everything "out there" no more than a construction of the human mind deriving its categories from the world of sensations and perceptions? Although an answer to this fundamental question will clearly never be possible, one of the important offshoots of the search for an answer has been a systematic form of inquiry into how the mind's products and the body's natural processes are interrelated.

SUGGESTIONS FOR FURTHER READING

Bergin, T. G. and Fisch, M. H. (1984). *The New Science of Giambattista Vico.* Ithaca: Cornell University Press.

Boysson-Bardies, B. de and Vihman, M. M. (1991). Adaptation to Language: Evidence from Babbling and First Words in Four Languages. *Language* 67: 297-319.

Bronowski, J. (1977). *A Sense of the Future.* Cambridge, Mass.: MIT Press.

Cox, M. (1992). *Children's Drawings.* Harmondsworth: Penguin.

Fiske, J. (1982). *Introduction to Communication Studies.* London: Routledge.

Griffin, D. R. (1992). *Animal Minds.* Chicago: University of Chicago Press.

Heisenberg, W. (1949). *The Physical Principles of the Quantum Theory.* New York: Dover.

Hudson, L. (1972). *The Cult of the Fact.* New York: Harper & Row.

Krampen, M. (1991). *Children's Drawings: Iconic Coding of the Environment.* New York: Plenum.

Lakoff, G. & Johnson, M. (1980). *Metaphors We Live By.* Chicago: University of Chicago Press.

McNeill, D. (1992). *Hand and Mind: What Gestures Reveal about Thought.* Chicago: University of Chicago Press.

Melzack, R. (1972). The Perception of Pain. In: R. F. Thompson (ed.), *Physiological Psychology*, pp. 223-231. San Francisco: Freeman.

Melzack, R. (1988). Pain. In: J. Kuper (ed.), *A Lexicon of Psychology, Psychiatry and Psychoanalysis*, pp. 288-291. London: Routledge.

Peirce, C. S. (1958). *Collected Papers.* Cambridge, Mass.: Harvard University Press.

Popper, K. and Eccles, J. (1977). *The Self and the Brain.* Berlin: Springer.

Saussure, F. de (1916/1966). *Course in General Linguistics.* Paris: Payot.

Schmandt-Besserat, D. (1978). The Earliest Precursor of Writing. *Scientific American* 238: 50-59.

Schmandt-Besserat, D. (1989). Two Precursors of Writing: Plain and Complex Tokens. In: W. M. Senner (ed.), *The Origins of Writing*, pp. 27-40. Lincoln: University of Nebraska Press.

Schmandt-Besserat, D. (1992). *Before Writing*, 2 vols. Austin: University of Texas Press.

Sontag, S. (1978). *Illness as Metaphor.* New York: Farrar, Straus & Giroux.

Sontag, S. (1989). *AIDS and Its Metaphors.* New York: Farrar, Straus & Giroux.

Uexküll, J. von (1909). *Umwelt und Innenwelt der Tiere.* Berlin: Springer.

Verene, D. P. (1981). *Vico's Science of Imagination.* Ithaca: Cornell University Press.

THE SIGNIFYING BODY!

Preliminary Remarks

It is now believed by some psychologists that we communicate over two-thirds of our ideas and feelings with the body. It is estimated that humans can produce up to 700,000 physical signs, of which 1,000 are different bodily postures, 5,000 are hand gestures and 250,000 are facial expressions. Consider, as well, the following facts (Axtell 1991: 9-16):

- In an elevator people usually lean against the walls of the elevator if several people are on board, and everyone invariably turns around and faces the door.

- According to some psychologists men and women unconsciously shrug their shoulders when they find each other attractive.

- In 1979, the psychologist Desmond Morris, together with several of his associates at Oxford University, examined 20 gestures in 40 different areas of Europe. The research team found some rather fascinating things. For instance, they discovered that many of the gestures had several meanings, depending on culture. A tap on the side of the head can indicate completely opposite things—"stupidity" or "intelligence"—according to cultural context. Morris and company also found that most of the gestural signifiers were used in many countries.

To a semiotician all this comes as no surprise. The expressions we make with our faces, the postures we assume, the gestures we make, how close we stand to each other, etc. are all part of signifying behavior. This chapter will look at bodily semiosis. Specifically, it will look at facial expressions, bodily posture and image, gesture and dancing. In the body/mind/culture nexus of semiosis, the body can function on its own as a signifier whose connection to a signified can be iconic, indexical or symbolic. It is hardly a "neutral" biological structure. Body parts, fluids, shapes, etc. all have connotations that we constantly use to generate meaningful and meaning-making texts. The word *text*, as it is used in this book, means something very specific. It is literally, a "putting together" of signifiers to produce a message, consciously or unconsciously, osmotically or mimetically. The text can be either verbal or nonverbal. In order for the text to signify or to be decoded, one must know the code to which the signifiers in the text belong. If one listens to a verbal language that one does not know, all one hears are "disembodied signifiers"— sounds, intonations, etc. that we intuitively know cohere into verbal texts that carry some intended meaning, but to which we have no access. The "embodiment" of the verbal signifiers occurs only when we come to know the language code to which they belong. This applies as well to all nonverbal texts, like clothing, bodily movements, gestures, and the like. Texts are semiotic reflexes of both individual and communal experiences. When these are understood or "appreciated" they take on meaning or signification. Musical performances, stage plays, common discourse exchanges, dance styles, religious rites, ceremonies, etc. are the texts that we regularly make, as individuals or groups, both to make meaning of the world and to make meaning within it. The word *context*, as its name clearly implies, is literally the surrounding, or "*con*-taining" environment in which a text is encoded and decoded.

Many of the social actions and routines that we commonly perform can also be thought of as texts, or "scripts," as cognitive scientists designate them. Script theory, especially as developed by Roger Schank (e.g. 1984), refers essentially to the knowledge structures used in typical social situations. These are dependent upon socio-semiosic texts or formats that equip us with the capacity to negotiate social actions successfully. The connection between social actions and textuality or scripting is implied in the following statement by Schank (1984: 125):

> When we read a story, we try to evaluate the reasoning
> processes of the main character. We try to determine why
> he does what he does and what he will do next. We
> examine what we would do in a similar situation, and we
> try to make the same connections that the main character
> seems to be making. We ask ourselves, *What is he trying*

to do? What's his plan? Why did he do what he just did?
Any understanding system has to be able to decipher the
reasoning processes that actors in stories go through....
Sometimes people achieve their goals by resorting to a
script. When a script is unavailable, that is, when the
situation is in some way novel, people are able to make up
new plans.

Facial Semiosis

To enhance bodily image, or the bodily text we present to others, we resort
typically to various forms of decoration or concealment. Young adolescents,
for instance, characteristically attempt to hide, camouflage or masquerade
facial blemishes and flaws such as pimples and oversized organs (noses and
ears). The wearing of eyeglasses is considered to be a detraction from a so-
called "cool" appearance during adolescence. Only "dorks" and "losers" wear
them, as the teenage parlance goes. In the case of female adolescents, facial
hairs are considered to be particularly detrimental to appearance; male teens,
on the other hand, perceive beard growth as enhancing their masculine
coolness. On the opposite side, some youth subcultures attempt to shatter
such models (e.g. punks) by decorating their body intentionally in "ugly" ways,
by letting facial hair grow, by highlighting their intended "ugly" features
through cosmetic emphasis, and so on. In semiotic terms, it can be said that
their bodily texts are often designed to be in paradigmatic opposition to the
mainstream form of adolescent coolness.

Underlying body image and especially the presentation of the face is, of
course, the emergence of sexual feelings. "Making out" (engaging in sexual
activity), in the jargon of teenagers, is achievable only by those who fit the
required models of bodily and facial attractiveness. This seems to imply that
in our society sexuality is especially susceptible to cultural shaping and to the
bodily texts that it generates.

Actually, the enhancement of the face, literally its "making up" for
presentation, is as old as civilization itself. The cosmetic "make-up" that we
use today has a long and unbroken connection with ritualistic fertility behavior.
It has a basis in sexuality: selecting colors, facial designs, and enhancements
of facial features are all latent sexual signifiers in the facial text. Red lipstick
appears to connote the redness associated with female genitalia; the wearing
of mustaches by males can be easily seen to connote pubic hairs; and the list
could go on and on. The point to be made here is that the human face is hardly

neutral semiotically. It is constantly being "made up" to convey messages ensconced in basic (factual) tendencies. As Helen Fisher (1992: 272-273) has aptly remarked, the sexually-constructed facial text is not a phenomenon restricted to modern humans. It probably was, as archeological evidence now seems to suggest, a characteristic feature of human artifactual semiosis that goes right back to our Cro-Magnon ancestors. It seems that they too spent hours decorating themselves, plaiting their hair, donning garlands of flowers in order to smell sweet, wearing bracelets and pendants, and decorating their tunics and leggings with fur, feathers, beads and red and yellow ocher. They also apparently strutted, preened and showed off for one another around the fire's glow. So, if Fisher is right, the contemporary cosmetic and clothing fashion industries would seem to be linked to innate biological tendencies in the human organism that transcend time and culture. They are artifactual and culturally-institutionalized reflexes of basic factual instincts, drives and feelings.

The face is also an osmotic and mimetic carrier of cognitive and feeling states. The work of Paul Ekman (e.g. Ekman 1985 and 1988) is highly relevant and useful to the topic at hand. In 1963 Ekman established the Human Interaction Laboratory in the Department of Psychiatry at the University of California at San Francisco. He was joined by Wallace V. Friesen in 1965 and Maureen O'Sullivan in 1974. The motivation behind Ekman's laboratory was the study of facial expression and bodily movement. Over the years, Ekman and his team have been able to link specific facial actions to different aspects of emotion. They have shown that the facial text can be broken down into its components: eyebrow position, eye shape, mouth shape, nostril size, etc. which in various combinations determine the expression of the face. It is, indeed, possible to write a "grammar" of the face which shows less cross-cultural variation than do language grammars. The following four iconic sketches of facial expressions show how easily it is to interpret them:

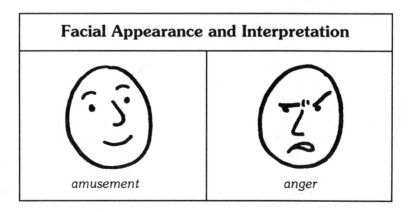

Facial Appearance and Interpretation

amusement   *anger*

surprise   *sadness*

Eye contact is particularly interesting as a signifying text. The occasion and length of time involved in making eye contact with someone are bearers of meaning. Staring can be interpreted as a challenge; "making eyes" at someone will be normally interpreted as flirtation; making eye contact early or late during a verbal exchange will indicate the kind of relationship one wishes to have with the interlocutor. We also detect eye movements unconsciously and react to them in appropriate ways. The pupil, for instance, becomes small during excited states, and we unconsciously pick this up. Narrow eyelids, on the other hand, communicate pensiveness. The eyebrows coming nearer also communicate thoughtfulness; when they rise they convey surprise. It should be noted, however, that although there are many universal aspects to facial semiosis, there is also much cultural variation involved in presenting the face. Eye contact texts, for instance, vary widely from culture to culture. Southern Europeans will tend to look more into each other's eyes during conversation than do North Americans.

Facial texts are typically constructed indexically and symbolically. But since we can also use the face to mimic something or someone, then they can be made to be iconic signs as well. Moreover, they can co-occur with other codes—e.g. language and gesture—or independently. The use of the face (consciously or unconsciously) as a conveyor of affective states is a phenomenon that cuts across all species. Many species of animals can combine different elements of facial expression in different ways so as to create a whole repertory of facial texts, each corresponding to a specific mood. All animals are predisposed by biology to use the ears, the eyes and the mouth to convey their inner states. Dogs, for example, prick their ears during an alert mode; lynxes twitch them in conflictual or agitated modes; and cats flatten them when they are in the protective mode. Eyes can be fixated to stare during an alert mode or to frown during a protective mode. Mouths can be tightened, made to gape and to pout in order to convey respectively states of hostility, aggression and amicability.

An interesting kind of facial expression documented by animal ethologists is the so-called *flehmen mouth*. This is a peculiar kind of facial expression shown by many mammals that follows intense sniffing, especially of a sexual nature. The head is tilted up as the neck stretches forward, and the top lip is curled upwards, exposing the upper teeth and sometimes even the upper gums. The mouth is slightly open and the animal appears to be momentarily lost in a kind of trance. The impression given is that the animal is inhaling deeply and enjoying the fragrance in the air.

As the example of the flehmen mouth shows, the mouth is a particularly versatile signifier. To see how this is so, look at the following two "circles" which are meant to represent the face iconically. These utilize two dots for "eyes", an angle figure for the "nose" and a straight line for the "mouth":

In this form, the two "faces" show no emotion. To convey happiness, all one has to do is to curve the line figure upwards in a U form; to show sadness— a paradigmatic opposite—all one has to do is to draw the reverse shape, an inverted U:

The "raising" or "lowering" of the mouth is, in fact, an act of semiosis intersecting with a natural biological tendency. All primate species are predisposed to display such features of facial expression in response to various stimuli or thoughts.

It is interesting to note that the relevant literature in psychology suggests that there are paradigmatic differences in male and female facial semiosis. In North America the documented gender-coded differences include:

Males	Females
They tend to avoid eye contact.	They are much more likely to make eye contact.
They tend to cock their head to the side and look at their interlocutors from an angle.	They tend to look directly at the other person.
They tend to stare more.	They stare much less.
They tend to smile less, and grin more.	They tend to smile more often, especially in the presence of males.
They are more inclined to "make faces" for comical effects.	They are more likely to keep their facial expressions composed.
They are conscious of detrimental facial aberrations such as acne, but less inclined to camouflage them.	They are more inclined to camouflage facial imperfections.

No doubt such paradigmatic contrasts are acquired in part because of biological differences between males and females, but in much larger part because of the osmotic acquisition of gender models in cultural context. Facial modeling, of course, can also be mimetic. This is what happens when we model our facial appearances after specific "heroes" in our culture, such as movie stars, television personalities, and the like.

Facial appearance is one of the primary means we use to enhance physical attractiveness. The psychological research has shown rather conclusively that judgments about social desirability are made first on the basis of facial appearance. No wonder, then, that we spend so much time preparing our faces for presentation. Of primary importance to facial presentation is hairstyle, which is meant to enhance the attractiveness of the face. We model our hairstyles after media prototypes or in accordance with context-specific grooming codes.

It is interesting to note, parenthetically, that specific individuals are responsive sexually to certain particular kinds of faces and not to others from puberty onwards. One explanation as to why such preferences surface at puberty is perhaps the presence of what some psychologists call "lovemaps" in the mind. These are mental images which determine the specific kinds of features—body, facial, etc.—that will evoke sexual arousal and love moods (such as infatuation) in an individual. Lovemaps are developed during childhood in response to various environmental experiences and influences. At adolescence, they unconsciously generate an image of what the ideal "sweetheart" should be like, becoming quite specific as to details of the physiognomy, build, race, and color of the ideal lover, as well as to his or her general demeanor.

Bodily Semiosis

Imagine the following scene. You are in an elevator with a few other people, all strangers to each other. There is silence in the enclosed moving cubicle. Perhaps you are looking down at the floor or at your watch, in order not to make eye contact with any of the others. All of a sudden your stomach sends out one of those uncontrollable "growls" that result from hunger, digestion or some other bodily process. What will your reaction be? If you are like others in North America, you will probably feel some embarrassment or unease, even if you know that you have no control over a sound manufactured naturally by your body. So, as a socially redeeming strategy you might either excuse yourself, make an ironic or facetious statement about the sound, attempt to hide it by making some other kind of "acceptable" noise, like clearing your throat, or ignore it completely as if it hadn't occurred.

Think, moreover, about other sounds made by the body—sneezing, coughing, burping, etc. Do they send out messages? Of course they do. And are we responsive to them in culturally-specific ways? Of course we are. The body is a powerful signifier. Its various parts, secretions and excretions invariably take on signification. We hide our genitals; animals do not. We attend performances—e.g. strip teases, "topless" dancing, etc.—when we desire to see the sexually-connotative parts of the human body that are normally hidden from view. We react strongly to bodily odors, imperfections, and size. We seem to be always preoccupied with "getting into shape." Being short or tall carries its own particular system of connotations. And the list could go on and on.

Consider, as well, the effects that touching has upon each one of us. Whom we touch, where we touch him or her, and when we touch him or her all convey a great amount of information about our relationship to him or her. How would you react if a stranger of the opposite sex were to touch you? What areas of your body would you consider to be more "touchable," which less touchable and which not at all? And what about bodily posture and orientation? Is it random, or does the way in which we angle ourselves to others send out messages about our relationships to them? Clearly, as you start to reflect upon questions such as these, you start to become consciously aware of the nature and power of the body as a signifying text. The study of bodily semiosis is known more technically as kin*esics*.

The body is indeed a powerful signifier. Consider, for instance, the sexual connotations that body parts have. Are they universal? It would seem, as Helen Colton in her book *The Gift of Touch* (1983) graphically describes, that sexuality turns out to be culture-specific. The situation she puts forward is as follows: Let us say you come upon a strange woman in her bath. What would her reaction be? According to Colton, it depends:

- An Islamic woman would probably cover her face.

- A Laotian woman would cover her breasts.

- A Chinese woman would hide her feet.

- A Sumatran woman would conceal her knees.

- A Samoan woman would cover her navel.

- A Western woman would cover her breasts with one arm and her genital area with the other hand.

Clearly, as Colton's examples reveal, the specific bodily parts that are perceived to be sexual or prurient differ widely from culture to culture. Michel Foucault argued—in fact, and correctly in my view—that sexuality is dependent upon cultural history and tradition (see Miller 1993). "Sins of the flesh" are, as a matter fact, a major concern of many cultures and religions. The Puritans of England saw sex as a kind of "necessary evil." "Temptation" is interpreted by many puritanical people in exclusively sexual terms. Television evangelists are continually attacking our "lack of morals" and the "scourge of sexual sins," even when they seem to be actively engaged in sexual activities behind the scenes, as was made obvious a few years back by the widely-publicized case of TV evangelist Jimmy Swaggart. On the other hand, many so-called "hedonistic" rites and practices exalt and glorify the same kinds of sexual activities. Obviously, what is "pornographic" or "obscene" behavior to some, is "natural" or "desirable" behavior to others. While sex and sexual urges belong to the universal world of biological factuality; sexuality is clearly a culturally-defined, artifactual state of mind. The body is indeed a powerful signifying text that we constantly prepare for others. It is one of the primary means at our disposal for making messages and meanings.

The first sign that body image is perceived to constitute a signifying text occurs when the child starts to become preoccupied at puberty with body size—slim vs. fat, tall vs. short, etc. The association of slim with attractiveness, for instance, is formed in part from media models (movies, ads, television, etc.). It is, in other words, partly a result of media mimesis. But in larger part it is due to social osmosis. In our culture we tend to perceive "fatness" in a negative light. Body size is often an issue of high moral, social and aesthetic value. All socioeconomic classes are highly affected by such body symbolism.

The *presentation* of the body, to use the term made popular by Erving Goffman (1959), is a powerful mode of social interaction. The inability to present a socially-acceptable body image can have rather dire consequences. The increase among female teenagers, for instance, in eating disorders such as anorexia nervosa and bulimia since the fifties is frightening. The presentation of Self, as Goffman calls it, has become an enormously problematic mode of social behavior indeed within our culture. Our concern over virtually every facet of bodily *persona* and semiosis—be it hairstyle, body size, etc.— reveals that the body has enormous value as personal statement, determining how we define ourselves and how the community defines us. Our body is as much symbol as substance. In contemporary Western society, the slim and lean look is a prerequisite for attractiveness for both males and females. The margin of flexibility from any idealized thinness model is larger for males than it is for females; but males must additionally strive to develop a muscular look.

In the case of females, the size of the breasts also becomes a problem in the building of body image. Adolescent girls are highly conscious of their breasts as being either too big or too small. The same kind of sensitivity is felt by male teenagers *vis-à-vis* penis size, with the general principle being "the bigger, the more masculine." This sensitivity to idealized body prototypes causes adolescents to become constantly discontented with their bodily appearance.

In the teenage subculture, smoking takes on great importance as bodily behavior. It constitutes a socially-symbolic act which can be used to illustrate how bodily semiosis manifests itself in a specific social context. As a signifying text it can be seen to provide valuable insights into the relationship between a code—smoking behavior—and the particular mindset of the teenager.

The structuring of smoking routines into discrete bodily movements and postures is determined by gender-coded perceptions of coolness. The teenager most likely to smoke is the one who desires to enhance his or her attractiveness to peers. To document the features of the smoking code, I brought together a team of five field workers at the University of Toronto in 1989. For two years each member was assigned to several high schools within Metropolitan Toronto. At key times during the day, when teenagers would typically mingle outside the school building to confabulate and engage in socially-meaningful actions, a field worker would sit in his or her car at a suitable distance from the group, recording the various features of the smoking scene and performance (bodily movements, postures, etc.). It is, of course, during such periods in the school day that teenagers group together to smoke. A feature grid was drawn up for each field-worker to fill-out during the observation periods. The grid contained a series of categories relating to specific bodily features. Two grids with these same features were used—one for males and one for females. The field workers were instructed to fill out each feature slot with their observations, focusing on either a male or a female subject per observation period. Over the two years of the project one hundred observation grids were filled out—50 for males and 50 for females—and several photographs taken. The observations of the field workers were then conflated into general descriptive statements that reflected the most fre-quently-recorded bodily patterns or schemas. A summary of the findings follows (see Danesi 1993 for a complete analysis).

It was found that females typically utilized a slow, deliberate movement to take the cigarette out of its package and to insert it into their mouths; males, on the other hand, tended to employ more abrupt, shorter-lasting movements, both to take the cigarette out of its package and to insert it into their mouths. The females used the thumb and the middle finger to remove the cigarette from its package, but changed to the index and middle fingers to insert it into the mouth in a slow, flowing motion. Males, on the other hand, used the thumb and middle finger both to take out the cigarette and to insert it into the mouth in an brusque, snappy movement. The only difference between females and males in lighting up the cigarette showed up in the rate of movement: the females tended to strike a match or lighter and to bring the flame towards the cigarette in a leisurely, drawn-out way, whereas males performed these same procedures with terse movements.

Females typically held the cigarette between the index and middle finger, guiding the cigarette to the lips in a slow, swooping, deliberate, quasi-circular arm movement. The cigarette was normally inserted into the middle of the mouth. When the cigarette was held between the fingers, females also typically flicked the ashes with the index finger, while holding the cigarette between the thumb and middle fingers. When not flicking, the females kept the hand holding the cigarette down by the side of the body. Males, on the other hand, held the cigarette between the thumb and middle finger, guiding it to the lips in a sharp, direct (short-arc) movement, inserting the cigarette to the side of the mouth (to the left or right in an asymmetrical fashion to the individual's handedness). Males either flicked their ashes in a way that was similar to the female flicking procedure (with the cigarette held between the thumb and middle finger while the index finger flicked the ashes), or, more typically, they shook their hand to force the excess ashes to fall down to the ground.

It was found that females normally took a longer time to inhale, drawing in the air through the nostrils slowly and gradually, then holding the smoke in the mouth for a relatively protracted period (rarely inhaling it down into the lungs), and finally exhaling it in an upward direction with the head tilted slightly back, often swinging or holding their hair back. Males, on the other hand, inhaled abruptly, holding the smoke in the mouth for a relatively short period (inhaling it down into the lungs more often than the females), and exhaling it in a downward direction (with the head slightly bent).

The females typically kept one leg back and one slightly ahead—their bodily weight being placed on the back leg. The head remained angled slightly to the side and looking upward with a frequent jerking motion of the hair (generally shoulder-length) so that it could be made to sway just before the insertion of the cigarette into the mouth. Males, on the other hand, kept both legs slightly apart—comparable to a "horseback" or "piggy-back" posture. They kept their heads taut and looking straight ahead during puffing motions.

Finally, it was found that females typically dropped the cigarette butt and stamped it out with a foot. Males, on the other hand, placed the butt on the thumb and hurled it away from them with the middle finger. They rarely stamped out the cigarette with their feet.

The picture that emerges from the above portrayals is that cigarette smoking in adolescence constitutes a gender-coded bodily text whose underlying message is sexual coolness. As a text, therefore, smoking is coherent, regular, predictable and anchored in socially-meaningful contexts (peer interaction). And, indeed, when asked why they smoke, teenagers typically give answers such as "Because the rest of my group smokes;" "It makes me look big;" "To feel sophisticated;" etc.

Above all else, the smoking text is a means by which perceptions of masculinity and femininity are conveyed through bodily semiosis. The slow, circular movements of the arm in females are enactments of bodily schemas that our cultural perceives as "feminine." The abrupt movements employed by the male teenagers, on the other hand, are performances of bodily schemas which are perceived as "masculine" by our culture. These schemas are, of course, reinforced by media images. The female and male smoking texts show a paradigmatic structure that reflects differences in perceptions of gender: e.g. the female exhales the smoke in an upward direction, the male in a downward direction; the female stands with one foot forward and one back (with the weight on the back foot), the male stands, "cowboy-style," with the legs apart; the female's arm movements are slow and sultry, the male's are abrupt and rough; the female holds the cigarette in a tantalizing manner between the index and middle fingers, the male holds it in a stiff and rugged way between the thumb and middle finger, or else makes it dangle on the side.

The female's bodily schemas are, in a nutshell, portrayals of feminine sexuality (sensuality, voluptuousness, sultriness, etc.); the male's bodily schemas are reflexes of masculine sexuality (toughness, roughness, coarseness, etc.). When the smoking text is performed in typical gatherings of teenage cliques, it can be said to constitute a kind of unconscious mating ritual that unfolds through bodily schemas that reflect culturally-coded perceptions of masculinity and femininity. During such performances, the cigarette seems to take on a fetishistic quality, with rather obvious phallic connotations. It becomes a sexual-erotic signifier that is manipulated unconsciously in paradigmatically complementary ways according to the sex of the teenager.

Like smoking texts performed in groups, so-called "hanging out" is a modern bodily-based phenomenon tied to courtship displays, not unlike those that characterize many other species. There are many types of specific bodily displays—leaping, dancing, twisting, turning, etc.—that animals perform at the start of the breeding season. Hanging out is a form of sexual display of contemporary youths. It is a controlled form of bodily movement, character-ized by an intense slackness and sleekness. Indeed, the term "hanging out" is an appropriate metaphor to describe the position of the arms left to hang or dangle on the sides of the body, the slackening of all bodily postures, and the conveyance of total bodily nonchalance, composure, indifference and insouciance.

In hanging out situations, the males try occasionally to look "tough" through aggressive posturing when other male peers or rivals approach the congregation. This toughness posture is put on to reinforce perceptions of masculinity. Its symbolism involves menacing facial expressions and language (with a profusion of swear words). Courtship displays in all species may look menacing or comical to outsiders, but to the species concerned they are a crucial communication device at a key stage in the enactment of reproductive urges. The modern shopping mall provides a particularly appropriate ambiance for hanging out performances. It provides the stage props (food outlets, smoking areas, etc.) and personages (other teens, adult spectators, etc.) that give emphasis and social meaning to them. No wonder, then, that adolescents are seen constantly at malls and shopping plazas, where they are rarely there to buy merchandise, but rather to congregate and enact courtship performances.

Gesture

Gesture can be defined simply as bodily semiosis involving the hands, arms and to a lesser extent, the head. Gestures constitute codes that can be used independently of speech. The more appropriate term used when gesture accompanies speech is *gesticulation*. Gestural codes include the many sign languages used in communities of the hearing-impaired, alternate sign languages used by religious groups during periods of imposed silence or for various ritualistic practices, the hand signals used to control traffic, the hand and arm movements used to conduct an orchestra and so on.

For many semioticians and linguists, gesture is considered a more fundamental form of semiosis and communication than verbal language. A pragmatic, anecdotal "confirmation" of this viewpoint can be ascertained when one doesn't speak the language of the people of a country one is visiting. In order to communicate with the people on the street, in a hotel, in a store, etc., one instinctively resorts to gesture and bodily semiosis in order to get a message across and to negotiate meaning. For example, if one were to describe an automobile to someone by means of gesture, one would instinctively use the hands to iconically portray a steering wheel and the motion used to steer a car, accompanying this gesture, perhaps, with an imitative sound of a motor. This anecdotal scenario not only suggests that gesture is a more fundamental mode of signification and communication, but also that its essentially iconic nature makes it a much more universal, and less culture-dependent, mode of message and meaning making.

Gesture spans the entire range of semiosis, from indexicality to symbolism. Pointing, for instance, seems to be a trans-cultural tendency in the human species. While the use of the index finger is the most common modality involved in pointing, the use of any body part that can be moved directionally (lips, nose, tongue, etc.) can be used to point out referents in the immediate environment, to indicate directions, etc. Pointing obviously constitutes a deictic/indexical code. Gestures can also be used iconically to characterize the features of some referent. For example, to describe some round object, one would tend to use both hands together moving in opposite—clockwise (the right hand) and counter-clockwise (the left hand)—directions. This simple example illustrates how gesture is fundamentally a kind of iconic "drawing" code which, of course, leaves no "traces," unless the characterizing manual movements are transferred by some drawing instrument onto some surface. Gestures can also be of a symbolic nature. In such cases, they are culture-specific. Most cultures agree upon the form and contents of gestural codes involved in signaling such referents as "greeting," "assent," "negation," "halting," etc. So-called "obscene gestures" are also culture-specific, although many of these can be deciphered at an iconic level.

Perhaps the greatest interest in gesture has been shown by anthropologists and linguists researching the origins of language and communication in the human species. Gestural theories posit that the use of the body, and especially of the hands, to refer to objects, beings, and events in the environment was the proto-form of communication and language. In this kind of "primal scene," it is easy to imagine preverbal hominids gesturing to attract attention, pointing out a particular object with a motion of the hand, imitating the shapes of things with hand gestures, etc. Eventually, by associating a gesture with the referent repeatedly these hominids extended it to situations in which the referent was not present. This would have constituted, therefore, the first act of representation. The transfer of this form of representation to the subsequently dominant audio-oral channel is explained in terms of an imitation and substitution process by which the gestural signs are transferred osmotically to the vocal apparatus.

The version of gesture theory that has become a classic "just so" story, as Rudyard Kipling called all attempts to explain the origins of things, was formulated by the French philosopher Jean-Jacques Rousseau (1712-1778) in the middle part of the eighteenth century. Rousseau became intrigued by the question of the origin of language while seeking to understand what he called the "noble savage." Rousseau claimed that the "cries of nature" that our early ancestors must have shared with the animals, and the gestures that they must have used simultaneously, led to the invention of audio-oral language. He explained the evolutionary transition as follows: When the accompanying gestures proved to be too cumbersome, their corresponding cries were there to replace them completely.

A while later, Richard Paget (1930) attempted to fill in the obvious evolutionary gap that Rousseau had left by putting forward the idea that manual gestures were copied unconsciously by positions and movements of the lips and tongue. The repeated association of gestures with vocal movements led eventually to the replacement of the former by the latter. So, for Paget human speech arose out of an unconscious mimetic gesture language made by the limbs as a whole, including the tongue and lips, which eventually became specialized in gestures of the organs of articulation, due perhaps to the fact that the hands were becoming continually occupied with the use of tools. The gestures of the organs of articulation were recognized by someone else because he or she unconsciously reproduced in the mind the actual gesture which had produced the sound.

From all the available evidence, and from common experience with communication, it would seem indeed that gesture is a more fundamental signifying system than is vocal language. As already mentioned, even in modern humans gesture can be seen to take precedence over speech in both language ontogenesis and in situations where vocal communication is impossible. Children invariably develop some form of gestural communication before audio-oral speech; and gesturing is the communicative mode we instinctively resort to with a speaker of a different language.

It is obvious that, apart from modern uses of symbolic gestural codes, gesture is tied fundamentally to iconicity. This process unfolds through a mimetic movement of the limbs, especially the hands, in order to represent some referent by resemblance. The ability to use the hands—the dominant limbs in the human species, given their physiological structure for grasping and pointing—was made possible by the fact that the first hominids walked upright (bipedalism). The liberation of the hands from the requirements of locomotion not only allowed early humans to make tools and to use fire deliberately, but also to use their hands for signing. The first "speakers" were really "hand signers". The capacity to point out and locate beings, objects, and events in the immediate environment, and to convey their existence and location to others, conferred upon our earliest ancestors a new and powerful control over their environment and over their own lives.

It was Charles Darwin (1872) who established the phylogenetic significance of gesture as a complex mode of communication expressing a broad range of iconic thoughts, from touching movements to affect displays. Gesture allowed the first signers to go beyond the indication of beings, objects, and events in the immediate environment to represent internal states and intentions: e.g. clenching could have conveyed anger; the opening of the hand could have communicated prohibition; and so on.

The form of representation that developed out of gesture is pictorial representation. The first inscriptions, cave drawings and other kinds of pictographic signs were the end result of the use of the hands to represent iconic thought. Pictorial representation is the most abstract form of iconic expression. The imitative hand movements used to portray shapes, for instance, were probably transferred to a cave wall or to an object by means of some sharp cutting tool. These portrayals constitute humanity's first genuine works of art.

The research literature on gesture is revealing and pertinent to the present discussion. It has shown, for instance, that children invariably pass through an initial stage of indexicality and gesture before they develop vocal language. Lieberman (1984: 87) points out that gestural communication in children seems to follow from the models of indication that they pick up from their environment. These are used for practical purposes (e.g. pointing to something desired) and are probably reinforced by osmosis with adult gesture. It is intriguing to note that, although vocal language eventually becomes the dominant form of communication, the gestural modality does not vanish completely. It remains a functional subsystem of human language that can always be utilized as a more generic form of communication when an interaction is otherwise impossible. As already mentioned, this happens typically when two interlocutors speak different languages. And, of course, in individuals with impaired vocal organs, gesture constitutes the only possible mode of communication. All such considerations suggest that iconicity is a fundamental force in symbol creation.

The intriguing work of McNeill (1992), moreover, has revealed that metaphors about language—called "conduit" metaphors—are typically accompanied by gestures which iconically depict the vehicles of these metaphors (the B in A is B). For example, when we say something like "Lay it out on the table," "Where did you get that idea?", etc. we tend to use an accompanying gesture consisting of the hand curved, up high in front of the face, with the fingers and thumb forward and apart, making the speaker appear to be holding onto something. With sentences such as "I gave him that idea," "It's hard to get that idea across," etc. the accompanying gesture consists of both hands extended, moving downward, making the speaker appear to be presenting an object to the other person along a conduit. And with utterances such as "Your words are full of meaning," "I can't get these ideas into words," etc. the accompanying gesture consists of both hands forming a cup, with the fingers curled and palms up, to show two containers.

McNeill's work gives us some idea of how the gestural-iconic modality intersects with the verbal one in normal discourse. As Frutiger (1989: 112) has put it, it would seem to be the case that accompanying gestures reveal an inner need to support what one is saying orally: "If on a beach, for example, we can hardly resist drawing with the finger on the smooth surface of the sand as a means of clarifying what we are talking about."

Dancing

Dancing is common to all peoples and cultures. As such, it is a signifying bodily text whose construction can range all the way from spontaneous movements in response to natural rhythms to "high art" dancing as in classical ballet. It can be said that the dancing texts which cultures commonly create and employ for various social reasons are artifactual transformations of factual bodily tendencies and needs.

It is virtually impossible to remain motionless for any protracted period of time. Indeed, when we are "forced" to do so, our body reacts against it. Imagine being at, say, a concert hall during the performance of a lengthy slow movement of a piano sonata. After a little while, it is almost impossible to keep yourself perfectly still or not to cough or make some other kind of sound. The need for almost constant movement during our waking hours is probably a residual tendency tied to an ancient survival mechanism—it is harder to attack moving prey! At the level of factuality, therefore, bodily movements once enhanced our biological survivability. It is when we organized at some point in time our bodily movements into patterned ones at the artifactual level that *dance* emerged as a signifying text, reenacting at this new level of mind and culture our basic bodily tendencies and needs. Indeed, with this model of semiosis, *art* of any type and modality (corporeal, visual, verbal, musical, etc.) can be thought of as an artifactual construction or transformation that converts factual (deep-level) sense and feeling structures into signifying cultural texts. Through these texts we attempt to extract meaning about life, ourselves and about the universe we inhabit. In many ways, art "brings us back down to our original or primordial feeling-states," so to speak. These are universal and beyond even the artifactual forms that contain the artistic text. This is the paradox, and power, of great art. Above all else, art is a form of semiosis that involves sense and feeling. It is, therefore, our most powerful means of message and meaning making.

At the artifactual level, dancing is closely linked to all forms of symbolic behavior. Religious rituals, ceremonies of all kinds (e.g. weddings), sexual mating rituals, etc. are normally accompanied, and literally "embodied," in dance texts of all kinds. People frequent discos, take dance lessons and enroll their children in ballet school because they feel that dance is closely linked with something basic. Dance *makes* meaning in ways that only humans know how. It can therefore be devised as art, work, ceremony, ritual, entertainment or a combination of any of these.

As an example of the signifying power of dance, consider the increase in blatant carnality in rock music, which often goes unnoticed by adolescents who acquire their musical preferences osmotically and therefore unconsciously. A classic example is Michael Jackson's 1983 *Thriller* album and rock video which sold some 22 million copies worldwide. The song *Beat It* from the album shows a group of young males—aggressive and angry—looking to rumble. As the fight begins, Michael Jackson intervenes and bursts into the catchy and powerfully rhythmic *Beat It*. Shortly after its release approximately 300 university students were asked how many times they had listened to the song. The 51% who had listened to it over 50 times were then asked if they knew what "beat it" means—it is, of course, a colloquial slang expression for male masturbation. Half of the aficionados did not know the meaning of the expression; the remainder attempted to rationalize the title—"the music beat," "to beat up someone," etc. The survey was repeated several times with the same results. The theme of masturbation simply escaped the conscious awareness of the listeners. The video even showed the dancers passing their right hands across their genital areas in a jerking, masturbatory motion. Incidentally, when told about the true meaning of the song, the informants invariably expressed disgust. The moral of this story is that people rarely notice the sexuality inherent in the rock music they listen and dance to. They simply respond to it osmotically.

Since its inception as a subculture mode of musical expression in the mid fifties, rock has always been associated with corporeality. Rock puts the body on display, to others and to oneself. Rock touches, fragments, multiplies and propels the bodies of its fans. The shift from radio to television as a primary source for establishing rock music trends occurred on August 1, 1981 when MTV—"Music Television"—was founded as a 24-hour all-music television network on US cable television. Music video programming has now become a major source for establishing musical and dance styles. MTV transmits images of immediacy, urgency, quickness, surrealism and above all else, coolness. The MTV look has become a ubiquitous one. It has given birth to a bodily language suited for communicating not complicated ideas but cool attitudes. This new vernacular constitutes a means aimed at grabbing the attention of a generation of viewers with reduced attention spans. MTV is performance without drama or narration. It is all pose and posture. But it is rather significant that MTV has itself fallen prey to the reduced attention spans it was designed to captivate. By early 1990, MTV had become all too familiar and boring. Teen generations and attitudes change rapidly, more rapidly than ever before. Keeping the new waves of teen viewers entertained homogeneously has become a huge problem even for those who intentionally attempt to shape teen attitudes to their own ways.

Concluding Remarks

The theme of this chapter has been that the body and the face are signifying texts. The universal, cross-cultural bodily reactions and facial expressions that are programmed into us by nature are being constantly converted into signifying texts at the artifactual level of mind and culture. Additionally, at the level of artifactual semiosis, many of these texts take on symbolic meaning. We use the body and the face constantly to signify and communicate intentions, roles, impressions, needs, etc. Gesture in particular constitutes a code, or more accurately, a set of codes that can represent the world indexically, iconically and symbolically. Indeed, in order to represent the world and to communicate effectively, the body and the face are all we really need. In hearing-impaired individuals, as a matter of fact, bodily semiosis is the primary means employed to communicate with others, even though such individuals also have access to the verbal codes of their cultures through writing. To unlock bodily semiosis is to unlock the essence of message and meaning-making in the human species.

SUGGESTIONS FOR FURTHER READING

Argyle, M. (1988). *Bodily Communication*. New York: Methuen.

Axtell, R. E. (1991). *Gestures*. New York: John Wiley.

Birdwhistell, R. (1970). *Kinesics and Context: Essays on Body Motion Communication*. Harmondsworth: Penguin.

Bremer, J. and Roodenburg, H. (eds.). (1991). *A Cultural History of Gesture*. Ithaca: Cornell University Press.

Colton, H. (1983). *The Gift of Touch*. New York: Putnam.

Danesi, M. (1993). Smoking Behavior among Adolescents as Signifying Osmosis. *Semiotica* 96: 123-159.

Darwin, C. (1872). *The Expression of the Emotions in Man and Animals*. London: Murray.

Ekman, P. (1985). *Telling Lies*. New York: Norton.

Ekman, P. (1988). Moving Faces: Facial Expressions and Emotion. *International Semiotic Spectrum* 10: 1-3.

Ekman, P. and Friesen, W. (1975). *Unmasking the Face*. Englewood Cliffs: Prentice-Hall.

Feher, M., Naddaf, R. and Tazi, N. (eds.) (1989). *Fragments for a History of the Human Body*. New York: Zone.

Fisher, H. E. (1992). *Anatomy of Love*. New York: Norton.

Frutiger, A. (1989). *Signs and Symbols*. New York: Van Nostrand.

Goffman, E. (1959). *The Presentation of Self in Everyday Life*. New York: Anchor.

Hall, E. (1973). *The Silent Language*. New York: Anchor.

Lieberman, P. (1984). *The Biology and Evolution of Language*. Cambridge, Mass.: Harvard University Press.

McNeill, D. (1992). *Hand and Mind: What Gestures Reveal about Thought*. Chicago: University of Chicago Press.

Miller, J. (1993). *The Passion of Michel Foucault*. New York: Simon and Schuster.

Morris, D. et al. (1979). *Gestures: Their Origins and Distributions*. London: Cape.

Nespoulous, J. L., Perron, P. and Lecours, A. R. (eds.) (1986). *The Biological Foundations of Gestures: Motor and Semiotic Aspects*. Hillsdale, N. J.: Lawrence Erlbaum.

Paget, R. (1930). *Human Speech*. London: Kegan Paul.

Royce, A. P. (1977). *The Anthropology of Dance*. Bloomington: Indiana University Press.

Schank, R. (1984). *The Cognitive Computer*. Reading, Mass.: Addison-Wesley.

Chapter 4

THE SIGNIFYING EYE!

Preliminary Remarks

The making of visual texts is unique to the human species. The capacity to draw and appreciate pictures, to represent the world through our ability to literally see it, is a fundamental source of signification and communication in our species. The paintings of animals found on cave walls and roofs, and the artifacts that exploded onto the scene in Europe 35,000 years ago, bear witness to the productivity of preverbal visual thinking. These are the "fossil records," so to speak, of humanity's first attempts at representation. The visual modality, and its ability to represent the world iconically, has also left its remnants in language. We commonly say that we *see* ideas, that we have *points of view*; that we have *insight*, that *seeing is believing*, etc. The testimony of *eyewitnesses* is considered to be more reliable than that of *hearsay* testimony. Such metaphors allude to the likely probability that language is tied etiologically to sense perception (especially vision). Phylogenetically, the visual mode of representation undoubtedly led the human organism to become aware of its own existence, to differentiate itself from other beings, to locate itself in relation to external objects. Dreams were particularly meaningful, because they could be recalled during waking hours with the help of the "mind's eye." The dream state unfolds in terms of iconically-presented episodes arranged into narrative sequences. The first form of consciousness was probably "visual," creating a mind-space that bestowed upon human beings the capacity to *intentionally* transcend their biologically-programmed instincts and reflex actions. The ability to summon up memorable images and models of life experiences, to reflect upon them, and to evaluate them allowed humans to direct and plan their bodily activities deliberately. Through such thinking, *intentionality* came to be the essence of humanness. The word *intention*, incidentally, derives from Latin *intendere* "to stretch," and, consequently, it reveals the metaphorical origins of our notion of intentionality as a kind of "stretching" of the mind in order to "see" into the future. The feelings and sense impressions that primitive humans were able to convert into iconic signs and to reuse for planning bodily actions and for recreating the external world within the mind must have filled them paradoxically with a sense of awe and power. This is why, as Julian Jaynes (1976) remarks, early humans must have thought that they saw and heard "gods" all the time. And indeed this is most likely why the Judeo-Christian Bible says that God created the world in His *image*, and that He allowed Adam to *name* it only later.

This chapter deals with how we represent the world for the eye to see. It is about pictures, drawings, diagrams, photographs, and all the other signifying means and codes we constantly employ to make messages and meanings for and through the eye. Specifically, it will look at visual perception and mental imagery, visual representation, visual art, and the visual media.

Visual Perception and Mental Imagery

What is a mental image? And how is it related to visual perception? These are questions that psychologists seek to answer, not semioticians. But their research and findings on these issues will be of obvious relevance to what semioticians do. It is beyond the scope of the present chapter to go into the relevant experimental work that has been conducted in this sector of psychology and to assess the ensuing debate it has generated. Suffice it to say that the field is divided into two camps—those who claim the "reality" of mental images and those who do not.

Semioticians, by and large, favor the claims and findings of the former. The reason for this is the persuasiveness of simple "empirical tests" like the following two: (1) Imagine a triangle. Can you *see* it in your mind? What *kind* of triangle is it? (2) Imagine a cat. Can you *see* the cat in your mind? What *kind* of cat is it? Most people would answer that they do indeed *see* the referents—a triangle and a cat—in their mind. What is perhaps more interesting is that most people (if not all) would describe the referents in ideal or prototypical terms. So, the kind of triangle that most people in Western cultures see in their minds is an idealized equilateral triangle (not a scalene, obtuse or any other kind of triangle). The cat that most people see mentally is the common house cat, not a lion, tiger or any other kind of feline.

Imagistic thought would seem to be a more fundamental form of cognition than is verbal, abstract, propositional thought. This is an implicit theme that can be extrapolated from a large portion of the research in developmental psychology. Vygotsky (1962), for instance, documented an "inner speech" stage in early childhood that is highly suggestive of an imagistic form of consciousness. It is only after the child has acquired language that "verbal thought" would seem to overlap with this more fundamental mode of thinking, becoming indistinguishable from it. From that point onwards, language gradually takes over as our primary bearer of thoughts.

The biological feature that made imagistic thinking possible was the emergence of what Julian Jaynes (1976) calls the "bicameral" mind. In modern humans, the brain is structured to carry out a symmetrical "division of labor." Its two hemispheres work cooperatively to produce mental functions. The left hemisphere (LH) is responsible for rational analytical thinking, speech and self-awareness. The right one (RH) balances out these functions. It is responsible for intuitive synthetic thinking, imagery and emotional states. The claim that imagistic thinking was the original form of consciousness posits that the RH once controlled most of human mentality, and that the left hemispheric functions emerged to assume more of the thinking load as the mind became more and more capable of abstraction.

In 1861 the French anthropologist and surgeon Paul Broca published a classic study of a patient who had lost the ability to articulate words during his lifetime, even though he had not suffered any paralysis of his speech organs. Noticing a destructive lesion in the left frontal lobe of the left hemisphere at the autopsy of this patient, Broca was thus able to present concrete evidence to link the articulation of speech to a specific cerebral site—which shortly thereafter came to bear his name. This discovery established a direct connection between a psychological function and a specific area of the brain. Broca was also responsible for suggesting that there existed an *asymmetry* between the brain and the body by pointing out that right-handed persons were more likely to have language located in the LH. Since 1861 the accumulated research in neuroscience has confirmed both that functions originate in one or the other of the two hemispheres and that the motor control system and sensory pathways between the brain and the body are crossed—i.e. that they are controlled by the contralateral (opposite-side) hemisphere.

In 1874 the work of the German neurologist Carl Wernicke brought to the attention of the medical community further evidence linking the LH with language. Wernicke documented cases in which damage to another area of the LH—which came to bear his name—consistently produced a recognizable pattern of impairment to the faculty of speech comprehension. Then in 1892 Jules Déjerine showed that problems in reading and writing resulted primarily from damage to the LH alone. So, by the end of the nineteenth century the research evidence that was accumulating provided an empirical base to the emerging consensus in neuroscience that the LH was the biological locus for language. Unfortunately, it also contributed to the unfounded idea that the RH was without special functions and subject to the control of the so-called "dominant" LH.

Right after Wernicke's observations, the notion of *cerebral dominance*, or the idea that the LH is the dominant one in the higher forms of cognition, came to be a widely-held one in neuroscience. Although the origin of this term is obscure, it grew no doubt out of the research connecting language to the LH and out of the conceptual link that has always existed in Western culture between language and the higher mental functions. As Springer and Deutsch (1985: 13) aptly remark, it nicely captured "the idea of half a brain directing behavior." The RH, in contrast, came to be designated as the "weak" or "minor" hemisphere. The nineteenth-century neuroscientists could not possibly have predicted the consequences of this infelicitous choice of terms for both education and science. It took the research in neuroscience most of the first half of this century to dispel the notion that only the verbal part of the brain was crucial for the higher forms of cognition, and to establish the fact that the brain is structured anatomically and physiologically in such a way as to provide for two modes of thinking, the verbal and the visual. Actually, the nineteenth-century British neurologist John Hughlings Jackson—paradoxically one of the authors of the dominance notion—was already casting doubts on the extreme view inherent in strict dominance theory by pointing out that patients suffering from Broca's *aphasia*—the partial or total loss of speech due to a disorder in any one of the brain's language centers—were nonetheless able to carry out basic communicative interactions, and by suggesting that nonverbal perception might be located in the RH.

Another landmark event in the history of neuroscience came a century after Broca's ground-breaking discovery. In 1967 Eric Lenneberg put forward his now classic "optimal age" hypothesis. On the basis of a large body of clinical studies, Lenneberg noticed that most aphasias became permanent after the age of puberty. This suggested to Lenneberg that the brain lost its capacity to transfer the language functions from the LH to the nonverbal RH after puberty, which it was able to do, to varying degrees, during childhood. Lenneberg concluded that there must be a biologically-fixed timetable for the acquisition of the language functions to the verbal LH and, consequently, that the critical period for the acquisition of language was before adolescence. Although his time frame has been disputed, Lenneberg's hypothesis that there is a fixed time period, a "critical period," during which the brain organizes its division of labor has not been seriously contested.

But this division of mental labor was not always the case. According to Jaynes (1976), in prehistoric times the brain was bicameral, not bilateral. The

LH was not the dominant one that it is in the modern brain. In early times the mind thought imagistically, not verbally. So it was up to the RH to plan, to concentrate for long periods and to solve problems creatively. It was hardly a "weak" or "minor" contributor to the human mind. The collapse of bicamerality led to the modern brain's complementary bilaterality. At that point, Jaynes maintains, humans developed rational thought and modern culture. In the modern brain, the RH is an equal partner of the LH in all aspects of neurofunctional organization. It is an "iconic" hemisphere that comprehends, produces and stores percepts and images. The RH must have played a much more crucial role in the formation of mind.

As it turns out, defining mental imagery neurologically is a difficult task. Does it really make any sense to think of individuals as having "pictures" in their brains? As mentioned above, psychologists are divided on this question. One camp—the pictoralists—believes that the brain generates visual information in the form of picture-like displays; the other camp—the descriptionalists—maintains that our so-called mental pictures are actually mental descriptions derived from our knowledge of how things are perceived. When we *say* that we think in *pictures*, we are using language to represent a nonverbal phenomenon. No wonder we get the two mixed up. All that can be said is that images *present* the stimulus and contextual conditions that evoked a sensory or affective response by the body in remarkably accurate form, although the stimulus is not a "replica." The conversion of experience into images is called "visual thinking" by Rudolf Arnheim (1969), in order to differentiate it from conceptual, or verbal, thinking.

It is important, above all else, to make a clear-cut distinction between an imagery theory of verbal meaning and simple imagery. The former attempts to explain why images can be evoked by language; the latter posits that images are more fundamental than verbal thinking. Imagine, once again, an equilateral triangle. Now, mentally put a dot in the middle of the triangle. Then, enclose the triangle in a square. What do you *see*? Clearly, all these modifications can be easily visualized by the mind.

The research that shows no imagery has been conducted on subjects who have been using language virtually since birth. In my view, this line of investigation has simply shown that the imagery system has become subordinate to the linguistic conceptual system. The constant use of language from early childhood onwards eventually diminishes the need to employ imagistic thinking. But, if one were asked to think of something totally imaginary, like a "winged table," then the imagery system reemerges to make such a verbal description literally "imaginable". It is almost impossible in the modern mind to separate imagistic from verbal thought.

Perhaps the most conspicuous flaw in imagery theories is that they often portray images as just "pictorial." Mental imagery is a kind of *Gestalt* or representation that need not be only "pictorial." It can also be musical and even verbal. One can literally *think up* melodies and words as easily as visualizable scenes. Note how easy it is for you to visualize such familiar sensations, sounds, etc. as the laugh of a friend, the sound of thunder, the feel of wet grass, the feel of a runny nose, the smell of fish, the taste of toothpaste, the sensation of being uncomfortably cold, the sensation of extreme happiness. A mental image, obviously, is a mental version of some sense impression or affective state. It can be a sound, a shape of an object, a smell, etc. Imagery would seem to share many of the same neural processes as the sensory perception system. This might explain why our vocabularies for visual sensation and mental perception share many elements. In actual practice, we rarely make a distinction between the two: sentences such as "I see the book on the table" (which implicates visual perception) are used in parallel with sentences such as "I see the point of your argument" (which implicates some abstract notion).

The topic of imagery has a long history in psychology. Individual differences in the ability to experience imagery were recorded already in the previous century. The research that shows how mental imagery can be elicited is actually rather straightforward and, in my view, unambiguous. People can recall faces and recognize voices accurately and quickly, rotate objects in their heads, locate imaginary places in terms of so-called "cognitive maps," and scan game boards in their minds with no difficulty whatsoever. While researchers might disagree on exactly what it is that their subjects "see," or "experience," in their minds, they concur that something is "going on" in the mind. Stephen Kosslyn (e.g. 1983) and a group of researchers have been investigating how the brain's imagery system might work. In a series of ingenious experiments, Kosslyn demonstrated how subjects can conjure up images of the arrangement of furniture in a room, of how to move a couch, of how to redesign a blueprint, etc. He has shown, in essence, how people construct elaborate mental images, search them out for specific purposes, and perform all kinds of visually-describable movements in their minds.

One of the most significant findings that has crystallized from the neuroscientific literature is the likelihood that the RH is a crucial point-of-departure for processing novel stimuli: i.e. for stimuli for which there are no preexistent cognitive codes or programs available. Neuroscientists suggest that the main reason why this is so is because of the anatomical structure of the RH. Its greater connectivity with other centers in the complex neuronal pathways of the brain makes it a better "distributor" of new information. The

LH, on the other hand, has a more sequentially-organized neuronal-synaptic structure and, thus, finds it more difficult to assimilate information for which no pre-formed categories exist.

An intriguing area of psychological research which shows how imagery and conceptualization overlap is color. What is color? Since color perception is a property of easily-observed sense data, it should ostensibly be independent from verbal labeling. But it does not turn out to be that way. Color terminologies are anything but universal. So, the question of how color is coded by languages is not a trivial matter—physicists point out that almost 8 million shades could potentially be discriminated.

The main evidence for color universals was provided in 1969 by Berlin and Kay who argued that lexical differences in color coding are only superficial matters which conceal general underlying principles of color categorization. Using the judgments of the native speakers of twenty widely-divergent languages, Berlin and Kay came to the conclusion that there were "focal points" in basic (single term) color systems which clustered in certain predictable ways. They identified eleven universal colors, or "focal points," which corresponded to the English words *red, pink, orange, yellow, brown, green, blue, purple, black, white* and *gray*. Not all the languages investigated had separate words for each color, but there emerged a patterning that revealed a fixed coding system. If a language had two colors, then the focal points were *black* and *white*. If it had three color terms, then the third one corresponded to *red*. A four-term system added either *green* or *yellow*, while a five-term system had both of these. A six-term system included *blue*; a seven-term system added *brown*. Finally, *purple, pink, orange* and *gray* were found to occur in any combination in languages which had the previous focal points. In other words, languages with, say, a four-term system consisting of *black, white, red*, and *brown* simply do not exist. Color perception appears to be a property of the brain, not of language.

The work on color was pursued vigorously and intelligently in the 1970s by the psychologist Eleanor Rosch (e.g. 1975). She demonstrated, for instance, that the Dani people of West Irian, who have a two-color system in their language code, were able to discriminate easily eight focal points. Using a recognition-memory experiment, Rosch found that the Dani were able to recognize focal colors better than non-focal ones. She also found that they were able to learn new colors in paired-associates tasks more easily when the names were paired with focal colors. Rosch's data thus established further that color perception is not a property of language. Although languages might provide a guide to the interpretation of color, they do not affect its perception in any significant way.

It would seem, therefore, that similarities among cultures far outweigh differences, despite considerable variation in how colors are labeled. But to this day the problem of color concepts has not been resolved in the minds of many psychologists. For one thing, the fact that the eleven focal points discovered by Berlin and Kay corresponded to the color terms of their own language (English) is bound to arouse suspicion. Could they have been predisposed by their own language to gloss all other terms as indicating what they themselves perceived? Was Rosch similarly predisposed to see English focal points as the only appropriate stimuli to be used in experimental conditions? Once a focal point has been identified to a subject, there is nothing that will stop that subject from perceiving it. But despite such questions, Berlin and Kay's 1969 findings have remained virtually unchallenged to this day. I too believe that their study was a valid one. But I read a different story in it than many psychologists do. The view that color categories are innate is, in my view, untenable. The Berlin and Kay data suggest, rather, a separation between the perceptual and conceptual levels of mind: i.e. *color percepts* are universal (factual); *color concepts*, on the other hand, are related to culture and language (artifactual). Color vocabularies were originally metaphorical. In Hittite, for instance, words for colors initially designated plant and tree names such as "poplar," "elm," "cherry," "oak," etc. Color concepts were thus born of metaphor which, by associating a feature of some object in the environment with all other objects that had this feature in varying degrees, was able to allow the human mind to extract a general pattern—*color*—from its particular manifestations. Percepts are manufactured to record sense impressions—in this case light frequencies. The number of percepts that the mind can generate which relate to variations in the color spectrum are infinite. It is only when metaphor connects them to some other perceived object or event in the world that displays the same light frequency pattern that a color concept emerges. This subsequently becomes sensitive to cultural contexts. In the artifactual mind, a color is just what the language says it is.

Visual Representation

The discussion of color leads directly to visual representation. Color words are the signifiers we use arbitrarily to refer to light-spectrum frequencies. But these words in no way have some visually-mimetic connection to such referents. To see how visual representation works, imagine doing the following: draw (1) a tree, (2) a ball, (3) a square. No doubt, you would have virtually no difficulty in drawing these with pen and paper. If you ask yourself what you did to draw, you will discover the constituents we commonly use to assemble visual signs and codes:

The first visual element used in sign-making is the *line*. A line is perceived as such if it remains narrow; once it is "thickened" it becomes a shape to our perception. Lines are versatile. They can be straight, round, curved, etc.; and they can be used in various combinations to make up signs. Three straight lines, for instance, can be joined up in various ways to make such visual signs as diagrams representing a triangle, the letter "H," a picnic table:

Lines can be used, additionally, to indicate movement and directionality. The vertical lines of Gothic cathedrals, such as the Notre Dame Cathedral in France, force the eye to look up toward the heavens, thus revealing the religious meanings of certain buildings.

Cathedral of Notre Dame, Amiens, France

Lines can also be used to deceive. For instance, the following two lines, one under the other, are obviously equal in length:

If I add "arrows" going in opposite directions to the two lines, notice what happens to your perception of each one. The bottom one now appears to be "longer." Such figures are known as optical illusions because they play on our perceptual modalities which, like Eco says of sign-making in general, can be easily deceived or duped by our sign-making.

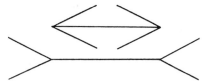

A classic optical illusion is the following one. Do you see a face? Do you see a vase instead? Do you see at times one and at times the other?

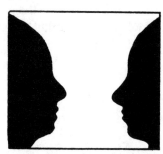

It is fascinating to consider that this automatic "shift" from one figure to the other is caused by a simple drawing: literally, a signifier constructed with lines and meaningful "shapes" corresponding to two signifieds. And, indeed, another basic visual element used in the construction of visual signs is *shape*. In order to be a shape the signifier must have an edge, no matter how irregular or indistinct it might be. Everything we see can be represented visually by lines and shapes: a cloud is a shape, a horizon is a line. So, like any other kind of signifier, lines and shapes force us to make an interpretation—denotative or connotative—of the referents they aim to depict.

Rudolf Arnheim (1969) points out that shape has character producing a feeling in an interpreter. For example, it is a documented fact that most people find the proportion in the "golden rectangle" to be "symmetrical" and "pleasing." The golden proportion is 5:8. Of the following rectangles, **E** is constructed with this proportion of sides:

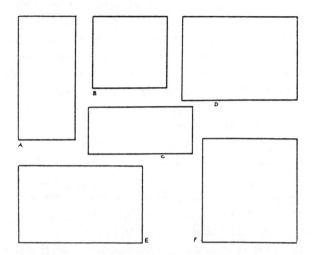

Other elements of visual signs include *value, color* and *texture*. *Value* refers to the darkness or lightness of a line or shape. It plays an important role in portraying varieties of dark and light contrasts. *Color*, as we have seen above, is a signifying element whose interpretation overlaps biological tendencies (perceptual) and the conditioning effect produced by culture-specific verbal labels. In visual representation, color covers a broad range of signification, from simple denotative reference—"stop" in traffic lights (as we saw in the first chapter)—to the evocation or conveyance of certain feelings in paintings. This is why we speak of "warm," "soft," "cold," "harsh" colors, for example. Connotatively, color often has culture-specific symbolic value: e.g. in our culture yellow connotes cowardice, in China it connotes royalty. *Texture* refers to our sensation of touch when we look at some surface. We react differently when looking at a smooth round figure like a circle, than when we look at a "jagged edge" figure:

circular figure
= "soft" texture

jagged edge figure
= "rough" texture

It is amazing to contemplate how a visual signifier, which cannot be felt by our sense of touch, can actually evoke a tactile sensation nonetheless. This is, in my view, strongly suggestive evidence that the senses are intermodal: i.e. that they interact in the act of perception and sign decoding. The term that best expresses the intermodality of sensation and interpretation is *synesthesia*—the sensation produced at a point other than, or remote from, the point of stimulation. When a visual figure evokes a tactile reaction, or when a sound evokes a visual signifier (color), the sensation is said to be synesthetic. Synesthesia refers as well to the juxtaposition of different sense modalities in semiosis. This is why we say that something is a "loud" color or a "bright" sound. The ability to evoke, and even replace, one sense modality by another explains why vision-impaired individuals can "see" objects by "touching" them. The term *aesthesia*, on the other hand, is commonly used to refer to the ability to experience sensation. When we call the appreciation of art an "aesthetic experience," we literally mean that we sense and feel the meaning of a work of art (factual interpretation), even though it has been constructed through some artifactual convention (musical forms, painting styles, etc.).

Consider how simple elements like lines, shapes, etc. create an illusion of depth. It is intriguing indeed to reflect on how a particular juxtaposition of lines, for example, will force us to see the ensuing "box" figure as three-dimensional:

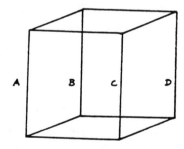

The figure has been drawn with straight lines drawn on a two-dimensional surface (the page). But we cannot help but interpret it as a three-dimensional box. Incidentally, this box is also an optical illusion. Ask yourself: Is line **B** in front of or behind line **C**? Now, keep looking at the box and you will see that the "perspective" (the position of line **C** vis-à-vis line **B**) with which you "see" the "box" will eventually change. In painting and drawing *perspective* refers to the ability to create an illusion of depth. Indeed, visual artists of all kinds, from painters to graphic designers, must know how to manipulate and guide perspective by means of lines, shapes, color, value, and texture so as to induce a specific range of interpretations to their visual texts. As a historical footnote, it should be noted that the craft of perspective drawing dates back to the Renaissance (from the fourteenth to the sixteenth centuries) when the Italian artist Filippo Brunelleschi (1377-1446) discovered and institutionalized this technique.

An interesting, and historically pivotal, example of the importance of visual representation for manipulating and, literally, extending our knowledge of the world is map-making. A map is an indexical (it indicates where places are), iconic (it represents places in topographical relation to each other) and symbolic (its notational system must be learned) code all at once. It represents direction, location and distance by means of basic visual elements (lines, shapes, etc.). It is therefore mind-boggling to think that such a simple visual text has made it possible to travel and explore the world with ease. Maps have allowed us to organize semiotically the *terra firma* which we inhabit.

Visual Art

Painting and sculpture are art texts constructed in the visual mode. As mentioned in the previous chapter, art can be thought of as an artifactual means for evoking fundamental feelings and sensations. The juxtaposition of artifact with feeling is a powerful means for making meaning in the world and for extracting meaning from it.

The earliest examples of "visual art" go back some 30,000 years. The art works of early *Homo sapiens* took two main forms: the vivid carvings of animals which cover the roofs and walls of caves, such as those at Lascaux in France and Altamira in Spain; and the small sculptures and relief carvings of animals and female figures found in caves throughout Europe. In all probability, visual art as we now know it probably originated when the hand movements used to draw simple concrete referents became more abrupt, allowing the first artists to gradually distance themselves from reproducing their objects. As a consequence, the figures they drew became more abstract. They took the first crucial step to *see* and, thus, to select and make objects representing something else; something existing in a different space and time or not existing at all.

What is the evolutionary significance of primitive art? I see no intrinsic connection between art and recent claims (as we shall see in the final chapter) that the mind's products are survival-enhancing strategies. What possible survival functions did the art works of 35,000 years ago serve? These represented animals engaged in some action or found in some physical state imbued with significance—e.g. a dying animal which had collapsed on the ground. I would like to suggest that primitive art, and art generally, reveals a fascination with consciousness. Children invariably start to draw as they discover their conscious thoughts. In adulthood, art penetrates the artifactual level of mind, reawakening in us our now largely unconscious perceptions of reality. It takes us back, in other words, to our imaginative origins.

Needless to say, the visual arts have changed dramatically over the centuries. The question "What is art?" is continually coming up in the media, as art galleries routinely put controversial "abstract" paintings and sculptures on display. Take, for example, the "art" of the late Andy Warhol. His painting of a Campbell's soup can (1964) really forces us to think deeply about the nature of art:

Campbell's Soup Can by Andy Warhol (1964)

What does this painting mean? Interestingly enough, when asked this question people will start to provide answers such as: "It is a symbol of our consumer society;" "It represents the banality and triviality of contemporary life;" etc. Recall the example of the crumpled cigarette package in the opening chapter. If seen lying on the street, we would interpret it unequivocally as "garbage;" if it is framed and hung from an art gallery wall, we tend to interpret it symbolically instead as "an example of a throw-away society." The reason for this is, of course, the context in which the object is placed. The art gallery context is conducive to a symbolic mode of interpretation *vis-à-vis* any of its displays. Warhol's "art" forces us to interpret common objects connotatively, both as signifiers with social meanings and, more importantly, as human-made objects in themselves. All our artifacts have their particular "beauty" or "ugliness," as the case may be. Perhaps there is no answer to what is art. As Warhol's work suggests, it might simply be the case that human-made things are interpreted as works of art because meanings and values are attributed to them by those who make them, by the society in which they live, and by those who look at them in later years. But, in my view, "art" that does not evoke our propensity for feeling and sensation is bound to have little "lasting" value. Only art that evokes basic human feelings will transcend the time-frame and culture in which it was created.

On the topic of artistic representation, it is also interesting to note that by the time of the first civilizations the imaginative part of the mind was collaborating with the conceptual part to produce what is, arguably, humanity's first great visual rationalization of reality—*geometry*. This wonderful product of the interactive workings of the rational (artifactual) and imaginative (factual) levels of mind gave the world its first spatial categories. There is nothing that is more aesthetically and logically pleasing, *at the same time*, than the visual order constructed by geometry. It is a metaphor of universal order. Our notions of space, as idealized by geometry, are rooted in our physiological selves, in our bodily experiences and perceptions. They are not *out there* in any objective sense. Geometric concepts are visual metaphors transforming our visual organization of the world into abstract experiences of space.

Visual Media

It is often said that we live in a visually-oriented world. By this, we mean that we tend to rely more than ever before on visual texts as primary message-making texts, and that we encode and transmit these texts through visually-based technological media such as photography, videography, television and cinema. And, indeed, our world would not be the same without such visual media. We are, in many ways, a "visually-mediated" culture.

The power of visual media such as motion pictures and television is that they have sequence and narrative qualities that simple drawings, paintings and sculptures do not. Such media are, therefore, similar to literary texts (novels, plays, etc.). But like plays and operas they are also "multisensory." Indeed, the juxtaposition of dialogue, music, scenery and action in a movie makes cinema a particularly effective means of aesthetic message- and meaning-making.

Photography too is a powerful medium of visual representation. Photographs capture a fleeting and irretrievable moment in time, extracting it from the flux of change that characterizes the space-time continuum. Such "captured" moments have strong appeal because they allow us literally to "freeze" time and "control" space. When this captured moment in space-time is associated with some emotionally signifying event or person, then the photograph becomes a powerful means of mnemonically-based signification. We literally "relive" the moment it captured, or "recall" a person in the photograph as he or she was at the time. The photographs that adorn our tables and walls in our homes are visual mementos and testimonials of who we are. They all have a stake in shaping and highlighting our memories. They are "memory signifiers," so to speak, and can be decoded by others as meaningful texts only if we provide them with the contexts in which the photographs were taken. Photographs are signs which acknowledge that we do indeed exist, that we have lived, that we have done something, etc. This signifying power of the photograph is brought out in Michelangelo Antonioni's 1966 movie masterpiece, *Blow-Up*. The search for "clues" to a crime in a blow-up of a photograph is a metaphor for the search for clues to our own existence in the iconography of our photographs. Photo albums are iconographic autobiographies of who we are, or more precisely, of who we think we are.

Movies grew out of the technical developments associated with photography. They "work" as conveyors of continuous visual sequences because our eyes see the sequences as a smooth, continuous *Gestalt*. This is because our eyes keep the same image in mind for a few seconds after the image has been removed from vision. So, instead of seeing moving-picture frames as individual units, we "overlap" them and maintain the illusion of motion. Television and videography involve the projection of "lines" on our television or video screens. Since our visual system keeps the impression of light for about one-tenth of a second after the light is removed, we do not perceive the images as being built up line by line, but rather as entire pictures or images moving smoothly in the same way that motion pictures do.

We perceive both cinema and television as story-telling media. This perception includes documentaries, news broadcasts, etc. which all unfold as narratives. More will be said about the penchant for narrative in the seventh chapter. Suffice it to say here that visual media are effective communicators of narrative messages. The difference between verbal texts and television or cinema texts is that the imagery generated in them is determined in advance by the television/movie producers, whereas in the verbal text it is up to the reader to generate appropriate mental images. Movies, therefore, have a more "common" appeal than do books, because they are perceived at a denotative level in virtually the same ways by everyone who sees them.

Concluding Remarks

The theme of this chapter has been that the sense of sight constitutes an important source of message- and meaning-making. Visual signification and communication are testaments to the fact that we use sensation (in this case visual) as the substance from which we make our signs. Visual sign-making is probably the oldest form of representation in the human species. There is no culture without visual art. And, in one form or other, all cultures have the equivalents of what we call diagrams, maps and drawings. Such artifacts bear witness to the fact that images are more fundamental to humanity than are concepts. The brain's ability to manufacture images is more important to cognition than is the presence of the verbal structures that we use to carry our thinking load. It was also pointed out that, as a result of technology, we have become a visually-mediated society: television, movies, photographs, etc. dominate our modes of receiving and producing information (messages and meanings).

It is interesting to note, in closing, that our need to literally "extend" our ability to see has been the motivating force behind the many scientific inventions that aim to extend human vision mechanically (the lens, the magnifying glass, the telescope, etc.). The world of vision-enhancing artifacts is, as mentioned repeatedly in this book, an extension of a particular domain of the factual level of experience. Our artifacts, physical and ideational, allow us to select sensations, urges, tendencies, etc. from the factual level and to convert them into signifying codes. The uniqueness of human nature lies in this incredible ability to make things that ultimately enhance our survivability, but more importantly, make us truly mysterious and "unexplainable" beings.

SUGGESTIONS FOR FURTHER READING

Arnheim, R. (1969). *Visual Thinking*. Berkeley: University of California Press.

Barthes, R. (1977). *Image-Music-Text*. London: Fontana.

Berger, J. (1972). *Ways of Seeing*. Harmondsworth: Penguin.

Berlin, B. and Kay, P. (1969). *Basic Color Terms*. Berkeley: University of California Press.

Dondis, D. A. (1986). *A Primer of Visual Literacy.* Cambridge, Mass.: MIT Press.

Dunning, W. V. (1991). *Changing Images of Pictorial Space: A History of Visual Illusion in Painting.* Syracuse: Syracuse University Press.

Jaynes, J. (1976). *The Origin of Consciousness in the Breakdown of the Bicameral Mind.* Toronto: University of Toronto Press.

Kosslyn, S. M. (1983). *Ghosts in the Mind's Machine: Creating and Using Images in the Brain.* New York: W. W. Norton.

Langer, S. (1957). *Problems of Art.* New York: Scribner's.

Lanier, V. (1982). *The Arts We See.* New York: Teacher's College Press.

Lenneberg, E. (1967). *The Biological Foundations of Language.* New York: John Wiley.

Rosch, E. (1975). Cognitive Reference Points. *Cognitive Psychology* 7: 532-547.

Saint-Martin, F. (1990). *Semiotics of Visual Language.* Bloomington: Indiana University Press.

Springer, S. V. and Deutsch, G. (1985). *Left Brain, Right Brain.* New York: Freeman.

Vygotsky, L. S. (1962). *Thought and Language* Cambridge, Mass.: MIT Press.

Chapter 5

THE SIGNIFYING TONGUE!

Preliminary Remarks

Since the dawn of civilization, human beings have had an abiding fascination with language—the ability to use the tongue, and the other organs of articulation, to represent the world through the sounds that the tongue and the organs make. The "signifying tongue" has served humanity well. All the world's cultures have composed myths and legends with it to explain their roots. Without it, culture as we know it would be impossible. Just think of all the verbally encoded knowledge that humanity has produced. The endless sea of written words contained in books, which have recorded human thoughts throughout the ages, and to which we can have access if we know the appropriate verbal codes, constitute a truly astounding achievement. If somehow all the books contained by the world's libraries were to be destroyed overnight, human civilization would have to start all over re-coding knowledge linguistically, by bringing together writers, scientists, educators, law-makers, etc. to literally "rewrite" knowledge.

Language, which derives incidentally from the Latin "tongue" *lingua*, has always been universally felt to constitute the feature that, more than any other, sets human beings apart from all other species. There is a deeply-felt conviction within us that if we were ever able to solve the enigma of how language originated in our species, then we would possess a vital clue to the mystery of life itself. The Western Bible starts off, as a matter of fact, with "In the beginning was the *Word*" (italics mine). Throughout the centuries, the debate on what language is has often focused on whether it was a *gift* from a divine source or a unique accomplishment of the human mind. In Ancient Greece, the term for "speech"—*logos*—designated not only articulate discourse but also the rational faculty underlying and inhering in speech. For the Greeks *logos* transformed the human animal into a rational animal. More recently, language is being blamed for many of the world's ills. It is now being claimed that the way we speak shows biases, produces evils, privileges one particular power group (be it males, whites, politicians or any other specific group), and does many other negative things. "Political correctness," as it is now called, is embedded in language perception. One cannot use words such as "janitor" or "mankind" without the feeling that they might "offend," because they are said to carry with them negative sociological, political or historical connotations. There is a widely-held belief that if we were to "reform" or "purify" language, we would be able set the world right. Rational cultures, such as ours, are caught indeed in a tangled linguistic web. This is one of the themes in Aldous Huxley's powerful and still meaningful 1932 novel *Brave New World*. Clearly, then, the topic of language is hardly a moot one for anyone interested in the study of message- and meaning-making.

This chapter will consider language from the strictly semiotic point of view, i.e. as a source of semiosis. The formal study of the properties of language—of its sound, grammatical, and semantic systems—is the task of the science of linguistics. A few classical linguistic texts are provided in the *Suggestions for Further Reading* section at the end of the chapter. Here, the focus will be on verbal semiosis and communication. The chapter ends with a brief discussion of writing and of verbal art.

What Is Language?

Language literally comes *naturally* to us. We acquire it without effort or training during our infancy. Indeed, the only requirement for learning any language, or languages, is adequate exposure to samples of it from age zero to about two. So natural is speech to us, in fact, that we hardly ever consider what it is that we are doing when we speak. We speak to others throughout the day. We read, write, type/input words, watch and *listen* to our television sets day in day out. The linguist Noam Chomsky (1986)—perhaps the most influential linguist of the last three and a half decades—has even gone so far as to view language as a truly *natural* phenomenon, i.e. as an endowment "from nature." He depicts it in fact, as a physical organ that is purported to be as innate as, say, flight is to a bird. So, for Chomsky, language came about in ways that are as explainable as, for instance, our ability to use our eyes and our noses for seeing and smelling. This is why attempts to teach language to the higher primates, who do not have such a language organ, have turned out to be unsuccessful, even though they seem to have developed a sophisticated form of manual signing. Is Chomsky right? In my view, he is partially correct. But he cannot be so easily dismissed. Given Chomsky's influence over the entire field of linguistics, it is necessary to look at his perspective with some scrutiny and discernment here. For, if Chomsky is *entirely* correct, then it would make all other forms of semiosis subordinate to, and dependent upon, the language capacity.

In 1957 Chomsky published an influential treatise titled *Syntactic Structures*. Soon after, the approach to the analysis of language that he laid out in that book became the mainstream one. The "Chomskyan paradigm" continues, to this day, to constitute a model with many adherents. For Chomsky, the speech faculty is determined by a set of "universal principles" present in the brain at birth that are subjected to culturally-specific "parameters" during infancy. The "parameter-setting" feature of Chomsky's theory assigns some role to experiential factors. But Chomsky maintains that the role of the linguist is to search out the universal principles which make up the speech faculty. This is the most recent version of Chomskyan theory, and it is one that has attracted a large following. Its epistemological orientation is evidenced by his choice of terms to refer to the language faculty in the brain. Several years ago he referred to it as a LAD, a "language acquisition device." He now calls it a UG, a "universal grammar," an inbuilt neurological generator of language structures.

Chomsky has always viewed the data collection and classificatory assemblages of linguistic facts by the linguists of the thirties and forties as interesting in themselves, but as ultimately useless for the development of a theory of language. Chomsky has thus worked to develop the abstract constructs and notions that he has always claimed would transform linguistics into a science akin to mathematics. But the image that his paradigm has produced is that of the mind as an automaton—an abstract machine that continually manufactures well-formed strings of linguistic symbols on the basis of neurologically-determined rules. Chomsky's inflexibility in maintaining this model has, understandably but unfortunately, made him a target of bitter criticism over the last two decades. The thrust of the Chomskyan paradigm is that the mind is programmed by nature to manipulate formal symbols which take on the structure of propositions in discourse, and so serve thought during speech. Cumulatively, they constitute the brain's UG—a neural system that manipulates symbols without considering what these might mean. Language is not seen as being tied necessarily to any experiential or social context. It consists simply of a UG which is present in the brain at birth and which equips humans by the age of two with the ability to develop the specific languages that cultures require of them. The psycholinguist Stephen Pinker (1990: 230-231) agrees:

> A striking discovery of modern generative grammar is that
> natural languages all seem to be built on the same basic

> plan. Many differences in basic structure but different
> settings of a few "parameters" that allow languages to
> vary, or different choices of rule types from a fairly small
> inventory of possibilities.... On this view, the child only
> has to set these parameters on the basis of parental input,
> and the full richness of grammar will ensue when those
> parametrized rules interact with one another and with
> universal principles. The parameter-setting view can help
> explain the universality and rapidity of language acquisi-
> tion: when the child learns one fact about her language,
> she can deduce that other facts are also true of it without
> having to learn them one by one.

In my view, the problem with using such constructs as "universal grammar" and culture-specific "parameters" is that they ignore a whole range of "lived" phenomena. Moreover, Pinker's analysis of language ontogenesis can be an acceptable interpretation, among many others, if it is restricted to accounting for the development of syntactic language, or grammar, in the child. But it is not a comprehensive theory, in my view, because it ignores a much more fundamental creative force in the child. The progression from iconic-sensorial to conceptual thought that was discussed in previous chapters makes it clear that there is a developmental link between bodily sense-making and language during infancy. Grammar emerges at the *end-point* of this progression, not at its *starting-point*.

Chomskyan models of language are based on studying the grammatical knowledge of an "idealized speaker-hearer," thereby licensing only a pristine, literal language as a legitimate object of study, and excluding, for instance, figurative language which, as we will see in the next chapter, is hardly an ornamental feature of language. Moreover, these models view the sentence as the basic unit of thought. So, they juxtapose "competence," or the speaker-hearer's knowledge of grammar, with "performance," or "the actual use of language in concrete situations." It is precisely the omission of performance factors from the purview of language study that has caused the contemporary rift in linguistics. By eliminating extremely problematic performance data from consideration, many linguists have reduced the corpus with which they work. But in so doing, they have failed to account for a number of important phenomena present in the entire corpus, such as social and regional variation, figurative language, pragmatically-shaped discourse, the strategic use of language and other context-based features. Grammatical systems are conceived as being machine-like generators of infinitely well-formed sentences insulated from the vagaries of human and social experience.

A large portion of the research in linguistics and developmental psychology today is being dedicated to discovering the form and content of Chomsky's UG and of determining the mechanisms that govern the mind's parameter-setting process. First and foremost, meaning is held to be objectively determinable in the syntactic structure of language. Accordingly, it is claimed that the goal of linguistics must be to establish the semantics of so-called "truth-conditions." These are seen as being intertwined solely with the syntactic properties of sentences. The question *vis-à-vis* UG theory that comes immediately to mind, therefore, is the following one: If the construct of a "universal grammar" is shown to be a plausible one, why restrict it to language? Why not also posit universal music, visual-aesthetic and humor "grammars," for instance? If the role of culture is simply to set the parameters that determine the specific "grammar" that develop in the child, could it not also set the specific melodic and harmonic parameters that determine the specific forms of musical knowledge that develops in the child? Could it not also set the specific visual-aesthetic and humorous parameters that determine the particular visual-aesthetic and laughter codes that the child learns? To restrict human beings to biological inheritors of language grammar is essentially a modern form of linguistic determinism.

There is growing evidence, moreover, that the phenomena which linguists have traditionally assumed to be abstract grammatical relations are, instead, dependent upon the ways in which we understand, or more precisely, experience the world around us. To see why this is so, consider the ways in which different languages treat weather verbs. In a Romance language like French, for example, the verb *faire* "to make" is used to convey a weather condition—*il fait chaud*, literally "it makes hot," *il fait froid*, literally "it makes cold." The condition of "hotness" and "coldness" is conveyed instead by the verb *être* "to be" when referring to objects—*c'est chaud* "it is hot," *c'est froid* "it is cold"—and by *avoir* "to have" when referring to people—*elle a chaud* "she is hot," *elle a froid* "she is cold." Theories based on abstract syntax have no way of accounting for such phenomena. A little reflection will show that the reason for the use of one verb or the other, *faire* or *être*, is motivated by an underlying experience of bodies and the environment as *containers*. So, the "containment context" in which the quality of "coldness" or "hotness" is located determines the verb to be employed. If it is *in* the environment, it is "made" by nature *(il fait froid)*; if it is *in* a human being, then the body "has" it *(elle a froid)*; and if it is *in* an object, then the object "is" its container *(c'est froid)*. Examples such as this suggest that the development of grammatical categories is motivated by experiential factors.

As a concrete example of how this experiential perspective might "explain" various other linguistic and conceptual phenomena, consider the use of the prepositions *since* and *for* in sentences such as the following:

(1)   I have been living in Toronto *since* 1980.
(2)   I have known Dr. Mary Jones *since* November.
(3)   I have not been able to sleep *since* Monday.
(4)   I have been living in Toronto *for* 15 years.
(5)   I have known Dr. Mary Jones *for* nine months.
(6)   I have not been able to sleep *for* five days.

An analysis of the phrases that come after *since* or *for* reveals that those that follow the former are "points in time," i.e. they are complements that reflect a conception of time as a "point" on a "timeline" which shows specific years, months, etc.: "1980," "November," "Monday," etc. Complements that follow *for* reflect a conception of time as a "quantity": "15 years," "nine months," "five days," etc. These two conceptual domains can be explained as "time is a point" and "time is a quantity". They are, clearly, conceptual domains that result from the ways in which English models time. They reflect the propensity to experience a phenomenon such as "time" in terms of something concrete. These conceptual domains can then be seen to have a specific *representational* effect at the level of language in terms of a grammatical dichotomy: complements introduced by *since* are reflexes of the conceptual domain "time is a point;" those introduced by *for* are reflexes of the conceptual domain "time is a (measurable) quantity."

This conceptualization of time is also present in such other symbolic systems as word problems in algebra. The only way to solve a problem such as the following is if the solver has access to the above conceptual domains:

> John is five years older than Mary. In four years from now,
> he will be twice her age. What is the present age of each?

This problem can be solved algebraically by setting up a so-called linear equation as follows: The letter symbol x can be used to represent Mary's present age. Therefore, John's present age can be represented by $x + 5$. The reason for this is because we have access to the conceptual domain "time is a point." John's age-point is "5 points" away from Mary's age-point, which can be considered the origin or "point 0" on the timeline:

0	•1	•2	•3	•4	•5
	Mary's				John's
	Age-Point				Age-Point

Identical reasoning can now be applied to represent John's and Mary's ages "in four years." We simply move their age-points "up by four" on the timeline. This translates into $x + 4$ for Mary and $x + 5 + 4 (= x + 9)$ for John. Now we shift to the conceptual domain "time is a quantity" to relate their ages. John's age is quantifiable as twice that of Mary's age. This is, of course, a relation that can be expressed by multiplying Mary's age by two: $x + 9$ [John's age] $= 2(x + 4)$ [twice Mary's age]. Solving this equation reveals that Mary is at present one year old and John six.

The point to be made here is that the unconsciously-embedded experience of time as a "point on a line" and as a "quantity" constitute the conceptual domains that have specific reflexes in English grammar and which undergird the capacity to solve word problems in algebra involving time.

So, if grammar (syntax) is not all there is to language, and if language is, arguably, not any more fundamental as a representational code than, say, a visual-iconic code, then *what is language*? Actually, in my view, the previous discussion provides some valuable clues for formulating an answer to this question. If syntax is iconically-motivated, i.e. if it reflects our direct perception of things in the world as they stand in relation to one another, then language must have originated as a kind of "replacement" for more fundamental iconic/indexical semiosic systems, becoming increasingly abstract over time. Consider the relation between an active and passive sentence such as *Sally ate the apple* vs. *The apple was eaten by Sally*. In traditional theories of syntax, especially of the Chomskyan variety, the passive is considered to be a derivative of the active: i.e. through some abstract mental rule anchored in a general principle of grammatical design, passives can always be reconstructed as actives. The implications for a theory of mind are obvious: active sentences are cognitively more salient than passives. Apart from the fact that it really does seem unlikely to think of active sentences as abstract forms "waiting" to be passivized by the demands of grammar or conversational style, there are sentences which are, seemingly, conceivable only as passive: e.g. The *Bible was written at the dawn of time*. When viewed from the vantage point of an iconic theory of grammar, on the other hand, the sentences *Sally ate the apple* and *The apple was eaten by Sally* reveal a different organization. In active sentences the subject is in the *foreground* of the mind's eye, while the object is in its *background*. The *action* implied by the verb is the link between the two. The overall "view" that such sentences convey is that of the subject as an agent, a "perpetrator" or "executor" of the action. A change from passive to active changes the position of the foreground and the background in the mind. The cognitive effect is to give more salience to the object as "receiver" of the action. The passive form literally gives us a different "angle" from which to see the world.

To use an insight from Susanne Langer (1948), it can be said that our first tendency is to feel the world, or some specific aspect of it, "presentationally," i.e. in its entirety as a global whole. The thought unit or *Gestalt* that subsequently forms in the mind is not linear, analytical or "syntactic," because it is not made up of "components." It is only when it is transferred to the "discursive" mode of representation that it takes on a linear, componential, and therefore "syntactic" quality. It is within the domain of language that it can be reshaped and remodeled syntactically. But no matter how many sentences are generated to explicate the original feeling-state, they will never be able to capture it in its globality. The whole is larger than the sum of its syntactically-remodeled parts.

As an illustration of how the presentational-to-discursive shift might unfold, consider the following situation. You have just heard a profoundly moving piece of music. Let us say that it was the first movement of Beethoven's intensely poignant "Moonlight" piano sonata. As you listened, you literally felt that there was something very profound in the music. You may have even been "moved" to tears. It is when you attempt to "express" your feelings in language that the shift to the discursive-syntactic mode forces you to dissect them, to relate them in a sequence, and so on. But, no matter how long you go on "talking" about your musical experience, you will never quite be able to capture it completely in words.

As Thomas Sebeok (e.g. 1991) has remarked, it is highly likely that language originally functioned as a "modeling device." This viewpoint is highly compatible with what is now known about the fixed chronological stages that the child passes through on his or her way to speaking, and it gives us a good account of how sentence composition reflects our experience of the world. Arnheim (1969: 239-242) presents a similar view of language. Words such as conjunctions and prepositions are claimed to be mere "formal devices" of grammar by mainstream linguists, i.e. they are not perceived as having any iconic motivation. But Arnheim gives a different and, in my view, more plausible explanation for their presence in language:

> I referred in an earlier chapter to the barrier character of
> "but," quite different from "although," which does not
> stop the flow of action but merely burdens it with a

complication. Causal relations...are directly perceivable
actions; therefore "because" introduces an effectuating
agent, which pushes things along. How different is the
victorious overcoming of a hurdle conjured up by "in spite
of" from the displacement in "either-or" or "instead;" and
how different is the stable attachment of "with" or "of"
from the belligerent "against."

It is my view, too, that language helps us model and reflect upon the world
in the same way that drawings do. I find it simply amazing that we can
appreciate great literature in virtually the same ways that we experience great
music or great paintings—not discursively, but holistically. In the same way
that a painting is much more than an assemblage of lines, shapes, colors, etc.,
verbal art is much more than an aggregate of grammatical bits and pieces.
Writers use grammatical elements to model the world in ways that parallel how
musicians use melodic elements and painters visual elements to model it.

Verbal Semiosis

In discussing verbal semiosis, a difference between *language* and *speech*
is in order. *Speech* is a physiological phenomenon. It involves the intentional
use of the organs of articulation and of the physical apparatus that contains
them. *Language*, on the other hand, is a mental phenomenon. It consists of
signs and structured relations among them. Language generally manifests
itself through the speech medium; but it can also be expressed through other
media, such as the visual-graphic and the gestural ones. One can have
language without speech (as do individuals with impaired vocal organs),
because it exists in the mind. But one cannot have speech without language,
because speech depends on the neurologically-defined categories of language
for its physical transmission.

There is a strong possibility that language develops before speech. It is
now a documented fact that around the age of 18 months to two years the
position of the larynx in human infants is high in the neck, as it is in that of
other primates. Infants breathe, swallow, and vocalize in ways that are
physiologically similar to gorillas and chimps. But, some time around the
second year of life, the infant's larynx descends into the neck, dramatically
altering the ways in which the child will carry out such physiological functions
from then on. Nobody knows why this descent occurs. It is an anatomical
phenomenon that is unique to humans. This new low position means that the

respiratory and digestive tracts now cross above the larynx. This entails a few risks: food can easily lodge in the entrance of the larynx; and humans cannot drink and breathe simultaneously without choking. But in compensation, it produces a pharyngeal chamber above the vocal folds that can modify sound. This is the key to our ability to articulate sounds.

The echoes of articulated words in the ears of our hominid ancestors, and the images of beings, objects and events that they conjured up, must have been interpreted as divine voices by the first speakers, as Julian Jaynes (1976) suggests. To this day, we feel the "power" of articulated speech: *obscene words, angry words, sweet words,* etc. are expressions which reflect how we react physiologically and emotionally to the mere uttering of words. In today's "politically correct" atmosphere, moreover, words are viewed to be as "magic" as they are in many religious contexts. "Word magic" is, in fact, the term used to describe how tribal medicine men would speak certain words in order to heal individuals.

Linguists have developed the concept of the *phoneme* to account for the capacity to keep words distinct. The phoneme is a unit of sound that the mind can identify as having some feature that keeps it distinct from other sounds and that allows it to enter into a referential relation with other sounds. Thus, what keeps words such as *sip* and *zip* meaningfully distinct is the first sound. The difference between s/z can be discerned in the vibration of the vocal cords in the larynx. If you put your index finger over your larynx and articulate these two sounds, you will see what I mean. The two sounds are otherwise articulated in the same way. The paradigmatic opposition between such sounds is designated phonemic. It seems that we learn almost from birth to make phonemic distinctions.

Take, as another example, the pair *pun/run*. The difference between /p/ and /r/—it is the practice in linguistics to symbolize phonemes by putting them between slant lines—is as follows. The former sound involves the sudden explosion of breath at the lips, while the vocal cords located in the larynx are kept taut. The latter involves a rapid vibration of the tip of the tongue against the palate, as the air escapes from the mouth. In the case of /r/ the vocal cords are allowed to vibrate. These articulatory differences are perceived by the hearing center of the brain and programmed through the motor pathways of the brain into a complex system of coordination between brain and vocal organs. The utilization of this psycho-physiological apparatus to imitate, reproduce or model the sounds associated with some referent is the essence of speech. There are 12 cranial nerves that link the brain with the head and neck. Some perform a motor function, controlling the movement of muscles, while others perform a sensory function, sending signals to the brain. Seven of these serve the process of speech production and hearing. They are the links between the brain and the vocal organs.

Above all else, the larynx must develop the ability to control the flow of air to and from the lungs, so as to prevent food, foreign objects or other substances from entering the trachea on their way to the stomach. It does this by means of a leaf-shaped cartilage known as the epiglottis, which is pulled across the entrance to the larynx as part of the swallowing procedure. This prevents substances from going in the wrong direction. Also, the ability to control the vocal folds makes it possible to build up pressure within the lungs and to emit air not only for expirational purposes, but also for the production of sound.

Neurologically, the ability to speak triggers a shift in hemisphericity from the RH to the LH—the latter being responsible for the motor and comprehension functions associated with speech (Broca's and Wernicke's areas). This entails a gradual shift away from an iconic form of mentality to an increasingly verbal form. The LH has an area to perceive sounds as being the same (recognition) or different (discrimination), and it has the capacity to focus on certain aspects of complex auditory stimuli and to ignore others (auditory attention). Without this capacity, it would be impossible for the mind to generate and utilize phonemic inventories.

On this topic, it is interesting to note the classic 1963 study of the ontogenesis of symbolic competence by Werner and Kaplan. These two researchers found that children start with a kind of iconic mentality in which referents are "objects of contemplation." From this stage they develop a system of motor-gestural depiction. This is followed by a stage in which onomatopoeic naming predominates. Finally, children develop linguistic expression by associating concepts to each other.

Phylogenetically, speech must have functioned as an audio-oral modeling system. Residual examples of this function continue to abound. We often use alliteration, or the repetition of sounds, for various effects: *sing-song*; *no-no*, etc. We commonly lengthen sounds for emphasis: *Yesssss!, Noooooo!*, etc. We regularly use intonation to express emotional states, to emphasize, to shock, etc.: *Are you absolutely sure? Noooooo way!* The language of cartoons and comic books is replete with sound-modeling effects: *Zap!*, *Boom!, Pow!*, etc. Verbal descriptions are, more often than not, sound-imitative—a mean individual, for instance, is typically compared to a snake as being *slithery, slippery, sneaky*, etc. The list could go on and on.

The use of speech to model the world can already be seen when the child reaches six months and starts to emit monosyllabic utterances (*mu, ma, da, di*, etc.). At eight months reduplications and imitative repetitions become more frequent; intonation patterns become distinct; utterances start to signal emphasis and emotions. By the end of the first year the first words emerge (*mama, dada*, etc.). At the completion of 18 months the child has a repertory of not more than 50 words. Comprehension is expanding rapidly. At the end of the second year the child begins to join vocabulary items together into two-word phrases. Communicative behavior increases rapidly.

The crucial period for the onset of language is when the child starts to utter so-called *holophrastic* (one-word) utterances around the first birthday. These are the first acts of true verbal semiosis. The holophrases have been shown to serve three basic functions: naming an object and event; expressing an action or a desire for some action; conveying emotional states. Holophrases are typically monosyllabic reductions of adult words—*da* for *dog*, *ca* for *cat*, etc. Over 60% will develop into nouns; and 20% will become verbs. Reduplication during the second year is also a well-documented phenomenon. Children typically double their monosyllables—*wowo* "water", *bubu* "bottle, etc.—probably because they are becoming aware of the phonemic value of sounds in word- and concept-formation.

In sum, it can be said that verbal semiosis is a sound-based form of meaning-making. Although the language that a group or culture speaks develops into a primarily symbolic code over time, there exists plenty of evidence—both in how the child learns to speak and in the nature of words themselves—that it was forged originally as a sound-modeling code. In his great 1939 novel *Finnegans Wake*, James Joyce makes the sound of words reverberate in our minds, thus stimulating in us memories of how they must have literally "sounded" to us when we first learned to speak. The power of Joyce lies in his ability to penetrate the deepest layers of verbal sound-making, and to put up to the light of consciousness its hidden experiences—the first fears, the first pleasures, etc. that it allowed us to encode. A single word in Joyce's narrative evokes a series of other words related to it via sound or rhythmic pattern. Words are stored by the mind not in terms of semantic fields or alphabetic categories, but in terms of what might be called "experiential contiguity:" i.e. words are related mnemonically to each other via sound and rhythm; a particular sound or rhythmic pattern in one word evokes that same sound or pattern in another. This is why Joyce coins words throughout his novel on the basis of sound and rhythmic resemblances to other words, thus evoking the primordial creative force of language. And this is why Joyce's syntax is not based on conceptual categories, but experiential ones. His "storyline" can only be "experienced," not "understood."

Verbal Communication

Perhaps the most useful description of the use of language for communication purposes is the one by Roman Jakobson (1960). His approach is to start by positing "constitutive" factors. These are as follows. An *addresser*, who recognizes that his or her verbal *message* must refer to something other than itself, sends the message to an *addressee*. For Jakobson the recognition of the message as referring to something other than itself is the *context*. Then he adds the idea of *contact*, by which he means the physical channel in which a message is uttered and the psychological connections between the addresser and addressee. The last factor is the *code*, the shared system of verbal signs and relations by which a verbal text is constructed:

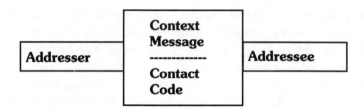

Jakobson then argues that each of these constitutive factors determines a different communicative function of language. According to Jakobson, there are six such functions:

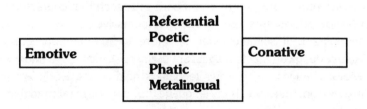

The *emotive* function refers to the fact that an addresser's emotions, attitudes, social status, etc. shape the construction of his or her verbal text. The emotive function varies in degrees according to type of message: poetic texts, for example, tend to be more emotive than referential ones. The effect— physical, psychological, social, etc.—that the verbal text has on the addressee is the *conative* function. The types of verbal texts that we construct can be *referential*, *poetic*, *phatic* and *metalingual*. A *referential* text is a straight-forward exchange of information ("Bloor Street is two blocks north of here"); a *poetic* text is aesthetically-constructed ("Roses are red, violets are blue, and how's it going with you?"); a *phatic* text allows for the establishment of contact ("Hi, how's it going?"); and a *metalingual* text is a verbal text that refers to itself or identifies the code being used ("This book is about semiotics").

Although the Jakobsonian model is the one that semioticians favor, there are other widely-accepted models of verbal communication, such as the ones put forward by Austin (1962), Joos (1967), Searle (1969, 1976), Hymes (1972), and Halliday (e.g. 1975, 1985) that are equally useful. Overall, the research on verbal communication has shown that discourse goes well beyond grammatically-based information transfers. It involves determining *who* says *what* to *whom*; *where* and *when* it is said; and *how* and *why* it is said. It involves, in other words, such factors as the setting, the message contents, the participants and the goals of each interlocutor. All these contextual factors are critical in determining the specific form a speech act will assume.

An interesting example of how psychological and social factors intersect in verbal discourse is the so-called "slang" spoken by North American adolescents. Teenagers "pick up" their ways of speaking from each other so as to demonstrate adherence and conformity to peer-acceptable and peer-sanctioned models of verbal behavior. Young people have always resorted to "code" words since the Medieval Ages in order to strengthen group identity and to set themselves apart from others. Medieval university students, for instance, used the word *lupi* "wolves" to refer to spies who reported other students for using the vernacular instead of Latin. For this reason, I prefer to call adolescent speech *pubilect*, a contraction of *puberty* and *dialect*. *Pubilect* can be defined simply as "the dialect of puberty" (Danesi 1989).

The peculiar intonations, words and modes of speech that characterize pubilect reveal how adolescents come to interpret themselves, others and their physical environment. It is little wonder, therefore, to find that pubilect is a highly unstable code, given that teenagers are themselves inclined to undergo rapid behavioral changes. The views teenagers hold of the world are in continual flux. So too, therefore, is the language they employ to talk and think about the world.

A few years ago, I undertook a research project on pubilect that consisted of two components. First, a research team of various investigators (other teenagers) was formed. In order to ensure that the adolescent informants were not aware of the fact that they were being recorded, each member of the team was instructed to keep a hidden microcassette recorder and to record the casual conversations they had with their peers whenever possible. Hundreds of hours of spontaneous discourse involving nearly 200 adolescents were recorded in this way. After the tapes were made the subjects were told about the project, and all agreed to allow me to use the tapes for the purposes of my research. However, for ethical reasons, the tapes have since been destroyed. The second component consisted of the direct interviewing of adolescents. The elicitation technique consisted in asking them to make comments about events in their daily lives, and to explain some of the words they were accustomed to using at the time: e.g. *slime-bucket, twit, bubble-head, dork, geek*, etc.

An analysis of the data collected in this way has led me to postulate three basic message- and meaning-making categories underlying the adolescent's speech: Emotive Language Programming (ELP), Connotative Language Programming (CLP), and Clique-Coded Language Programming (CCLP).

I coined ELP to refer to the common tendency among adolescents to speak with intensified language markers (exaggerated rates of speech delivery, too fast or too slow, overwrought intonation features, expressive voice modulations, etc.). For instance, utterances such as "He's sooooo cute!" "She's faaaaar out!" "That's amaaaazing!" exemplify the common ELP pattern of overstressing highly emotional words by prolonging their tonic vowels. Utterances such as "We called her up (?) (intonation like a question)...but she wasn't there (?) (same feature)...so we hung up (?) (same feature)" show regular rising contours (as if each sentence were interrogative). This is a common ELP discourse trait that probably indicates the need to ensure the full participation of the interlocutor. ELP also manifests itself in the abundant use of interjections, exclamations and grunts ("Yuch!" "What's happening?" etc.), which reflect the adolescent's need to draw continual attention to his or her feelings, opinions or attitudes. Swear words are also manifestations of this feature. Exaggerated irony or facetiousness ("Get off my case!") and the use of "like" ("Like, I called him up, but, like, he wasn't sure, if he, like, could come..."), reflecting an unconscious hesitancy in expression, are other manifestations of ELP. Essentially, ELP reveals a strong tendency in adolescents to project their feelings. This category was found on both the spontaneous conversation tapes and the interview session tapes, suggesting that ELP is a dominant category in the adolescent's programming of discourse.

CLP was coined to refer to the tendency of adolescents to coin descriptive words, or to extend the meaning of others, in highly connotative ways. Connotation is at the core of the adolescent's socioaffective modeling of reality. In the mid eighties words such as *loser, gross out, air-head, slime-bucket*, and others were in widespread use in Toronto.

Perhaps the most revealing finding came during the interview sessions. Several adolescents were asked, during one specific project, to explain, in their own way, the semantic differences among *nerd, dork* and *geek*. One informant defined *nerd* as "a social outcast...male, greasy, studies chemistry all night long...someone I would never talk to." Another described a *dork* as "more socially acceptable, although he always bumps into people and drops things." "Dorkness," another informant added, "is not a permanent state." A *geek* is "someone who doesn't take showers, who is slimy, greasy and drippy." One informant pointed out that there was a particular kind of *geek*, known as a *leem*, in her school, who was particularly odious. He was described as someone "who just wastes oxygen."

CLP reveals that adolescents are keenly sensitive to bodily appearance and image, as well as to the perceived sociability of peers. At puberty the dramatic changes in physical appearance, and the emotional changes that accompany them, are traumatic. Teenagers become inordinately concerned about their appearance and behavior, believing that everyone is constantly observing them. This is why they talk continuously about how others act, behave and look. Language, dress, musical tastes and other signifying codes become means for identifying with peers. During childhood the individual's modes of interaction with the environment are centered upon a constantly-developing consciousness of Self. The child is typically concerned with learning about how the Self fits into the scheme of things. At puberty, however, the child's social consciousness emerges and begins to dominate his or her thinking and actions. While human beings of all ages are influenced by their consciousness of others, and tend to conform to behavioral models that are acceptable to their peer groups, teenagers are particularly susceptible to this kind of influence, simply because their social consciousness emerges for the first time on the developmental timetable as a powerful mental *Gestalt*. The CLP phenomenon is a symptomatic manifestation of its power over cognition during adolescence.

The CCLP category refers to the fact that adolescent language constitutes a means for peer-group identification. The life of a typical teenager is anchored within the social cosmos of the high school. It is here that he or she strives to gain and maintain social status primarily through actions and behaviors that are deemed socially advantageous by the peer group. In the contemporary high school community students tend to become part of clan-like cliques which impose specific behavioral codes (in dress, in hairstyle, etc.) for membership. Teenagers gain overall acceptance, status and prestige within the high school through a skillful manipulation of the symbolic codes that characterize so-called "coolness." Language constitutes one of these codes. The CCLP category refers to the kinds of discourse that each clique engages in. Adolescents will talk mainly about what is of direct interest to their clique members. The themes that surface most frequently in the speech samples collected are the following: quantity of alcohol consumption, the "doing" of drugs, music preferences within a clique, party-related activities, the strategic use of physical aggression, dress, sexual promiscuity and prowess, automobile ownership, physical appearance. In a nutshell, the domain of teenage discourse is centered around the immediacy of present events and the specific interests of the clique. This restricted discourse range is a product of peer communicative interaction within the clique.

The research on adolescents that I started several years ago has made me realize, more than ever before, that verbal communication is rarely a script-based, disembodied, information-transfer process. Pubilect, like many other discourse phenomena, leads me to believe, on the contrary, that verbal communication almost always involves what Goffman (1959) has appropriately called "strategic interaction," a mode of human interactive behavior that unfolds in terms of the enactment of ego-centered agendas, goals and affective states.

The study of how people speak strongly suggests that human beings enter into verbal communication primarily to draw attention to their feelings and attitudes. The verbal messages we construct daily implore addressees to focus momentarily on our ego-states or feelings. Our utterances make an emotional claim of sorts on everyone in the social situation. Our affective responses to the world seem to dictate, or at the very least guide, the choice of the words and structures we continually make in discourse. Like a novel where the author's feelings and perspective shape the form and contents of the storyline, our verbal messages are woven together with the semiosic thread of our emotional states.

To see what this means, consider the following situation. Let us assume that you are a university student and that you have just picked up an essay from a professor whose reputation for toughness is legendary. You look at the grade on the essay and you see an A⁺. I am willing to bet that you will find a way to work the fact that you got a high grade into the substance of the discourse you are going to have with the next person you run into, even if that person may have no connection whatsoever to the "essay situation." You simply will not be able to hold back from verbalizing your elation.

Writing

If language is an audio-oral modeling code, then what is the relation of speech to writing? Is the latter simply a graphic means of recording speech? So natural is the association of speech with writing in literate cultures that we rarely make a distinction between the two. From a phylogenetic perspective, the possession and utilization of an alphabet could only have been achieved by a highly-evolved and abstract rational intellect, capable of reflective and conscious thought. No wonder, then, that knowledge of the alphabet, or *literacy*, has always been considered to be the primary condition for the formal coding of knowledge.

How did alphabets come about? Here is a hypothetical scenario. Recall from the previous chapter that early humans had apparently mastered drawing long before the advent of the first civilizations. As primitive art proliferated, it must have been used eventually for recording and communicating thoughts. The hand movements employed to record thoughts in this way must have gradually become abbreviated. From these condensed iconic representations a pictorial form of writing emerged. This led to the invention of *writing*. The earliest writing systems were all independent of speech and were not alphabetic or syllabic in character but were all pictographic or iconically representational. Early writing, therefore, was conventionalized artistic expression.

The first examples of pictographic—as opposed to alphabetic—writing are actually rather recent. In the ancient civilization of Sumer around 3,500 BC, pictographic writing was used to record agricultural transactions and astronomical observations. Most of the pictographs represented nouns for stars and animals with a few qualifying adjectives for "small," "big," "bright" and the like. A few centuries later, verbs were introduced into the pictographic writing system: *to sleep*, for example, was represented by a person in a supine position. To facilitate the speed of writing, the Sumerians eventually streamlined their drawings and transformed them into symbols for the actual sounds of speech. These were written down on clay tablets with a stylus in a form of writing known as *cuneiform*.

By about 3,000 BC the Ancient Egyptians used a kind of script—known as *hieroglyphic*—which consisted of symbols that stood for parts of words. These allowed the Egyptians to record their hymns and prayers, to register the names and titles of individuals and deities, and to annotate various community activities—*hieroglyphic* derives from Greek *hieros* "holy" and *glyphein* "to carve." Such developments bear witness to a very advanced stage of mental and cultural evolution. Once writing became a flourishing enterprise, it began to appear without pictures, producing the first written verbal *texts*—writing without pictures.

By about 1,000 BC the Phoenicians had invented an alphabet. This became the primary means for recording audio-oral speech. The Phoenicians had finally severed the iconic relationship between pictures and referents, creating an abstract system for recording phonetic values. The Greeks adopted the Phoenician alphabet and called each symbol by such words as *alpha, beta, gamma*, etc., which are imitations of Phoenician/Semitic words: *aleph* "ox", *beth* "house", *gimel* "camel", etc. They also introduced symbols for vowel sounds, thus producing the first true *alphabet*, in the modern sense of the word.

Writing is a truly remarkable achievement. It has made possible the recording and transmission of knowledge. Indeed, in Western culture to be *literate* is to be *educated*. The first schools were a logical outgrowth of the invention of cuneiform writing. So close has the link between the two been forged that today we can scarcely think of knowledge unless it is recorded in some textual form and preserved in some library for posterity. But in every alphabetic symbol that we now use to record our thoughts, there is an iconic history and prehistory that has become "dim" or virtually "unseeable" because our eyes are no longer trained to extract iconic meaning from it.

Verbal Art

Like any art, verbal art is an artifactual means by which we try to make sense of the world. The great poems, novels and plays of all cultures are verbal crystallizations of our search for meaning to life. There is no culture, for instance, without poetry. The use of words to reproduce natural sounds, to evoke feelings, to provide insight into the nature of things is a truly remarkable accomplishment. More will be said about this in the seventh chapter.

The philosopher Vico, who was introduced in the second chapter, saw poetry as the primordial form of language. Vico called the first speakers "poets," which etymologically means "makers," because their first words were verbal inventions. At first, what will eventually become an abstract concept is formed as a god or a hero. Vico says of the ancient Greeks that they could not form the concept of "valor." So, like poets, they formed what they meant by it through the character of Achilles. Children acquire concepts in identical ways—through god-like and heroic story characters who embody them. But these embodiments are not merely fanciful nor principally subjective.

Concluding Remarks

With this chapter, which dealt with what is perhaps the most powerful source of message- and meaning-making available to us—verbal semiosis—the first part of the book (how we make messages and meanings) is completed.

Detailed and complementary discussions of the various topics treated in this part can be found in the suggested readings at the end of each of the five chapters.

Language results from audio-oral semiosis. It is not, in my view, a kind of innate mental organ, as some linguists claim. Indeed, if we were somehow to shut off subsequent generations from language, there is virtually no doubt that it would disappear. Physical organs, on the other hand, would continue to develop as they do now. Language, like all other semiotic codes, must be transmitted to subsequent generations. What we do inherit from our biological heritage is the capacity for semiosis.

SUGGESTIONS FOR FURTHER READING

Arnheim, R. (1969). *Visual Thinking*. Berkeley: University of California Press.

Austin, J. L. (1962). *How to Do Things with Words*. Cambridge, Mass.: Harvard University Press.

Bloomfield, L. (1933). *Language*. New York: Holt.

Chomsky, N. (1957). *Syntactic Structures*. The Hague: Mouton.

Chomsky, N. (1966a). *Topics in the Theory of Grammar*. The Hague: Mouton.

Chomsky, N. (1966b). *Cartesian Linguistics*. New York: Harper & Row.

Chomsky, N. (1986). *Knowledge of Language: Its Nature, Origin, and Use*. New York: Praeger.

Danesi, M. (1987). *Robert A. Hall and American Structuralism*. Lake Bluff, Ill.: Jupiter Press.

Danesi, M. (1989). Adolescent Language as Affectively Coded Behavior: Findings of an Observational Research Project. *Adolescence* 24: 311-320.

Farb, P. (1974). *Word Play*. New York: Bantam.

Goffman, E. (1959). *The Presentation of Self in Everyday Life*. Garden City: Doubleday.

Halliday, M.A.K. (1975). *Learning How to Mean: Explorations in the Development of Language*. London: Arnold.

Halliday, M.A.K. (1985). *Introduction to Functional Grammar*. London: Arnold.

Hymes, D. (1972). Models in the Interaction of Language and Social Life. In: J. Gumperz and D. Hymes (eds.), *Directions in Sociolinguistics: The Ethnography of Communication*, pp. 34-45. New York: Holt, Rinehart & Winston.

Ingram, J. (1992). *Talk, Talk, Talk: An Investigation into the Mystery of Speech*.

Harmondsworth: Penguin.

Jakobson, R. (1960). Linguistics and Poetics. In: T. A. Sebeok (ed.), *Style and Language*, pp. 34-45. Cambridge, Mass.: MIT Press.

Jaynes, J. (1976). *The Origin of Consciousness in the Breakdown of the Bicameral Mind.* Toronto: University of Toronto Press.

Joos, M. (1967). *The Five Clocks.* New York: Harcourt, Brace and World.

Langer, S. (1948). *Philosophy in a New Key.* Cambridge: Harvard University Press.

Pinker, S. (1990). Language Acquisition. In: D. N. Osherson and H. Lasnik (eds.), *Language: An Invitation to Cognitive Science*, pp. 191-241. Cambridge, Mass.: MIT Press.

Sapir, E. (1921). *Language.* New York: Harcourt Brace.

Saussure, F. de (1916/1966). *Course in General Linguistics.* Paris: Payot.

Searle, J. R. (1969). *Speech Acts: An Essay in the Philosophy of Language.* Cambridge: Cambridge University Press.

Searle, J. R. (1976). A Classification of Illocutionary Acts. *Language in Society* 5: 1-23.

Sebeok, T. A. (1991). *A Sign is Just a Sign.* Bloomington: Indiana University Press.

Tannen, D. (1989). *Talking Voices.* Cambridge: Cambridge University Press.

Werner, H. and Kaplan, B. (1963). *Symbol Formation: An Organismic-Developmental Approach to the Psychology of Language and the Expression of Thought.* New York: John Wiley.

Part 2

Making the Human World

Chapter 6

"LOVE IS SWEET" IS MORE THAN A METAPHOR!

Preliminary Remarks

If a very young child were to ask you "What is love?" how would you answer him or her? One thing you would not do for sure is to give the child a "dictionary" definition of love. What you are more likely to do is to relate the "experience" of love to something that is familiar to him or her: "Well, you know, love is like...when mommy or daddy kisses you...and you feel good about it, don't you?" What you have done is something very familiar that reveals something rather fundamental about how we think. You intuitively knew that the child could relate the abstract concept of *love* to a feeling with which he or she is familiar. You have discovered, incidentally, the reason why we tell stories to children all the time to explain morals, ideas, difficult concepts, etc. to them. These relate concepts to the world of experience. This "relational process" is the essence of *metaphor*.

Despite the enormous amount of interest in metaphor among scholars in the last few decades—in 1979, Booth remarked that if one were to count the number of bibliographical entries on metaphor published in the year 1977 alone, one would be forced to surmise that by the year 2039 there would be "more students of metaphor on Earth than people"—by and large people still think of "metaphor" as a rhetorical device used by poets and writers to decorate or render their messages more effectively or ornately. Nothing could be farther from the truth. If the recent work on metaphor is even partially correct, then metaphor is a fundamental form of thought. This is what we constantly discover when we attempt to "explain" concepts to children. Metaphor underlies the way we conceptualize the world. It is the cognitive phenomenon that converts factual feeling—states into artifactual conceptual structures. It allows us to literally create the artifactual world of culture.

Consider, again, the concept of *love*. To find out what we "mean" by love, all we have to do is "talk" about it. Here are a few of the ways in which our culture talks about, and therefore conceptualizes, love (from Lakoff and Johnson 1980: 49):

(1)   There were *sparks* between us.
(2)   We are *attracted* to each other.
(3)   My life *revolves* around her.
(4)   I am *magnetically drawn* toward her.
(5)   Theirs is a *sick* relationship.
(6)   Their marriage is *dead*; it can't be *revived*.
(7)   Their relationship is *in good shape*.
(8)   I'm *crazy* about her.
(9)   I'm constantly *raving* about her.
(10) He's gone *mad* over her.
(11) I've *lost my head* over her.
(12) She *cast* a spell over me.
(13) The *magic* is gone.
(14) She has *bewitched* me.
(15) I'm *in a trance* over her.

The first four sentences reveal that we commonly think of love as a physical force (gravitational, electromagnetic, etc.); sentences 5-7 indicate that we also think of love as a patient relation; sentences 8-11 disclose that we conceptualize love, at other times, as a madness; and the sentences 12-15 suggest that we experience love as well as a kind of magical force. *Love* is indeed a metaphor, as the poets have always known. But to say that it is a metaphor has, clearly, many more implications than might at first seem.

The origin of the concept *love* is to be found in instinctive responses such as increases in blood flow, muscle tension, salivation, etc. which are registered as memorable percepts. *Percepts* are immediate units of knowing derived from sensation or feeling. These are then organized into a model of feeling to which all humans can intuitively identify and respond. At this factual level "love" is a perceived state. Through the workings of cultural sense-making, some of the constituents of this state are then connected metaphorically to each other to form the concept *love*. At this higher level *love* is a force, a patient, a madness, etc. In our culture, it is often thought of as a gustatory reaction: *You're so sweet, She's my sweetheart*, etc. The transformational process from affective state to conceptualization has now been completed.

"Love" has been transferred from the world of affective states to the world of conceptualization. A *concept*, therefore, can be defined as any "connection" made by the human mind within specific cultural contexts. So we probably feel love in similar ways the world over, but we think about it in culture-specific ways. It is interesting to note that once a concept has been formed in this way it can then be extended beyond the language system to shape cultural institutions and behaviors. Rituals of love-making in our culture invariably involve metaphorical thinking, such as the *love is sweet* metaphor: e.g. sweets are given to a loved one at St. Valentine's day; matrimonial love is symbolized at a wedding ceremony by the eating of a cake; we "sweeten" our breath with candy before kissing our loved one; etc.

The purpose of this chapter is to look at metaphor and metonymy as fundamental signifying forces in the human species. Specifically, it will attempt to answer what metaphor and metonymy are, and how they literally allow us to *make* concepts and culture-specific *models* out of feeling-states. Metaphor is the feature of the human mind that transforms factual World 1 and 2 states into artifactual World 3 ones:

World 3 = Artifactual World

The human-made world of concepts, cultural models. *Love* **is now "thought of" as sweetness, a physical force, a state of madness, etc.**

Metaphor

Converts World 1 and 2 factual states into World 3 states.

(A is B)

World 1 and 2 = Factual World

The biologically-inherited world of feelings, urges, and sentiments, etc. *Love* **is felt as entailing certain physical and affective states.**

What Is Metaphor?

As can be gleaned from the discussion above, *metaphor* is essentially an **A is B** relation. It is a tendency of the human mind to think, or experience, one thing in terms of another. The **A** is usually something abstract or unfamiliar, and the **B** something concrete or familiar. The model which has become the basic schema to discuss metaphor is the *topic-vehicle-ground* model put forward by Richards in 1936, and then refined by Wheelwright (1954) and Black (1962). After Black, this model has come to be known as the "interactional model." The *topic*, also known as the *tenor*, is what is talked about in the metaphor (the **A-referent)**. It is the thing that our mind literally wants to know more about. The *vehicle* is that part which makes a comment on the topic (the **B-referent)**. It is the part that "explains" the **A** to us in terms of concrete or familiar notions. The *ground* is the meaning that is generated by the "interaction" between tenor and vehicle. Thus, in the metaphor *Time is money*, "time" is the tenor, "money" the vehicle, and the meaning—which would obviously require an extensive paraphrase—is the *ground.*

Recent work in linguistics and psychology has shown that metaphor operates at various levels of complexity and abstraction. *Seeing is believing* is both a simple verbal metaphor, but also a much more encompassing cultural model of how we conceptualize time, as can be seen in the following examples:

(16)   There is more to this than *meets the eye.*
(17)   I have a different *point of view.*
(18)   It all depends on how you *look* at it.
(19)   I take a *dim view* of the whole matter.
(20)   I never *see eye to eye* on things with you.

A little reflection should convince you that this embedded metaphorical pattern permeates all aspects of the way we think. This is why we constantly say that we have a *world-view*, *insight*, an *image* to maintain, etc. So, *seeing is believing* is at one level a simple metaphor: **A is B**. But at a higher level it is a model—an overriding metaphorical formula—of how *believing* is perceived to unfold. The vehicles that instantiate this model can take on any form, verbal and nonverbal. We say, for instance, that *justice is blind* and represent it by statues built outside or inside courtrooms with blindfolds to symbolize this metaphor. The metaphorical expression *the scales of justice*, too, is commonly symbolized by corresponding sculptures of scales near or inside justice buildings. The instantiations of the vehicle are always evident in a discourse or poetic text, while the topic may or may not be mentioned. This view of verbal metaphor extends it beyond the sentence level to encompass discourse, textuality and cultural sense-making.

Although interest in metaphor is as old as Aristotle (384-322 BC), the experimental study of its relation to cognition and communication is a relatively recent phenomenon. Since the seventies interest in metaphor on the part of many scholars has become so intense that it is virtually impossible to skim even the surface of the empirical findings it has generated. What stands out most from this research domain is that metaphor is now viewed by many to constitute an intrinsic feature of how we represent the world and, subsequently, of how we construct cultural models of it. Indeed, without the capacity to metaphorize, culture would not exist.

Metaphor evokes as many perceptions among people as it does definitions. Aristotle is the one who, in his _Rhetoric_ and _Poetics_, coined the term— itself a "metaphor" (_meta_ "beyond" + _pherein_ "to carry")—to refer to the common verbal phenomenon of implicit comparison (**A implies B** or **A is B**). Aristotle's view has come to be known as the _comparison_ theory of verbal metaphor. He noticed that metaphors revealed something fundamental about the human mind: "Midway between the unintelligible and the commonplace, it is metaphor which most produces knowledge." However, Aristotle did not pursue this line of thinking. He simply acknowledged that metaphorical language was psychologically powerful, but affirmed that it was, in essence, an ornamental or stylistic option to more basic literal ways of thinking and speaking.

The literalist view of meaning has survived practically unaltered since Aristotle's time. It posits that metaphors are derivatives of literal, propositional modes of semantic programming (e.g. **If A...then B**). Some go even further, viewing metaphors as _deviations_ from semantic rules. But in the last few decades such views of metaphor have come increasingly under attack. Since the seventies the scientific investigations of metaphor have been proliferating. In 1977, for instance, a study by Pollio and his associates (Pollio, Barlow, Fine and Pollio 1977) showed that metaphorical language was an all-pervasive force in cognition and communication. They found that speakers of English uttered, on average, 3,000 novel verbal metaphors and 7,000 idioms per week. It became clear from their study that verbal metaphor was hardly a mere stylistic option to literal language. Since 1977 the number of volumes, symposia, courses and article-length studies on metaphorical language programming in the cognitive and social sciences has reached astronomical proportions.

Literalist and deviationist models of verbal metaphor are of no particular relevance here. Both claim, essentially, that literal speech is primary and that metaphors are extensions, deviations or anomalies. As mentioned, this view is really no longer tenable. Aristotle's comparison theory is still, in my opinion, the basis for any discussion of metaphor. Over the course of the centuries, the Aristotelian model has been rejected or expanded. But its basic premise, expressed in the formula **A is B**, has never been completely discarded. The comparison view implies an analogy between two concepts or entities. Verbal metaphor is construed, in effect, to be a condensed simile. Similarly, so-called *substitution* theories, which are versions of comparison theories, assume an analogy that is said to remedy gaps in literal expression. They claim that the speaker employs an expression which actually refers to something else. The comparison and substitution explanations of metaphor can be seen, in actual fact, to offer different perspectives on the same phenomenon. The metaphorical capacity inheres in the ability to establish similarities among phenomenologically-dissimilar things—at times by comparison, at others by substitution—to create models of the world that the mind can utilize in many diverse ways. Metaphor is a "tool" that the mind constantly enlists to explore reality and to give order and coherence to our otherwise chaotic experiences. In fact, metaphor can be said to fabricate similarity and resemblance in the world of human experience. The only way we can conceptualize "similarity" or "resemblance" is metaphorically.

Vico defined *metaphor* as a "fable-making" capacity that allowed the first humans to make connections and, therefore, to literally create new, context-free associations. The primordial function of metaphor inhered in what Verene calls an "isness" relation (Verene 1981: 60-100). Traditionally, metaphor has been viewed as tied to analogy, i.e. as an operation that makes out something to be "like" something else. For Vico, on the other hand, the primordial operation of the metaphorical capacity established an "isness" among things. Vico claimed that *Jove* was the first name created by humans as they became conscious of the first thundering sky. Once this sky was called *Jove*, all other experiences of the same phenomenon were "found again" in this name. This is how metaphor works.

Lakoff and Johnson (1980) relate imagery to metaphor by means of what they call *image-schema* theory. Johnson (1987: 79) defines *image schemas* as "those recurring structures of, or in, our perceptual interactions, bodily experiences and cognitive operations." For Lakoff (1987: 444) *image schemas* involve a largely unconscious process that portrays locations, movements, shapes, etc. in the mind. Lakoff (1987: 444-446) illustrates image-schema theory as follows. If someone is asked to explain an idiom such as *spill the beans* in terms of its associated imagery-content—"Where are the beans before they are spilled?" "How big is the container?" "Is the spilling on purpose or accidental?" etc.—then, Lakoff suggests, even those speakers who claim not to have a conscious image of the idiom can answer such questions in remarkably uniform ways: e.g. the beans are supposed to be kept in a container; the container is always described as being about the size of the human head; etc.

To get a firmer sense of how metaphorical formulas underlie the ways in which we perceive, think and act, consider how we conceptualize arguments (Lakoff and Johnson 1980). The most commonly-used vehicle for conceptualizing arguments in our culture is "war":

(21)   Your claims are *indefensible*.
(22)   You *attacked* all my *weak points*.
(23)   Your criticisms were *right on target*.
(24)   I *demolished* his argument.
(25)   I've never *won* an argument.
(26)   She *shot down* all my points.
(27)   If you use that *strategy*, I'll *wipe you out*.

What does talking about argument in this way imply? It means that we actually "win" or "lose" arguments, and that our reactions are parallel to those experienced in physical battle. In fact, we experience and conceptualize an argument as we would a battle: we attack position, lose ground, plan strategy, defend or abandon a line of attack, etc. The *argument is war* metaphor structures the actions we perform when we argue. In fact, it might even be said that arguments "exist" because we conceptualize them in this way.

Now, take *time is money* as it is reflected in English:

(28)   I'm *wasting* too much time.
(29)   That will *save* you hours.
(30)   I've *invested* a lot of time in her.
(31)   That mistake *cost* me several hours.
(32)   He's living on *borrowed* time.

What this formula clearly reflects is the value that money has in our culture. Subsequently, this metaphorical formula can be used in concomitance with others—*time is a limited resource, time is a valuable commodity*—to produce increasingly complex cognitive models of "time."

This kind of thinking seems to permeate the entire artifactual domain of concepts. Here is just a sampling of how metaphor underlies conceptualized models of the world:

- *Happiness is up/Sadness is down*

(33)   I'm feeling *up*.
(34)   She's feeling *down*.
(35)   That *boosted* my spirits.
(36)   My mood *sank*.
(37)   That gave me a *lift*.

- *Health and life are up/Sickness and death are down*

(38)   I'm at the *peak* of my health.
(39)   He *fell* ill.
(40)   Life is an *uphill* struggle.
(41)   Lazarus *rose* from the dead.
(42)   He's *sinking* fast.

- *Light is knowledge/Dark is ignorance*

(43)   I was *illuminated* by that professor.
(44)   I was left in the *dark* about what happened.
(45)   That idea is very *clear*.
(46)   That theory is *obscure.*
(47)   His example *shed light* on several matters.

- *Ideas are buildings*

(48)   That is a *well-constructed* theory.
(49)   His views are on *solid ground.*
(50)   That theory needs *support*.
(51)   Their viewpoint *collapsed* under criticism.
(52)   She put together the *framework* of a theory.

- *Ideas are plants*

(53)   Her ideas have come to *fruition.*
(54)   That's a *budding* theory.
(55)   His views have contemporary *offshoots.*
(56)   That is a *branch* of mathematics.

- *Ideas are commodities*

(57) He certainly knows how to *package* his ideas.
(58) That idea just won't *sell.*
(59) There's no *market* for that idea.
(60) That's a *worthless* idea.

It is interesting to note that all scientific theories are metaphors. This was Black's (1962) brilliant demonstration. The Bohr theory of atomic structure, for instance, is presented as a tiny "universe," with a nucleus ("sun") and orbiting planets ("electrons," "protons," etc.). The end result is a theory of atomic structure that is conceptualized in terms of something familiar. Everything that I have written in this book, too, has been structured by specific metaphorical vehicles. Just read it with this perspective in mind and you will be able to pick out the vehicles that have served me well in exposing the subject matter of semiotics. So, too, with every verbal text. Next time you listen to a news broadcast, read a textbook, a newspaper article, etc. pay close attention to *how* the message is structured, and you are bound to discover the work of metaphor lying beneath the surface. Next time you have an opportunity to listen to and watch a television evangelist, listen carefully to his sermon, and you will discover the power and force that metaphor has over people's minds. When the preacher talks about the need of being "cleansed," "purified," etc., he is utilizing the concrete force of the *sex is dirty* metaphor to impart a feeling of "uncleanliness" to his believers.

All this really could not be otherwise. Metaphor reflects the nature of human cognition. Our thinking is apparently structured in an **A is B** way. This is how we make conceptual meaning and how we come to understand the world around us. This does not mean that icons and indexes, for instance, are metaphors in the strict sense of the word. But, in a referential sense, we can see how the mind relates things in an **A is B** way even at this fundamental sign-making level. When semioticians say that "something stands for something else," they are really saying that the **A** (be it a signifier or a representamen) **is** (stands for) **B** (something else/the referent). So, in a certain fundamental sense, semiosis is itself a metaphorical process. This, incidentally, is the great insight to be learned from reading Giambattista Vico's monumental *New Science* of 1725 (Danesi 1993).

Metonymy

The study of metaphor has fallen traditionally within the discipline of *rhetoric*, the field that studies the techniques used in all kinds of discourses, from ordinary conversation to verbal aesthetic texts. Within this domain, metaphor is viewed to be one of the many *tropes*—figures of speech—to be studied. But if the recent work in psychology and linguistics is correct, then *metaphor* is much more than "just a metaphor." So the practice today is to use this term to refer to the study of all figurative language and to consider the other tropes as particular kinds, or stylistically-shaped manifestations, of metaphor. Within this new analytical framework, *personification*, or the figurative endowment of inanimate objects or qualities with human attributes ("Life has caught up with him"), for instance, can be easily seen to have the general **A is B** structure. In this case the underlying conceptual unit is always **A is a person**. The same kind of reasoning can be applied to most of the other classical tropes—catachresis, hyperbole, etc.

But there is one type of metaphorical process that is regularly considered separately from metaphor. This is *metonymy,* or the use of an entity to refer to another that is related to it. Here are some examples of this interesting phenomenon (Lakoff and Johnson 1980: 35-40):

(61) She likes to read *Dostoyevski* (= the writings of Dostoyevski).
(62) He's in *dance* (= the dancing profession).
(63) My mom frowns on *blue jeans* (= the wearing of blue jeans).
(64) New *windshield wipers* will satisfy him (= the state of having new wipers).

There is a special subtype of metonymy, known as *synecdoche*, which is particularly productive in cognition. This is the signifying process by which the part represents the whole:

(65) The *automobile* is destroying our health (= the collection of automobiles).
(66) We need a couple of *strong bodies* for our teams (= strong people).
(67) I've got a new *set of wheels* (= car).
(68) We need *new blood* in this organization (= new people).

Particularly fruitful in our culture is the metonymic formula *the face is the person:*

(69)   He's just another *pretty face.*
(70)   There are an awful lot of *faces* in the audience.
(71)   We need some new *faces* around here.

This metonymic concept also crystallizes in nonverbal behaviors. It underlies the reason why portraits, in painting and photography, focus on the face. We look at a person's face first, and, as we saw in the third chapter, preparing and decoding the face is a primary act of signification. In fact expressions such as *saving face, face the music,* etc. highlight the prominent role the face has as a metonym for personality.

Concepts

Metaphors vary in force and novelty. A conventionalized metaphor is automatic, effortless, and established by community consensus. To say that *ideas are geometrical objects*—that they are *parallel, circular, diametrically opposite,* etc.—is a reflex discourse pattern that we have acquired from our culture. But other metaphors are conceptually new and thus require us to reshape the way we think. These are highly characteristic of poetry. Metaphor involves a thought process by which we understand one kind of thing experientially in terms of another.

Lakoff and Johnson's (1980) idea of "conceptual metaphors" is indeed a crucial one in understanding how communal, World 3, sense-making is based on metaphor. These are really "cognitive formulas" that our cultures have made available to us. They have crystallized from the repeated associations made between a specific tenor and a class of vehicles—vehicles belonging to the same vocabulary theme known as a *lexical field.* The result is a conceptual domain that associates the entire lexical field to the tenor. So, for instance, if the tenor *ideas* is continually conceptualized in terms of different geometrical figures and relations (*points, lines,* etc.) a new category of conceptualization eventually emerges: *ideas are geometrical figures and relations* ("Those *ideas* are *circular,*" "I don't see the *point* of your *idea,*" "Her *ideas* are *central* to the discussion," etc.).

Conceptual metaphors or formulas, as Lakoff and Johnson (1980) have persuasively argued, underlie culture-specific models of reality. They are, of course, artifactual signs. This is why it is now possible to write computer programs to generate conceptual metaphors *à la* Lakoff and Johnson (Martin 1990). But it must not be forgotten that they are the end-products of a more fundamental creative force. The latter can never be simulated computationally.

To see why this is so, consider the following hypothetical reconstruction of the origin of the cognitive formula *more is up/less is down*. In the deep factual level of mind, image schemas are being continually generated by our bodily system interacting with the environment. The schema "verticality," for instance, is probably forged out of our perceptual experiences connected with standing upright, climbing stairs, looking up, etc. Let us assume that a certain individual might have spontaneously used this schema during a conversation in association with a "quantity" schema. This individual might have said something like "Prices keep going up." Then another individual might have appropriately added "Yes, and my earnings have fallen." Such associations between verticality and quantity in routine communicative exchanges led eventually to the concept *more is up/less is down*. Only after this has transpired can a computational algorithm for generating instantiations of this formula be envisaged. Of course, a computational algorithm can be devised to make random associations between different tenors and vehicles, and therefore to generate "novel" metaphors just like the individuals of my hypothetical story did. But for these random metaphors to become meaningful, and therefore communicatively usable, it takes a human mind in a specific social context to *interpret* them, i.e. to truly "metaphorize" them.

It is interesting to note that the relevant research on verbal metaphor has shown that it has a content-related locus in the RH and a form-related one in the LH. The evidence for this comes primarily from the study of brain-damaged patients. The experiment that has become a classic point-of-reference on the neurological programming of metaphor is the one by Winner and Gardner (1977). These two researchers presented a series of verbal metaphors to various subjects asking them to select one of four response pictures which best portrayed the meaning of the metaphor. For the sentence "A heavy heart can really make a difference" the subjects were shown four pictures from which to choose: (1) a person crying (= metaphorical meaning); (2) a person staggering under the weight of a huge red heart (= literal meaning); (3) a 500-pound weight (= a representation emphasizing the adjective *heavy*); (4) a red heart (= a representation emphasizing the noun phrase *red heart*). The subjects were divided into aphasics (i.e. subjects with LH damage), patients with RH damage, and a normal control group. Normals gave five times as many metaphorical responses; but the RH patients could respond only with equal frequency to metaphorical and literal cues. Winner and

Gardner thus established a link between the ground of a metaphor and the RH of the brain, making it possible to hypothesize that the ground is programmed by the RH.

Since the early eighties the evidence in favor of an RH involvement in metaphorical language programming has been steadily mounting. The picture that emerges from the research, therefore, suggests that the RH is the locus for the content-structure, or ground, of a metaphor, and that the LH is responsible for its form-structure and ultimate conceptualization. In novel metaphors it is highly likely that the neurological flow goes from the RH to the LH.

There are a few caveats that must be made *vis-à-vis* the idea that metaphor is the crucial mechanism that transforms the world of factual-sensory experience into an artifactual-conceptual one. First, whether or not all concepts are structured metaphorically or based on image schemas is a question that is open to research and debate. It is, nevertheless, certainly judicious to entertain the possibility that many concepts are metaphorical in structure. Second, even if this were so, it must not be forgotten that there are many aspects of language and cognition that are not conceptual. These may be perceptual, iconic, indexical or denotative, for instance. But I agree with Lakoff and Johnson that many of the concepts encoded by a language reveal a metaphorical form in their underlying structure. Moreover, their approach to language through the level at which it coincides with conceptualization seems to me to be much more revealing than the undue emphasis on syntax that characterizes mainstream linguistics. If nothing else, the plethoric research conducted on the world's languages during the last century has amply documented that syntactic systems are remarkably alike and rather unrevealing about the nature of how a message or a thought is programmed verbally. It has shown, in my opinion, that syntax constitutes a kind of organizing grid for the much more fundamental conceptual-semantic plane. This, on the other hand, is the level at which languages show significant differences, revealing the modeling systems that sustain their uses in communication.

In the last few decades the research on the comprehension and production of metaphor has made it insupportable to assign figurative meaning to some subordinate category *vis-à-vis* other semantic systems. Research on so-called anomalous strings (e.g. "Colorless green ideas sleep furiously"), for instance, has shown that the metaphorizing capacity forces people to extract meaning from virtually any well-formed combination of words (e.g. Pollio and Smith 1979). If people are required to interpret such strings, then they will do so, no matter how contrived the interpretation might appear. This suggests that metaphorical thinking is a dominant and ever-present option in discourse, and that literal thinking might actually constitute a special, limited case of communicative behavior. In the absence of contextual information for an utterance such as "The murderer is an animal," we are immediately inclined to apply the metaphorical mode in interpretation. It is only if we are told that the so-called "murder" was committed by a biological animal that a literal interpretation becomes possible. This is probably due to the fact that literal speech is tied to the verbalization of the finite universe of *actual worlds*, whereas metaphor extends discourse into the infinite universe of *potential worlds*.

Cultural Models

Language and discourse result when deep-level factual activities become part of *communal* sense-making. Human thought starts off at a factual, *common-sense* (i.e. universal) level as a system of feeling-states. But through the workings of metaphor, a surface artifactual form of cognition eventually crystallizes. The particular characteristics of this communally-forged mentality constitute the source of differences among persons and among cultures. Although it evolved out of the deep level, it has come to be the dominant form of mentality in the discursive mind. *Syntax* is definable, therefore, as a surface-level system that has emerged to arrange and organize the increasingly complex structures that the concept-generating mind has invented. Syntax produces a stable *conceptual* system. Deep-level sense-making gives pattern and continuity to human *experience*. Surface-level syntax gives pattern and stability to *concepts*.

Besides transforming deep-level units into surface-level ones, metaphor continues to do its work within the confines of the surface level of mind (World 3) to produce increasingly abstract symbolic structures. These result from the connections that we make metaphorically among different *concepts*. The concept forged by a metaphorical connection in the deep level between percepts can be called a *first-order* concept. Metaphorical associations among first-order concepts in the surface level can, therefore, be called *second-order* concepts. If a first-order concept has the structure **A is B**, and another **D is F**, then a second-order concept will have the underlying structure **[A is B] is [D is F]**. This process of concept-formation constitutes the "blueprint" for the whole "architecture" of abstract cognition, and eventually for its propositional or computational structure. At this level, language structures feed the new abstract, rational form of cognition. The chief property of this form is syntax which organizes *n-order* concepts into relations of concatenation and subordination.

As a general working model, it can be posited that a concept starts out as a percept i.e. as an iconic model of some aspect of experience or reality. *Models* are the result of the process of taking in and *re*-forming the information emanating from our sensorial and affective responses to the world. Once such models are connected metaphorically, we come to "conceptualize" them, i.e. to think of them in terms of other models or image schemas. This process constitutes our *re*-presentational cognitive mode.

In such an approach to meaning-making, conceptualization is viewed as a largely unconscious strategy that maps sensory experience onto the inner world of cognition via metaphor. As an example of how this strategy might work "creatively" in discourse programming, consider the following hypothetical situation. Let us say that someone is practicing the piano at home. It is a rainy day and that person is bound to be playing a sad piece of music on such a day. Someone else walks into the room and asks the pianist how he or she feels. The sad music and the rain outside have put the pianist in a frame of mind that leads him or her to make a commentary on his or her mood. Seeing raindrops on a nearby window, the pianist might answer the interlocutor with "I'm feeling *drippy.*" The utterance makes perfect sense because of the experiential context in which it was produced and because it reflects an underlying metaphorical model of mood—*mood is an environmental state* (as in "I'm feeling under the weather," "I'm in a stormy mood today," etc.).

In a fundamental sense, therefore, conceptual meaning is closely linked to the ways in which a culture organizes its world on the basis of experience. It inheres, as Lakoff and Johnson (1980: 5) remark, in "understanding and experiencing one kind of thing in terms of another." Common concepts, ranging all the way from love to justice, seem typically to be grounded in metaphor, and since communication is based in large part on the same conceptual system that we use in thinking and acting, then language is an important source of evidence of what that system is like.

As a final consideration, take the following two North American cultural models of thinking: *thoughts are movable objects* and *thinking is visual scanning*. These models are instantiated frequently in common discourse by utterances such as the following:

- *Thoughts are movable objects*

(72) *Work it over* in your mind.
(73) *Turn* that thought *over* in your mind.
(74) You should *rearrange* your thoughts carefully.

(75)   You should *put* your previous thoughts *in order* before going forward with your plans

•   *Thinking is visual scanning*

(76)   You must *look over* what you've written.
(77)   I must *look into* what you've told me a bit further.
(78)   She *saw right through* what you told her.
(79)   I'm going to *see* this thing completely *out*.

These sentences suggest that the mind probably conceptualizes thought processes as extensions or analogues of physical objects and events. Thoughts, like objects, can be moved, arranged, located, etc. They can also be seen, looked into, etc. Often, this involves pre-established conceptual domains, such as, for instance, Euclidean geometry:

•   *Thoughts are geometrical figures*

(80)   I don't *see* the *point* of your argument.
(81)   Their ideas are *diametrically* opposite.
(82)   Their ideas are *parallel*.
(83)   That's an example of *circular* reasoning.
(84)   His thinking is rather *square*, isn't it?

In these examples the experiential *Gestalt* is already inherent in the geometrical concept. These examples show that there are different degrees or "orders" of concepts. The *thinking is visual scanning* model, for example, is a first-order concept because it connects a perceptual *Gestalt—seeing—*to an abstraction—*thinking*—directly. But first-order concepts can become themselves the vehicles of higher-order concepts. So, the *thoughts are geometrical figures* model reveals a second-order conceptualization, since geometrical figures and notions are themselves concepts.

Concluding Remarks

In sum, it would seem that there is more to metaphor than "meets the eye," if you pardon my metaphor. Indeed, metaphorical concepts are so deeply ingrained that it is virtually impossible to say or write anything, even a chapter on metaphor, without them. The traditional, and still mainstream, literalist perspective posits that we think syntactically when we are about to utter a sentence. The experientialist one claims instead that we think conceptually, and that, ultimately, conceptual thinking derives from a more fundamental form of sensorial cognition. I conclude by adding that, unlike the approach taken by Lakoff, Johnson and other experientialist linguists, I believe that there are various levels or layers of meaning in addition to the metaphorical-conceptual one that need to be taken into consideration in a more comprehensive experientialist approach to semantics. At the most basic level of signification there are those processes that are tied to the sensory system. These produce our most fundamental signs—e.g. indexes and icons. Denotation, in this approach, would be defined as the coding of perception by indication (indexical signs) or by some form of osmosis or mimesis (iconic signs). These signs are built from basic image-schemas—our acquired mental models of space, time, emotions, etc. Once this fundamental experiential level of cognition is established within the mind, metaphorical connections transform it into one of conceptualization in ways that have been discussed in this chapter. Percepts register our physiological and affective responses to the signals and stimuli present in the environment; concepts give form and meaning to these responses. The particular characteristics of the metaphorically-fabricated artifactual World 3 universe constitute the source of differences among persons and among cultures. Although it evolved out of a more fundamental and universal experiential level of mind, it has come to be the dominant form of mentality. Free from sensory control, conceptual structures gradually come to dominate purposeful thinking. The mind's conceptual cognitive system is a truly powerful one. It can be projected onto the external world of reality to partition it, organize it, classify it, and explain it, as we have seen in previous chapters.

For most of the twentieth century the systematic study of the mind has concentrated on the ways in which the rational part carries out its computational tasks—deduction, inference, problem-solving, etc. Seldom, if ever, have scientists of the mind asked themselves where this kind of thinking comes from, and how it is related to other ways of thinking. The experientialist approach is beginning to show how our system of concepts is tied to bodily schemas.

There are, of course, many questions that the study of metaphor raises for semiotics that will need to be answered. How are concepts related to more fundamental forms of representation (indexical and iconic)? Is the conceptual system separate from the grammar of language? Or does it reflect it? What is the mind? Is language a product of metaphor? Are abstract thoughts end-products of metaphor? And the list could go on and on. Obviously, metaphor opens up a fertile field for semioticians to explore and cultivate in their quest to understand how we *make* the world of culture.

SUGGESTIONS FOR FURTHER READING

Black, M. (1962). *Models and Metaphors*. Ithaca: Cornell University Press.

Booth, W. (1979). Metaphor as Rhetoric: The Problem of Evaluation. In: S. Sachs (ed.), *On Metaphor*, pp. 47-70. Chicago: University of Chicago Press.

Danesi, M. (1987) (ed.). *Metaphor, Communication, & Cognition*. Toronto: Toronto Semiotic Circle.

Danesi, M. (1993). *Vico, Metaphor, and the Origin of Language*. Bloomington: Indiana University Press.

Hausman, C. R. (1989). *Metaphor and Art*. Cambridge: Cambridge University Press.

Johnson, M. (1987). *The Body in the Mind: The Bodily Basis of Meaning, Imagination and Reason*. Chicago: University of Chicago Press.

Kövecses, Z. (1986). *Metaphors of Anger, Pride, and Love: A Lexical Approach to the Structure of Concepts*. Amsterdam: Benjamins.

Kövecses, Z. (1988). *The Language of Love: The Semantics of Passion in Conversational English*. London: Associated University Presses.

Kövecses, Z. (1990). *Emotion Concepts*. New York: Springer.

Lakoff, G. (1987). *Women, Fire, and Dangerous Things: What Categories Reveal about the Mind*. Chicago: University of Chicago Press.

Lakoff, G. and M. Johnson. (1980). *Metaphors We Live By*. Chicago: University of Chicago Press.

Lakoff, G. and Turner, M. (1989). *More than Cool Reason: A Field Guide to Poetic Metaphor*. Chicago: University of Chicago Press.

Langacker, R. W. (1990). *Concept, Image, and Symbol: The Cognitive Basis of Grammar*. Berlin: Mouton de Gruyter.

MacCormac, E. (1976). *Metaphor and Myth in Science and Religion*. Durham, N. C.: Duke University Press.

Martin, J. H. (1990). *A Computational Model of Metaphor Interpretation*. New York: Academic.

Pollio, H. and M. Smith. (1979). Sense and Nonsense in Thinking about Anomaly and Metaphor. *Bulletin of the Psychonomic Society* 13: 323-326.

Pollio, H., J. Barlow, H. Fine and M. Pollio. (1977). *The Poetics of Growth: Figurative Language in Psychology, Psychotherapy, and Education*. Hillsdale, N. J.: Lawrence Erlbaum Associates.

Richards, I. A. (1936). *The Philosophy of Rhetoric.* Oxford: Oxford University Press.

Sontag, S. (1978). *Illness as Metaphor.* New York: Farrar, Straus & Giroux.

Sontag, S. (1989). *AIDS and Its Metaphors.* New York: Farrar, Straus & Giroux.

Verene, D. P. (1981). *Vico's Science of Imagination.* Ithaca: Cornell University Press.

Wheelwright, P. (1954). *The Burning Fountain: A Study in the Language of Symbolism.* Bloomington: Indiana University Press.

Winner, E. (1988). *The Point of Words: Children's Understanding of Metaphor and Irony.* Cambridge, Mass.: Harvard University Press.

Winner, E. and Gardner, H. (1977). The Comprehension of Metaphor in Brain Damaged Patients. *Brain* 100: 717-729.

Chapter 7

IT'S MORE THAN A MYTH!

Preliminary Remarks

Imagine being on a "first date." You and your partner are at a restaurant. You have just finished ordering your meals. Now, what will you do? Typically, you will start by being inquisitive about your partner, as he or she will, no doubt, want to "know" more about you. This normally leads to the telling of life stories: "I was born in Toronto. I've lived here all my life. I majored in mathematics and the University of Toronto. I now work at IBM..." The ways in which you will put the strands of your autobiographical text together will, of course, be strategically-motivated, strewn together in such a way as to be appropriate to the situation.

This telling of stories is a fundamental feature of the human mind. Our life is, in fact, perceived to constitute a story, and we tell it as such. The details of the telling change from context to context, just as stories do. It would be no exaggeration, in fact, to say that the mind seems to have a "narrative" structure that manifests itself extrinsically in the form of the stories, myths and mythologies that all individuals and cultures invariably create.

The study of how mythical narratives describe and portray the origin and basic experiences of a culture is probably as old as civilization itself. In ancient Greece there emerged a debate over myth and story-making versus reason or *logos* as a reliable means for producing accounts of what is happening and of what is going to happen in the world. Xenophanes, Plato and Aristotle, for example, criticized myths trenchantly as symbolic tools for explaining reality, exalting reason instead as the only trustworthy means for gaining access to the outer world of reality and the inner world of human experience. But the ancient debate, and the advent of the rational scientific method, did not eliminate the need for story-making in Western civilization. On the contrary, throughout our history there has always been an urgent propensity to produce and rely on narrative accounts—factual and fictional—to explain who we are and why we are here. Even in the domains of inquiry that we call "scientific" or "technological," there is (and probably has always been) a deeply-felt suspicion that the narrative mode of explanation plays a fundamental role in constructing the whole edifice of rational science.

In this chapter, I will first look at the nature and function of the narrative mode of representation. Then I will discuss the meaning of myths in culture and the role of what Roland Barthes (1957) calls *mythologies* in the building of cultural modes of thought and representation. Finally, I will illustrate the concept of mythological thinking with a semiotic analysis of commercially-produced *toys*.

But before starting, it is necessary, for the sake of clarity, to constrain the definitions of several recurring terms that semioticians constantly use when talking about narrativity As used here, the term *narrative* refers to something narrated—i.e. told or written—such as an account, a story, a tale and even a scientific theory. The narration may be purely fact-based, as in a newspaper report, a psychoanalytic session, etc., or fictional, as in a novel, a comic strip, a film, etc. Needless to say, it is often difficult, if not impossible, to determine the boundary line between the factuality or fictionality of any single narrative, given the interplay of the many cognitive and social factors that coalesce in the production of narratives. The term *narrativity* designates the innate human capacity to produce and comprehend narratives. The term *narrative mode* refers to the use of narrativity as the cognitive means by which something is conceptualized and then expressed—"narrated"—in verbal or nonverbal ways. Finally, the term *narratology* refers to the branch of semiotics that studies narrativity.

The Narrative Mode of Representation

The idea of "fictional narration" (from Latin *fingere* "to form, make, put together") emerges in the late Middle Ages. It was at this turning point in human history that cultural modes of interaction started to come under the formative influence of a story-like, fictional textuality. The advent and spread of fiction as a mode of representation changed the ways in which we perceive and understand the world permanently. This was the era that invented romances, novellas, and, a little later, the novel. Before the Middle Ages, human cultures did indeed create stories—myths, legends, etc. But these were not forged *fictionally*. The first myths and legends were descriptive accounts of world events and figures. Even the ancient dramas were not "fictional" in the Medieval sense. They were enactments or portrayals of perceived human or supernatural actions and events. They were anchored in the mimetic mode of representation, rather than in a fictional-narrative mode.

This does not mean that there was no telling of "untruths," of things that were not, in Antiquity. Indeed, the need to tell stories is as old as civilization. To quote Ashley (1984: 11):

> The compact and realistic *novella* of the Italians and the poetic and romantic French *roman* (related to "romance," but today the French word for "novel") both developed along separate but related lines from the desire to tell a story, a desire already old when, two or three millennia before Christ, papyri recorded the pleasure that the sons of Cheops gave their father with their little narratives. Sir Edmund Gosse traced the modern novel at least as far back as Aristides who, two centuries before Christ, wrote a kind of *Winneburg, Ohio* collection about his hometown, Miletus, called the *Milesiaka*. Then followed pastoral tales and the Syrian Helidorus' *Aethiopica* and the Greek love story of *Daphnis and Chloë* and *The Golden Ass* of Apuleius in Latin.

But, notwithstanding Ashley's use of the term "narratives" to describe ancient stories, there is no evidence to suggest that the concept of "fiction," as we have come to know it since the Middle Ages, existed in the ancient world. There was "artifice" in this world, not "fiction." The creation of fictional worlds did not become a narrative craft until the authoring of texts such as the *Chanson de Roland*, the *Roman de la rose*, and Boccaccio's *Decameron*. In the ancient world the term *narration* did not have the connotations that it took on in the Middle Ages. It did not emerge in a context related to storytelling, the invention of tales, or well-crafted narration, as we understand the term today. Rather, it was a technical rhetorical term that designated the part of an oration immediately following the statement of the argument.

What is germane to the discussion here is that the fictional creations of Medieval writers have had a great impact on how we have subsequently come to view human nature and mentality. The great fictional works of the modern era are their offspring. At an intuitive level, we accept these as telling us more about the nature of mind and reality than do the reams of research papers written by cognitive and social scientists.

The narrative mode also continually projects meaning onto a series of what would otherwise be perceived to be random actions. A few years ago, there was a popular program on American television called the *The Wild*

Kingdom. The show purported to explain animal behavior in scientific terms. Each week, a film would be made of specific animals eating, hunting, mating, etc. Unedited, the actions of the animals caught on film would hardly make up a meaningful storyline. But, with the help of film editors and script-writers the program produced an intriguing account—a narration—about the actions dispersed randomly on the unedited film. The result was a weekly "story" of animal behavior put together by the program's film editors, directors and script-writers. Although they may have extracted their ideas from ethological and zoological sources, the particular ways in which the animals' actions were "explained" by the narrator constituted an anthropomorphic storyline. The result was a weekly dose of human signification projected onto the world of animal behavior. My aim here is not to criticize *The Wild Kingdom* or other television "animal" programs. In their own quaint way, they are interesting programs. But they belong to an artifactual world generated by the narrative mode of cognition.

Among the very first attempts to identify and single out narrativity as a distinguishing trait of the human species is Plato's (c. 428-c. 347 BC) effort in his *Republic* to define it in terms of content. Plato distinguished between pure narrative *(diegesis)* and imitation *(mimesis).* But the "scientific" study of narrativity traces its roots to the study of myths as theories of human and cultural origins in the eighteenth century. Modern interpretations of myth-making, and hence of narrativity, probably begin in 1725 with the publication of Giambattista Vico's *New Science* (Bergin and Fisch 1984). Vico was reacting to the emerging view of his times that only the rational, objectivist approach of the physical sciences would lead to an understanding of the human mind. And, indeed, only a few decades later, a new "scientific" discipline emerged—psychology—declaring its autonomy from philosophy by developing and institutionalizing what it claimed to be a rigorous empirical approach to the study of mind. The precise observation and measurement of mental behavior gave the fledgling enterprise its "scientific" personality. Incidentally, the practice of "controlled" experimentation, the use of randomization in subject selection to comply with the requirements of Gaussian statistical theory, and the utilization of artificial tasks for subjects to perform under laboratory-like conditions are its modern-day descendants. In our culture there continues to exist a propensity to accept mathematically-reported observations as somehow more significant, or "real," than other kinds.

Vico's conception of what a science of mind would entail was essentially narratological. Vico explained the origin of the narrative mode of cognition as a response to a fundamental need to represent the world in a coherent connected fashion. Through the workings of the imagination, Vico suggested that humans come to connect world events in the form of narratives. The imagination is thus the source of all knowledge; the latter, therefore, is a human product This proposal has come to be known as the *verum-factum* principle—we can know only what we ourselves have made (literally "the truth is made").

For Vico, the primordial form of cognition was a "poetic" state of mind from which the first human cultures took shape, developing the first institutions, especially religious, burial and marriage rites. The organization of early cultures was universally "poetic," i.e. it was based upon, and guided by, conscious bodily experiences that were transformed into generalized ideas. The course that humanity runs, according to Vico, goes from a poetical age, through a heroic one, to a rationalistic one. Each age has its own kind of mentality and language. The poetic mentality, for instance, generates myths; the heroic one, legends; and the rational one, rational history. Rationality, according to Vico, is humanity's greatest achievement. But, unlike Cartesian philosophers, he did not see it as an innate "given." He considered it to be a point-of-arrival, achievable only in a social ambiance. Human beings do not inherit rationality from their biological legacy. Stripped of culture, which is a kind of collective memory system, human beings would be forced to resort to their poetic, or corporeal, imaginations to make sense of the world all over again.

The study of narrativity was pursued seriously in the first half of the present century when Propp (1928), Cassirer (e.g. 1946) and Lévi-Strauss (1958: 206-231) argued successfully that language and myth shared the same cognitive structures. Propp was among the first in this century to pay special attention to the narrative structure of ordinary discourse, and especially to the minimal units of narratives and their organization into what he called a "plot grammar." Propp also discovered, during his work on the folktale, that there existed a relatively small number of "narrative units" (plot themes) which went into the make-up of a "plot grammar." Cassirer pointed out that ordinary cognition and cultural mythologies sprang from an unconscious grammar of experience, whose categories were not those of logical thought, but rather of an archaic mode of sensorial thinking that continues to exert enormous control over our routinized thought processes. Lévi-Strauss showed how the semantic constituents of cultural symbolic codes are derived from sensorial experience. For Lévi-Strauss these are to be viewed as the conceptual tools for coming to grips with the more abstract concerns with which human cultures must grapple.

Thus, at about mid-century, the narratological mode of inquiry was starting to crystallize in semiotics, philosophy and the social sciences. Narratology was thus born as an interdisciplinary field of semiotic investigation. Today it encompasses the study of verbal and nonverbal narrativity in all cultural contexts. There is now even a rather influential school of thought within developmental psychology which makes the basic claim that children develop conceptual structures primarily through story formats. As Wells (1986: 194) has aptly put it, the proponents of this school of thought have, for at least a decade, been gathering data which suggest that "constructing stories in the mind is one of the most fundamental means of making meaning; as such it is an activity that pervades all aspects of learning."

Stories of all kinds do seem indeed to allow children to make sense of the world. This general finding strongly suggests that the narrative structure of the stories children are able to produce and comprehend betrays the actual structure of human cognition. Current psychological research has, in fact, been showing that children will grasp new concepts only if these are presented to them in the form of narratives. Stories provide the intelligible formats that mobilize the child's natural ability to learn from context. In a fairly recent study, Jerome Bruner (1986) has persuasively argued that culturally-shaped narrative thinking underlies how we come to understand ourselves and the social world in which we live. Beginning with the acquisition of language, narrative thinking brings the developing human organism into the arena of human culture. It is the form of thinking that gives pattern and continuity to human perception and experience.

It is clearly beyond the scope of the present discussion to go into the details of the relevant research in psychology. Suffice it to say here that the narrative sequences found in children's stories would seem to constitute a primary medium for knowledge acquisition across a broad range of cultural settings. As Wells (1986, pp. 193-213) points out, the research on child development indicates the existence of a timetable in the development of narrativity. Since it is not a deliberate or intentional activity, the emergence of narrativity suggests strongly that the mind works narratively. To understand and tell a story entails selecting and bringing together various events. In the case of two-year-olds this involves assistance from an adult if "the original impulse to link events in a narrative structure is to come to fruition" (Wells 1986: 197). By four or five, children are able to manage and negotiate narratives by themselves, especially during play when narratives function to create a framework within which the child's actions can be interpreted by others watching. It is here that fundamental social roles come to the fore in structuring the story and enabling participants to join into the child's narrative universe.

Myth

The word *myth* derives from the Greek *mythos*, "word," "speech," "tale of the gods." It can be defined as a metaphorical narrative that seeks to give order and coherence to experiences and perceived events. In the beginning stages of human culture, myths were genuine "theories" of the world. Mythical narratives continue to form the basis for imparting knowledge of the world to children. There are no cultures without stories, fables and legends. All cultures have created them to explain their origins: the Zuni Indians, for instance, claim to have emerged from a mystical hole in the earth, thus establishing their kinship with the land; Rome was said to be founded by Romulus and Remus, two humans reared by wolves; and the list could go on and on. Myth-creation and story-telling in general reveal something rather unique about humans. Unlike other animals, humans possess the capacity to invent stories of all kinds, true or not. Narrativity appears to be a fundamental sense-making operation of the mind, and would seem to be universal throughout humanity. It is a common experience that we remember stories more easily and vividly than we do isolated concepts and words.

The narrative structure of the myths of early cultures allows us to reconstruct the *forma mentis* of that people. The crucial thing to note is that the first myths have not disappeared. As psychoanalysis has maintained for years, there seems to be a kind of "mythic unconscious" in humanity embedded in a mental substratum shaped by our first stories. The "unconscious" mind, in turn, would seem to be a powerful shaper of conscious activity. This is, after all, the reason behind the use of so-called "subliminal" techniques in advertising. Whether or not the psychological effectiveness of such methods has ever been established empirically is beside the point. The fact is that ad creators continually attempt to tap specific "mythic" or "archetypal" structures, as Carl Jung (1956) called them, in the unconscious mind. No wonder, then, that there now is such considerable interest in the semiotics of advertising. If there is one theme in this new line of inquiry that is of specific relevance to the present discussion, it is that many ads are interpretable at two levels—a discursive surface one, and a deep mythical one. The surface level narrates the ad, both verbally and visually. But this narration is both a "reflex" of, and a "trace" to, the mythical level: i.e. the surface elements cohere into a *signifier* that has an underlying mythic or archetypal *signified* that works at a subthreshold level.

As Key (1989: 149) has recently put it: "Humans label consciously, but symbolic significance remains at an unconscious level." Cosmetic ads, according to Key (1989: 149), "create archetypal genital symbolism, powerfully attractive both to men and to other women." The effectiveness of such symbolism, according to Key and other media psychologists, lies precisely in the fact that it works at an unconscious mythic level. Indeed, when the underlying meaning structure is consciously recognized, subjects tend to become alarmed and even repulsed by the ad in question. More will be said about this in Chapter 12.

Particularly relevant to the present discussion is the notion that archetypes make up the thematic substance of common folk stories and of dreams. According to some scholars of mythology (e.g. Campbell 1969, Heinberg 1989) our primordial acts of conscious social activity (hunting, gathering, etc.) constitute the source of many archetypal structures in the unconscious mind. As Campbell (1969: 59-60) has observed, many of these structures encode fear and awe of the world of nature itself. The paleographical and archaeological record suggests rather unambiguously that human societies progress through a series of stages. During the primitive stages of all societies there is evidence that myth is the primary mode by which cultures come to establish communal sense-making. Not possessing the knowledge to understand or "explain" environmental events, the first humans ascribed them to awesome and frightful "gods" or "divine" creatures, thus producing humanity's first myths, stories and archetypes (literally, an original model of something). In a succeeding stage of cultural evolution, societies then tend to look toward their own "human contexts" for the symbolic means to explain phenomena in the world. Out of these emerged the first "human dramas" with the "heroes" of the evolving culture as the major players in these dramas. Cognition was structured primarily by the mimetic mode, but the overlapping narrative mode transformed these dramas into legends and history. At this secondary stage of cultural development, contextuality—the capacity to locate deep-level thought patterns into a context—began to play a crucial role in the formation of a rational cognition. It was only at an advanced stage of cultural evolution, however, that rationality, or "discursiveness," became the dominant mode of cognition and social action.

Vico's search for the origins of a specific culture was based on the proposition that the first thoughts of that culture could be reconstructed from the concrete meanings of the words, symbols and myths used to express them. Myths were created to allow the humans living in groups to make sense of the world together, and their narrative structure can be seen to betray the actual metaphorical structure of cognition. There is no irony, for example, in early myths and cultures. For Vico, irony is the characteristic feature of a highly abstract rationalistic state of mind. Irony is one of the four tropes that he identifies as fundamental to human language—metaphor, metonymy, synecdoche and irony—and he claims that it is the one that develops later, both phylogenetically and ontogenetically. Irony unfolds only in an advanced cultural context: i.e. it is a surface-level cognitive feature that emerges at the level of culture, not of primordial thought.

The choice of four tropes as the main types of verbal figuration was a practice that Vico inherited from the Renaissance. He saw it as a late-stage metaphorical process that combines a concept, **A**, with its opposite **-A** by implication, **A implicates -A**. In this conception, irony is the end of culture and the reflective mode in which modern science and history must be written.

Mythologies

Think of the term *teenager*. It might seem to you that it has been around since time immemorial. As it turns out, it is a relatively recent one. It is of course true that even the earliest civilizations differentiated between *young* and *old* as biologically- and socially-significant categories. But the idea of making *adolescence* a specific period for psychologists to study was forged at the turn of the present century when they decided to pay more attention to the developmental phase that began with puberty and ended with adulthood.

And, indeed, it was not until the end of World War I that *youths* and *young adults* came to be viewed as distinct *personae* belonging to a new recognizable subculture. The first to portray the newly-fashioned *persona* of the teenager in fiction was J. D. Salinger in his still popular and controversial novel, *The Catcher in the Rye*, published in 1951. During the fifties, the culturally-constructed image of the "sweet sixteener" was being constantly enshrined in books, magazines, songs, television programs and movies. Songs of that era, with titles like *Sixteen Candles*, *Happy Birthday Sweet Sixteen*, etc., bear witness to the arrival upon the scene of a new social being with a new social character. By the mid fifties, the adolescent's sixteenth birthday party was felt implicitly to signal the end of adolescence. It was during this turning point in North American cultural history that the term *teenager* gained general currency in the mainstream culture, providing verbal evidence that a new sociological reality had crystallized. The breakpoint of "sixteen" was extended by a few years during the "hippie" sixties and early seventies to encompass the entire high school period. Today, many of the behaviors that once surfaced and were constrained to the high school years can be observed to continue way past the individual's sixteenth or seventeenth birthday. Cases of "terminal adolescence" seem to be cropping up throughout our society!

The extension of the teen years has been carefully nurtured and vigorously reinforced by adult institutions (the marketplace, the media, etc.). The social empowerment of the modern adolescent has been brought about by the world of adults. If we sometimes worry about the results, we really have no one to blame but ourselves. The very survival of the current economic structure depends in large part on the conservation of adolescence as a social reality. Without it, work related to schooling, to a large chunk of the music and cinema industries, to the faddish clothing business, to the fast food commercial empire and the list could go on and on would virtually disappear.

The very idea of the *teenager*, and of the social connotations that this term has come to have, is a twentieth-century construct. It is what semioticians call a *mythology*. Nature segments the life continuum into three biological periods: pre-reproductive, reproductive and post-reproductive. The first crucial dividing line is, of course, *puberty*—the period during which an individual becomes physiologically capable of reproduction. Any other segmentation of this continuum has a social origin. Categories such as *childhood*, *adolescence*, *adulthood* and the like are discrete segmentations that are reflective of the ways in which cultures organize, or represent, what is essentially a continuous biological *Gestalt*—the life span of a human being.

The term *teenager* itself first appeared as a colorful term in the 1943-45 issue of the *Reader's Guide to Periodical Literature*. The term *adolescens* ("adolescent") was used as far back as the Middle Ages to refer to any boy, irrespective of age, who began to work independently. But in no sense did it have any of the psychosocial connotations that it has today. The basis for being categorized as an *adolescens* in Medieval Europe was purely that of economic independence. Moreover, *adolescentia* ("adolescence") was considered to be an early period of maturity, not of transition, that lasted well into one's twenties and thirties.

Anthropologists have found that in many cultures the kinds of behaviors that we associate with North American teenagers simply do not emerge. By mid century, the anthropologist Margaret Mead had assembled a large corpus of data on Samoan society which showed that the adolescent experiences of North American culture were not unavoidable. Mead discovered that Samoan children followed a continuous growth pattern, with no abrupt changes from one age to the other. Simply put, the traditional Samoan culture might be said to have juveniles capable of reproduction, but it does not have the kinds of individuals whom we immediately recognize socially as *teenagers*.

The crystallization of the teenage *persona* and of a supporting teenage subculture can be traced to the fifties. In most of the Western world, the appearance of this new "social animal" has led to significant changes in social structure and economic behavior. It has also had notable consequences on the processes that characterize the child's psychosocial development at puberty. As a social construct, "teenagerhood" has generated its own distinct and easily recognizable *mythology*, or modalities of symbolic thinking and acting that children approaching puberty acquire unconsciously from their social environment. Here are some of its characteristic features.

Hanging out after school to socialize with peers constitutes a daily event. The Saturday night party with school friends is an event of great significance to the social life of the teenager. The rituals performed at such a social gathering include the smoking of cigarettes, the consumption of alcohol and a casual engagement in sexual activities. Missing a Saturday night party is perceived to be a blight on a teenager's reputation on the Monday after at school.

Teenagers have their own music, *rock & roll*, a term which clearly connotes the verve and bodily rhythms of pubescence. The birth of rock is usually traced to the 1955 hit song by Bill Haley and the Comets *Rock Around the Clock*. By 1956, with the emergence of Elvis Presley as the first rock deity, it became clear that rock & roll was much more than just a new form of musical entertainment. It was, and continues to be, clothing and hairstyle, social criticism and an agent of change. The first true "mythical heroes" of the teenage subculture were rock & roll artists.

Perhaps no one embodied the new mythology more than Elvis Presley. At every one of his live performances, teenage girls screamed, fainted, languished and attempted to reach and touch Elvis on stage. After appearing on the *Ed Sullivan Show* in 1956, he became an instant teen idol—a "Vichian hero"— in the eyes of teenagers throughout North America and, at the same time, a menacing evil force in the eyes of countless parents. Elvis Presley also became the first model of male *coolness*. His bodily movements, facial expressions (especially his peculiar raised lip twitch), hairstyle verbal drawl, became the discrete features of coolness for male teens. Many of Elvis' fifties fans, who are still alive today, continue to cling on to his model of physical appearance. Since Elvis' death in 1977, the "King of Rock &Roll" lives on as a mythology, worshipped and venerated through television shows, Elvis impersonators, reissues of his records and memorabilia.

Madonna, a female teen mythology, came onto the scene in 1983. Her songs introduced a reactionary tinge to the feminist movement in North American society. Songs such as *Like a Virgin, Material Girl,* and *Dress You Up,* which blatantly portrayed females as objectified sexual beings topped the hit-parade charts to the chagrin and dismay of leading feminists in the eighties. Madonna combined a Marilyn Monroe "sex-kitten" pose with a compelling and urgent sensuality. But it was an aloof and distant form of sexuality that

Madonna displayed. It had (and continues to have) a mediated, peep-show quality suited for a voyeuristic society that seems to prefer a mediated form of sexuality to the real thing.

It should be obvious that categories such as *childhood* and *adolescence* are reflective of the ways in which cultures perceive biologically-significant stretches on the life continuum, and of the ways in which they set their conceptual boundaries. In other words, such categories are attempts to relate our biological heritage to communal sense-making.

Once cultures establish conceptual limits and spaces on the life continuum there is a tendency to associate idealized, prototypical characteristics to those who occupy any one of them. These cohere into *mythologies*, each with its themes, motifs, etc. that are felt to express significant truths about human life or nature. *Childhood* was forged as such a mythology during the Romantic movement, when goodness, love and justice were attributed to humans uncorrupted and untainted by civilization. These "noble savages" were purported to be the "children" of humanity. Such notions did not exist in previous eras, nor are they found to be universal even today. Children are younger human beings undergoing growth in body, mind and personality. These are *different* from those of adults, not any better or worse. Children may lack adult social, cognitive and linguistic skills, but their behavior ranges considerably. The images of children as "pure," "innocent," etc. are part of a mythology, not a psychology or sociology of childhood. A child has no awareness whatsoever of being pure or innocent. It is not merely a question of the historical construction of the category, nor of its ambiguous relation to other categories preceding adulthood. Youth is a question of chronology, sociology, style, attitude.

According to Roland Barthes (1957), cultural mythologies such as childhood are reflexes of mythic dichotomies. Childhood connotes "innocence," old age "wisdom." Mythologies are anchored in mythic connotation. In early Hollywood westerns, for instance, the mythic "good" versus "evil" dichotomy was portrayed by having heroes wear white and villains black. Sports events are mythical dramas juxtaposing the "good" (the home hero or team) versus the "bad" (the outsider or visiting team). The whole fanfare associated with preparing for the "big event," like the World Series of baseball or the Superbowl of American football, has a ritualistic quality similar to the pomp and circumstance that ancient armies engaged in before going out to battle and war. Indeed, the whole event is perceived to be a mythic battle. The symbolism of the "home" team's (army) uniform, the "valor" and "strength" of star players (the heroic warriors) and the capacity of the coach (the army general) all have a profound emotional effect on the fans (one of the two warring nations). The game (the battle) is perceived to unfold in moral terms: it is a struggle of "righteousness" and "beauty" against the forces of "ugliness" and "baseness." Sports figures are exalted as heroes or condemned as villains. Victory is interpreted in moral terms as a struggle of good versus evil. The game is, as the television and radio ads constantly blurt out, "real life, real drama!"

Mythologies have, clearly, great connotative power in all cultures. Without them, cultures would be hardly "human-made," restricted to carrying out only survival functions at a denotative level. Sports events replace great battles, spectacles re-enact our need for ritual and dramatic performance, sweet sixteen birthday parties signal a "rite of passage," and the list could go on and on. The human-made world is a mythological one.

The Mythology of Toys

Closely tied to the mythology of childhood is the mythology of toys. Why do we give toys to children? Consider what happened back during the 1983 Christmas shopping season (see also Solomon 1988: 77-93). If you have forgotten, that was the period of the "Cabbage Patch" doll craze. Hordes of parents were prepared to pay almost anything to get one of those dolls for their daughters. Scalpers offered the suddenly and unexplainably "out-of-stock" dolls (a marketing ploy?) for hundreds of dollars through the classified ads. Grown adults fought each other in line-ups to get one of the few remaining dolls left in stock at some mall toy outlet.

How could a toy, a simple doll, have caused such mass hysteria? To a semiotician, only something with great mythological signification could have possibly triggered such intense commotion. To see why this is so, let us investigate the semiotic nature of toys. Why do we give toys to our children at all? What sorts of toys do we give them and why?

Consider, for example, the humanoid toys we give our children—dolls and action hero toys. It is instructive to note, incidentally, that the Cabbage Patch dolls came with "adoption papers." This is a concrete clue as to what the dolls really signified. Each doll was given a name —taken at random from 1938 state of Georgia birth records—which, like any act of naming, conferred upon it a personality and human reality. And, thanks to computerized factories, no two dolls were manufactured alike. The doll became alive in the child's mind, as do all objects with names. The dolls provided the precious human contact that children living in nuclear families with both parents working desperately need. Dolls are "people substitutes." In some cultures, one is purported to be able to cause some physical or psychological effect on a person by doing something to a doll constructed to resemble that person. In our culture, children, and adults for that matter, "talk" to their dolls. These invariably lend a receptive ear to their owners' needs and frustrations. Dolls answer a deep need for human contact. No wonder, then, that the Cabbage Patch episode was such an hysterical one. Parents did not buy a simple doll, they bought their child a sibling.

This brings us back to the nature of myth and mythologies. As mentioned above, our culture thinks of childhood in mythological terms. In a certain sense, "children," as we now think of them, did not exist until recent centuries. In medieval and Renaissance paintings and portraits there are no "children," at least not in the way we think of them. The "babes" and "children" that do appear occasionally in such portraits look more like "midgets" than they do "children."

Before the Industrial Revolution of the eighteenth and nineteenth centuries, most people lived in agricultural communities or settings. Children barely out of infancy were expected to share the workload associated with tending to the farm. There was, consequently, little distinction between childhood and adult roles—children were perceived, apparently, to be adults with smaller and weaker bodies. During the Industrial Revolution the center of economic activity shifted from the farm to the city with the repercussion of many moving into the city (urbanization). This also led to the construction of a new social order with different role categories and assignments. The result was that children were left with few of their previous responsibilities, and a new mythology emerged, proclaiming children as vastly different from adults, needing the time to learn at school, to play, etc. Child labor laws were passed and public education became compulsory. Protected from the harsh reality of industrial work, children came to assume a new pristine identity as innocent, faultless, impressionable, malleable organisms. To this day, we think of children as living in some Walt Disney world, in some "Fantasyland." In reality, children are hardly ever "pure," "good," "kind," etc. Just watch small children play together. Their behaviors towards each other are hardly to be construed as kind or generous!

Mythologies work, as we have seen, in dichotomic fashion. So, a mythology of "gender," for instance, is based upon and leads to stereotypical views of men and women: "men are rational/women intuitive," "men are active/women passive," "men are aggressive/women caring," etc. The reality, of course, is different—human behaviors do not fall into discrete paradigmatic categories. Men, too, are intuitive, passive at times, caring at others, etc.; and women are rational, active at some times, aggressive at others, etc.

The mythology of toys fits in rather nicely with the mythology of childhood. Children have always "played" with objects. Objects take on signification in any way we wish to assign it to them: broom handles can be imagined to be swords, rocks can be thought of as balls, and so on. Objects with memory value (e.g. objects given as gifts from some loved one) have great signifying power. If they are somehow "misplaced" (e.g. taken away from a bedroom), the result can be literally "felt" as a violation or rape. This is because our *persona* is projected into our objects. They are extensions of ourselves. Toys, as the logo for a major toy chain states, are indeed us *(Toys 'R Us)*. We give toys to children as we would give ourselves. In many ways, this act of giving soothes our sense of guilt for not being able to be with our children more often. We give them toys because we have no more time to give ourselves to them. Moreover, the *type* of toy we give is synchronized to any mythology of gender that is in place at the time of giving: a few years ago, little girls were given Barbie dolls and little boys Rambo dolls to keep the gender dichotomy between males and females operative. Barbie dolls connoted our culture-specific view of femininity (passiveness, interest in bodily glamour, etc.), while Rambo toys connoted our views of masculinity (aggressiveness, toughness, patriotism, etc.). As our mythologies of gender and childhood are bound to change, there is no question that the signifying value of toys will change correspondingly. Such is the nature of human culture.

Concluding Remarks

In this chapter, I have argued that the propensity for narrative manifests itself at all levels and evolutionary stages of culture. The narrative mode is operative as well in the development and life of the human person. We are, in a real sense, our autobiography. Narratives do not only recount states and events; they interpret them. They do not simply mirror what happens; they explore and predict what can happen. Narrativity gives order to the chaotic flux of events in the passage of time. As G. Prince (1982: 60) aptly puts it, "narrative illuminates temporality and humans as temporal beings."

One way perhaps to think of narrativity is in terms of the well-known dichotomy of memory into episodic and semantic systems (Tulving 1972). The former specifies and stores past events as unconnected "episodes." It is useful for getting on with the practical matters of life—recognizing faces, friends, family members, telephone numbers, etc. It makes up a kind of *annales* of events. The semantic memory system, on the other hand, is involved in providing meaning structures to the events of life. It shapes stored information into meaningful wholes. It has an inbuilt system for converting episodes into *chroniques* and *histoires*. Narrativity is tied to the semantic system. It can, in fact, be claimed that the global structure of the human mind is reflected in the structure and contents of our myths, stories, works of art, and other products of our narrative mode. The human mind thinks in terms of stories, as it seeks to organize experience and to generate explanatory models of the sequence of events. Reality is, in a fundamental sense, a narrative fiction.

One of the manifestations of mythic thinking is in what have been designated cultural mythologies. These reflect what I have designated in the previous chapter second-order metaphorical thinking (*childhood is innocence, toys are people, etc.*). They show, in other words, that the metaphorical mode of cognition is at the basis of cultural behavior and at the foundation of our cultural institutions, just as Giambattista Vico pointed out over two and a half centuries ago.

SUGGESTIONS FOR FURTHER READING

Ashley, L. R. N. (1984). *The History of the Short Story*. Washington, D. C.: U. S. Information Agency.

Bal, M. (1985). *Narratology: Introduction to the Theory of the Narrative*. Toronto: University of Toronto Press.

Barthes, R. (1957). *Mythologies*. Paris: Seuil.

Bergin, T. G. and Fisch, M. (1984). *The New Science of Giambattista Vico*. Ithaca: Cornell University Press.

Bruner, J. (1986). *Actual Minds, Possible Worlds*. Cambridge, Mass.: Harvard University Press.

Campbell, J. (1969). *Primitive Mythology*. Harmondsworth: Penguin.

Cassirer, E. (1946). *Language and Myth*. New York: Dover.

Genette, G. (1988). *Narrative Discourse Revisited*. Ithaca: Cornell University Press.

Greimas, A. J. (1987). *On Meaning: Selected Essays in Semiotic Theory*, trans. by P. Perron and F. Collins. Minneapolis: University of Minnesota Press.

Greimas, A. J. and Courtés, J. (1979). *Semiotics and Language*. Bloomington: Indiana University Press.

Heinberg, R. (1989). *Memories and Visions of Paradise*. Los Angeles: J. P. Tarcher.

Jung, C. (1956). *Analytical Psychology*. New York: Meridian.

Key, W. B. (1989). *The Age of Manipulation.* New York: Henry Holt.

Leitch, T. M. (1986). *What Stories Are: Narrative Theory and Interpretation.* University Park: Pennsylvania State University Press.

Lévi-Strauss, C. (1958). *Structural Anthropology.* New York: Basic Books.

Liszka, J. J. (1989). *The Semiotic Study of Myth: A Critical Study of the Symbol.* Bloomington: Indiana University Press.

Perron, P. and Danesi, M. (1993). *A. J. Greimas and Narrative Cognition.* Toronto: Toronto Semiotic Circle.

Polanyi, L. (1989). *Telling the American Story: A Structural and Cultural Analysis of Conversational Storytelling.* Cambridge, Mass.: MIT Press.

Prince, G. (1982). *Narratology: The Form and Functioning of Narrative.* Berlin: Mouton.

Propp, V. J. (1928). *Morphology of the Folktale.* Austin: University of Texas Press.

Ricoeur, P. (1983). *Time and Narrative.* Chicago: University of Chicago Press.

Solomon, J. (1988). *The Signs of Our Time.* Los Angeles: Jeremy P. Tarcher.

Stahl, S. (1989). *Literary Folkloristics and the Personal Narrative.* Bloomington: Indiana University Press.

Sutton-Smith, B. (1986). *Toys as Culture.* New York: Gardner.

Toolan, M. J. (1988). *Narrative: A Critical Linguistic Introduction.* London: Routledge.

Tulving, E. (1972). Episodic and Semantic Memory. In: E. Tulving and W. Donaldson (eds.), *Organization of Memory*, pp. 23-46. New York: Academic.

Turner, M. (1991). *Reading Minds: The Study of English in the Age of Cognitive Science.* Princeton: Princeton University Press.

Umiker-Sebeok, J. (ed.). (1987). *Marketing Signs: New Directions in the Study of Signs for Sale.* Berlin: Mouton.

Veyne, P. (1988). *Did the Greeks Believe in Their Myths?* Chicago: University of Chicago Press.

Weir, L. (1989). *Writing Joyce: A Semiotics of the Joyce System.* Bloomington: Indiana University Press.

Wells, G. 1986. *The Meaning Makers: Children Learning Language and Using Language to Learn.* Portsmouth: Heinemann.

CLOTHES MAKE THE PERSON!

Preliminary Remarks

Imagine yourself in the following situation. Let us suppose that you have a twenty-some-year-old brother who has an important job interview at the head office of a bank. Your brother has never been a good dresser. So it has been decided that you are going to help him get dressed appropriately for the situation. In semiotic terms, what you are going to do is to make use of the dress code for "male office employees" in order to come up with an "apparel text" befitting the occasion.

Let's go through the code in order, starting with hairstyle (a kind of semiotic extension of clothing) and ending with shoes. Here are the kinds of selections and options at your disposal within the framework of the code in question:

Dress Code for "Male Office Employees"	Selections and Options
Hairstyle	well-groomed, neatly cut, short hair
Shirt	a white, long sleeves, no designs
Tie	conservative: colors must match the suit
Jacket	gray or blue
Pants	matching gray or blue
Shoes	black (preferably with shoe laces)

There is, needless to say, some latitude to the options and selections you can make, but not very much. You know for certain that your brother cannot dress "outside" of this code, for if he does (if he decides not to wear a tie, if he decides to put on sneakers, etc.) the chances are very good that he would not even get past the door of the job interviewer with whom he has an appointment. Although conformity with the dress code will not guarantee him a job, it will at least get him past that door. Dressing for the occasion is indeed a social requirement. The dress code you suggested to your brother does not apply when, say, eating at a fast food restaurant, going out to a party with friends, going out to see a movie, etc. It is constrained by a specific context—the office scene.

Now, let's switch the situation from the standpoint of gender. Let us suppose that this time it is your twenty-some-year-old sister who has an important job interview at the head office of a bank. Your sister, too, has never been a good dresser. So now you are going to help her get dressed appropriately for the situation. Once again, in semiotic terms, you are going to make use of the dress code for "female office employees" in order to come up with a suitable apparel text for the occasion:

Dress Code for "FemaleOffice Employees"	Selections and Options
Hairstyle	well-groomed, neatly cut, relatively short hair
Blouse	soft colors, preferably white
Jacket	gray, blue or some other conservative color
Skirt	color must match the jacket
Shoes	preferably with high or semi-high heels

Although there are some paradigmatic opposites in the female dress code *vis-à-vis* the male one (e.g. pants versus jacket), you will also notice many similarities. This suggests that the type of job cuts across gender categories. Such commonality of classification and perception in some area of cultural behavior is invariably reflected in context-specific codes associated with it, such as the dress code.

As this simple illustration clearly suggests, clothes literally *make* the person—your brother and sister were "made" to look like prospective bank employees through the deployment of the appropriate dress codes. No wonder, then, that semioticians have such a keen in interest in clothes. Dress is more than mere bodily covering and protection. It is a signifying system through which we make messages and meanings about ourselves—about our feelings, attitudes, social status, political beliefs, etc. This is why uniforms are required by special groups like sports teams, military organizations, religious institutions, etc. The association of clothing with ritual behavior is character- istic of all the world's cultures. Clothing is a source of powerful signification in human culture. This chapter will look at the following themes connected with clothing: at the meaning of clothes in semiotic terms, at the kinds of messages that clothes allow us to make, at the paradigmatic opposite of clothing, *nudity*, and at the nature and function of fashion.

From Clothing to Dressing

At a fundamental, "biological survival" level, clothes have a very useful function indeed—they enhance our survivability considerably. They are, at this factual level, human-made "extensions" of the body's protective resources and systems designed to counteract environmental fluctuations (e.g. weather changes). They are "additions" to our protective bodily hair, skin thickness, etc. At this level, *clothes* constitute universal, trans-cultural items that have a unitary meaning—they improve our ability to survive. As Werner Enninger (1992: 215) aptly points out, this is why clothes vary according to geography and topography: "The distribution of types of clothing in relation to different climatic zones and the variation in clothes worn with changes in weather conditions show their practical, protective function." It is only when clothes are transformed into *dress* (from the Old French *dresser,* "to arrange, set up") that they take on culture-specific connotations. In the artifactual realm of culture, therefore, clothes become signifiers that are associated, by connota- tion and various metaphorical and metonymic processes, with a whole range of signifieds. This "transformational" model of cultural signification applies to any object, substance, etc. that is mapped from the factual level (Popper's World 1) to the artifactual one (Popper's World 3) via signifying processes (Popper's World 2):

World 3 = Artifactual World

The object, item, substance, etc. takes on signifying power. *Clothes* are transformed into *dress* code.

World 2 = Signifying Processes

Connotation, metaphor, etc.

These convert World 1 factual objects into World 3 signifying codes.

World 1 = Factual World

Objects, items, substances, etc. are adapted to enhance survivability.

These are "extenders" of bodily functions.

Clothes extend the body's invironmental protection system (bodily hairs, thick skin, etc.

As has been argued throughout this book, semiosis is a complex process that transforms the world of physical, perceptual-organismic reality, into one of reflective, conceptual-cognitive reality. The factual mind inheres in a biological program based on signal interpretation that the human organism can apply to environmental events and objects so as to employ them for some adaptive advantage. The making of clothes at this level does indeed enhance survivability. We would hardly be able to get through a Canadian winter, for instance, without appropriate clothing. When this human-made fabric—*cloth*—is transformed by some signifying process (connotation, metaphor, metonymy, etc.) within a specific cultural context, a new constellation of meanings is assigned to it. The particular characteristics of this new artifactual meaning system will differ among persons and among cultures. Although it evolved out of the factual level, in the artifactual world of culture clothing is subject to much variation and interpretation. To someone who knows nothing about Amish culture, the blue or charcoal _Mutze_ of the Amish male is just a jacket. But to an Amish the blue _Mutze_ signals that the wearer is between 16 and 35 years of age, the charcoal one that he is over 35. Similarly, to an outsider the Russian _kalbak_ appears to be a brimless red hat. To a Russian, it means that the wearer is a medical doctor. Indeed, going back to Eco's definition of semiosis as the capacity to lie and deceive (Chapter 1), we can even use clothing to lie: con artists and criminals can dress in three-piece suits to look trustworthy; anyone can dress like a policeman, whether or not he or she is an officer of the law in reality; and so on. To avoid the possibility of deceiving via clothes, some societies have even enacted laws that strictly define dress codes. In Ancient Rome, for instance, only aristocrats were allowed to wear purple-colored clothes; in medieval Europe peasants were required to wear their hair short, because long hair was the privilege of the aristocracy; in many religiously-oriented cultures, differentiated dress codes for males and females are regularly enforced; and the list could go on and on.

Clothing as Message-Making

Clothing is a rich source of social semiosis, spanning the whole range of cultural message-making from political-ideological statement to job-related conformity. Clothes are powerful signifiers of gender, sexuality, identity and group values. A few decades ago, females in our culture did not wear pants. The one who "wore the pants" in a family meant, denotatively and connotatively, that the wearer was a male. With the change in social role structures during the sixties, women too began to wear pants regularly, with many of the social connotations that this entailed. The reverse situation has never transpired. Except in special ritual-related circumstances—e.g. the wearing of a Scottish kilt—men have never worn skirts in modern rational cultures. If they do, then we label it as an act of "transvestitism," with the particular kinds of negative connotations that this act elicits.

The association between clothing and sexuality is an ancient one. As Helen Fisher (1992: 253-254) aptly observes, even in the jungle of Amazonia Yanomamo men and women wear clothes for sexual modesty. A Yanomamo woman would feel as much discomfort and agony at removing her vaginal string belt as would a North American woman if one were to ask her to remove her underwear. Similarly, a Yanomamo man would feel just as much embarrassment at his penis accidentally falling out of its encasement, as would a North American male caught literally "with his pants down."

During the fifties, the clothes worn by the first rock stars and by television personages such as the dancers on *American Bandstand* became the dress models for teens. Female teens wore "bobby socks," which had actually originated in the thirties; cool male teens wore leather jackets. With the fragmentation of the teen subculture into cliques from the mid sixties onwards, a corresponding diversification of clothing styles has also taken shape. Since the seventies teen dress styles have become coded according to the particular ideological and behavioral characteristics of the clique to which the teen belongs.

In the mid seventies, punks dyed their hair with bizarre colors and cut it in unconventional ways, they wore unusual clothes and they used various kinds of props (e.g. safety pins stuck through their nostrils) to send out their counter-culture message. Although the punk movement started as a political statement from working class youths in England, by the time its symbolism was acquired osmotically by a larger segment of the teen subculture, the punk dress code ended up being all things to all classes: e.g. the fascist insignia used by English punks lost its ideological overtones becoming a "put on" aimed at provoking those of a middle-class, bourgeois mentality. The punk dress code was also used, and continues to be used, strategically to intimidate other cliques and individual teen peers.

Dress codes are indicators of personal style. The punk dress code, for instance, started out as a barbaric style. And although it retains some of this symbolic value, it now also conveys images of mockery and negligence, and above all else, intimidation. Teens who become punk rockers concomitantly become more inclined to be aggressive, belligerent, bold, destructive and offensive.

During one observational period I spent at several high schools in the Toronto area several years ago, I became capable of differentiating rather markedly among the various dress codes adopted by specific cliques. The main clothing features of the members of several cliques of a few years ago can be summarized as follows:

Clique Name	Association	Dress Code Features
Housers	*Housers* grew out of an association with the so-called *House* music and the dance club scene connected with it.	Typically, they copied the clothing and hairstyle of the music-makers they listened to. Bell-bottom pants and large belts were the distinguishing features of the *Houser* dress code. These matched the short, well-groomed hairstyles of the males, and the long flowing hairstyles if the females.
Rockers	The origins of so-called *Rockers* (also called *Hard Rockers*, *Metalloyds*, or *Metallurgists*) lie in the Hard Rock music styles of the late sixties and seventies of such rock groups as Pink Floyd, Led Zeppelin and The Doors. Knowing the songs of those groups and wearing apparel that band members wore are the primary requirements for clique membership.	The dressed in a unisexual way with old, ripped jeans, leather boots, long scruffy shoulder-length hair, T-shirts, and leather jackets.
Mods	*Mods* traced their origins to the *New Age* music of the mid-eighties and to the *Punk Rock* movement.	Both male and female *Mods* wore black clothes, especially black leather jackets, and dyed their hair pitch black.
Bat Cavers	*Bat Cavers* were teen aficionados of the *Rocky Horror Picture Show*.	They wore black clothes in a gothic style.
B-Boys	The *B-Boys* were teens who listened to rap.	They wore baseball caps pointing backwards, sports T-shirts, running shoes and (often) shorts. The wearing of baseball caps started out as part of the apparel worn by many male rap musicians who wore the caps generally witht eh bill out to the side or facing backwards.

The clique provides a specific context within which teenagers can bond with their peers. It performs the crucial function of drawing together specific members of the teen subculture and of keeping outsiders out. A specific individual will tend to choose the clique that provides opportunities for status-achievement which are compatible with his or her natural abilities, attributes, or preferences: e.g. a physically-powerful teen will tend to join a clique that perceives physical aggression as prestigious. The high school community can be seen to exemplify a small-scale model of status-achievement within society at large. It shows that status is configured symbolically by specific traits. The person most likely to climb the teen status-scale, so to speak, is the one who can best manipulate the shared meaningful symbols of status and power in the high school.

There is nothing especially innovative about the kind of terminology employed by contemporary teen cliques. Its aim is to define a clique metonymically, i.e. in terms of a single attribute. In the sixties and seventies, terms such as *Jocks*, or teenagers actively involved in sports, *Motorheads*, or adolescents who spent most of their time driving or repairing cars, and *Fleabags*, or teenagers who consumed drugs regularly, were common. Belonging to a clique has become a powerful form of socialization within high school communities throughout North America.

When people put clothes on their bodies, they are primarily engaged in making images of themselves to suit their own eyes, and to conform to various ideological and lifestyle codes. There are two main trends that have occurred from the seventies onwards *vis-à-vis* clothing. First, mainstream teens have been developing increasingly expensive clothing tastes. Designer jeans, costly running shoes, expensive T-shirts and the like have become the norm for many affluent middle-class teens. Second, there would now seem to be a "meta-code" in teen clothing styles: i.e. a generalized model of dress in the teen subculture at large which is an extrapolation and recombination of the specifics of various single-clique fashion props and accouterments. As I write, some of these include earrings for males, multiple earrings for girls, shaved sides of the head with designs or letters carved into the hair, torn jeans, baggy jeans, jeans worn backwards, baggy pants, unlaced sneakers and baseball caps worn backwards. This meta-code excludes such single-clique fads as nose rings for both males and females, multicolored hair and makeup for both sexes and brassieres and other lingerie worn on the outside by females. The diversity, eclecticism and unisexual nature of the current meta-code cannot but be reflective of the diversity and pluralism of North American society at large.

Nudity

If dress is a means of meaning- and message-making in a cultural ambiance, then its paradigmatic counterpart, *nudity*, is bound to acquire great signification as well in the same ambiance. We are, in fact, the only animal that does not "go nude," so to speak, without triggering off some form of social repercussion (unless, of course, the social ambiance is that of a so-called "nudist camp"). Indeed, nudity can only be defined culturally. We are all born "nude," but we soon learn that this has special negative connotations during our childhood years. Moreover, what is considered "exposable" of the body will vary significantly from culture to culture, even though the covering of genitalia seems, for the most part, to cross cultural boundaries.

To see how powerful the symbolism associated with clothing and nudity is, consider the "art" of strip-teasing (male and female). A semiotician would ask immediately: Why do we attend (or desire to attend) performances whose sole purpose is the removal of clothing to reveal the human body, particularly the genitals, and, in the case of female strip-teasing, the breasts? The semiotician would, of course, seek an answer to this question in the domain of signification: What does clothing connote? And what does its paradigmatic complement, nudity, signify?

The act of "clothing-removal" in an audience setting has, first and foremost, something of a pagan ritualistic quality to it. The dark atmosphere, the routines leading up to the performance, the predictability of the performance itself with its bodily gyrations and mimetic emphases on sexual activities and the cathartic effects after the performance are all suggestive of a pagan rite worshipping our carnality and sexuality. There is no motive for being at such performances, really, other than to indulge in our fascination with sexuality. This is, in a certain basic sense, our "nature," as the psychoanalyst Sigmund Freud (1856-1939) claimed. Freud believed that the unconscious mind has a powerful influence over the conscious mind. He suggested that the latter tries constantly to cover up the largely unconscious sexual feelings that constantly seek some form of expression. Clothing not only covers the body for survival, as discussed above; at the cultural level it also covers our sexuality. This is why clothing is often associated with religious and moral codes aimed at repressing our "Freudian" urges. Clothing is invariably connected with mythological and ritualistic corporeal behavior. Just think of the glorious signifying power of dress during Christian Easter rites: the colors worn on Easter Sunday by clergy and believers alike are veritable eye-fillers. These rites are the Christian counterparts to the pagan rites of seasonal re-birth (just think of the meaning of the word "spring").

Covering the body is an act of modesty. But, paradoxically, by covering the sexual organs, clothes have in effect imbued them with a kind of "secret" existence and desirability below the covered surface. The genitals are always there in the back of our minds, if Freud is correct. So, at a strip-tease performance, the shedding of clothes does several symbolic things at once: it removes our imposed moral restrictions on sexuality; it "reveals" those hidden and "secretive" bodily parts that have taken on such great significance; it brings us down, so to speak, from our artifactual mode of thinking and behaving to more basic sensory and carnal ways of feeling and expressing ourselves; and it evokes ancient archetypes of body symbolism and ritual. To this semiotician at least, there's more to strip-teasing than an act of purported male masturbatory "gazing," as some have naively portrayed it.

The Freudian perspective might also explain why Western visual artists have always held a fascination for the nude. In the same way that we are captivated by body symbolism at strip-tease performances, so too do we seem to be fascinated by visual depictions of the body and of sexual activities. The Ancient Greek and Roman nude statues of male warriors, Michelangelo's powerful *David* sculpture, Rodin's nude sculpture of the thinker are all suggestive of the brutal power of male nudity. In these depictions, the male body is always strong, aggressive, potentially dangerous. It is these characteristics that enhance the sexuality of male genitals, not the "size" of the genitals (as is popularly believed). On a "weakling" body, male genitals are hardly ever perceived as "sexual," no matter what size they are. On the other side of this semiotic paradigm, the female nude has typically been portrayed as soft, sumptuous and submissive. Whatever psychological or sociological significance one might want to read into this dichotomy in visual representation (and many do!), one thing is for certain for the semiotician: these iconic models reflect a mythology of masculine and feminine sexuality.

The modern-day fascination with erotic materials, magazines and videos is a contemporary testament to our fascination with nudity as a signifying phenomenon. Those who see exploitation in such materials, and seem to be prepared to become everyone else's "moral guardians" by censoring them, are probably more overwhelmed by the connotative power of nudity than the "consumers" of such materials. Censorship is a dangerous thing. It is an attempt to control the form and contents of the artifacts we produce, by claiming to have the best interests of society in mind. In actual fact, it reveals a desire to control our moral codes of behavior to suit particular ideologies or perspectives. Censorship imposes limitations on the process of meaning- and message-making by prejudging the effects and value that the signification process might entail. "Gazing" at the human body depicted in sexual poses or activities reveals, in my opinion, the signifying value that nudity and sexuality have in our culture, no more no less. Only when such depictions are repressed does a perilous fascination with nudity surface. In the world of symbolic behavior, nudity is indeed a very powerful signifying phenomenon.

Fashion

What is fashion? And why are television shows like *Fashion TV* so popular the world over? The answer is to be found, as discussed in this chapter, in the signifying power of clothes.

Let us return briefly to the dress code with which the chapter started—the business suit—to see how fashion trends are formed and institutionalized. The subtext message underlying the apparel text you selected for your brother is, of course, *dress for success*. How did this message crystallize in our culture? A look at the history of the business suit provides an interesting answer to this question..

In seventeenth-century England there existed a bitter conflict in social ideologies between two forces—the Royalist "Cavaliers," who were faithful to King Charles I, and the Puritans, who were followers of Oliver Cromwell, and who controlled the House of Commons in the English Parliament. This conflict was a battle of styles, as the two warring camps sought to gain political, religious and cultural control of English society. The Cavaliers were aristocrats who only superficially followed the teachings of the Anglican Church. Their main penchant was for fashion. They dressed flamboyantly and ornately. They wore colorful clothes, feathered hats, beards and long flowing hair. The image of the Cavalier has been immortalized by novels such as *The Three Musketeers, Cyrano de Bergerac* and by contemporary movie versions of these. The Puritans, on the other hand, frowned on such ostentation and pomp. Known appropriately enough as the "Roundheads," Cromwell's Calvinist followers cropped their hair very closely (a prototype of the modern "brush" or "crew" cut), forbade all carnal pleasures and prohibited the wearing of frivolous clothing. They wore dark suits and dresses with white shirts and collars. Their clothes conveyed sobriety, plainness and rigid moralism.

The Cavaliers were in power throughout the 1620s and the 1630s. During this period the Puritans escaped from England and emigrated to America, bringing with them their lifestyle and rigid codes of conduct. However, in 1649 the Puritans, led by Cromwell, defeated the Royalist forces and executed the King. Subsequently, many Cavaliers also emigrated to America—while the Puritans set up colonies in the northeast, the cavaliers set up colonies in the south. The King's son, Charles II, escaped to France to set up a court in exile. For a decade, England was ruled by the Puritans. Frowning upon all sorts of pleasurable recreations, they closed down theaters, censored books, enforced Sunday laws, etc.

With Cromwell's death in 1658, the Puritans were eventually thrown out of power and England welcomed Charles II back. Known as the Restoration, the subsequent twenty-five year period saw a return to the lifestyle and fashions of the cavaliers. For two centuries the Puritans had to bide their time. They were excluded from holding political office, from attending a university, from engaging in any socially-vital enterprise. Throughout the years they maintained their severe lifestyle and dress codes.

By the time of the Industrial Revolution, the Puritans had their revenge. Their belief in thrift, diligence, temperance, and industriousness, which some have called the "Protestant work ethic," allowed them to take advantage of the new socioeconomic climate with its new set of lifestyle demands. In America and in England, Cromwell's descendants became rich and eventually took over the economic reins of power. Ever since, English and North American culture has been influenced by Puritan ethics in the work force, especially after the defeat of the Cavalier south in the American Civil War. The origins of modern corporate capitalism are to be found in those ethics.

The Puritan triumph in the socioeconomic order came to entail a victory in lifestyle and dress codes. The belief that hard work and "clean living" were necessarily interrelated, and that this combination led to wealth and prosperity, had become a widespread one by the turn of the present century. To this day, there is a deeply-felt conviction in our culture that hard work and strict living codes will lead to success in both this and the next life.

The business suit is a contemporary version of Puritan dress codes. The toned down colors (blues, browns, grays) that the business world demands are the contemporary reflexes of the Calvinist's fear and dislike of color and ornament. Features such as the wearing of ties, which literally keep the shirt "tied up" so that the chest will not be exposed, the cutting of one's hair short, the wearing of a jacket even in sweltering heat, etc. are all Puritan signifiers of solemnity and self-denial. During the so-called "hippie" sixties and early seventies, the office scene came briefly under the influence of a new form of fashion. "Cavalierism," with the wearing of colorful suits, of turtleneck sweaters rather than of white shirts, of longer hair, of sideburns, of Nehru jackets, of medallions and of beards, made its pitch to take over the world of corporate capitalism. But this fashion experiment was bound to fail, as the "Cavalier" sixties were overtaken by conservative neo-puritanical forces in the late seventies and eighties. The "gray flannel suit" model has become once again the business dress code for all of corporate North America, with only minor variations in detail.

The story of the business suit is a long and intriguing one. But nowadays fashions seem to come and go overnight. So how de we know today whether an article of clothing is fashionable or not? Do we simply watch *Fashion TV* or consult current fashion magazines? Who decides what is fashionable? Who are today's Cavaliers and Roundheads?

Actually, it is not an item of clothing in itself, but its details that define a fashion trend. Take, as an example, the length of skirts for females in our culture. The mini, maxi and normal length skirts are alternatively in and out of fashion. One year the mini is fashionable, another it is not. Evidently, a detail such as length of skirt is, in itself, meaningless. What appears to count is what it implies about the ever-fluctuating perceptions of femininity. When the mini is "in," it might imply an increased emphasis on sexuality in the culture at large. When it is "out," then it might imply the opposite—a decreased emphasis on sexuality in the culture at large. Whatever the case may be, the point to be made here is that the specific elements and features of the dress code will invariably have connotative value that is interwoven with larger connotative frames and codes within the culture. Fashion is a reflection of cultural values and attitudes. When some fashion detail is emphasized in the media (in magazines, television programs, movies, etc.), then a fashion trend normally ensues.

Fashion is also ideological statement. Young people who see themselves as antisocial and iconoclastic will convey this through their clothing selections. The hippies dressed to emphasize "love" and "freedom;" punks dress to convey "toughness" and "nonconformity;" and so on. Uniforms, on the other hand, have great social and symbolic significance. Military dress connotes patriotism and communal values. The wearing of military uniforms for fashion can be construed as a counter-culture statement—a kind of dress parody of nationalistic tendencies—, as a statement of "military toughness," or as some other type of statement. One thing is for sure. Clothing communicates. Like language, it can be endearing, offensive, controversial, delightful, disgusting, foolish, charming and the list could go on and on. But you can be absolutely sure that no one will make a fashion statement in the nude. Those who attempt to do so—the so-called "nude streakers" who occasionally run across baseball and football fields, for instance—are quickly chastised or punished in some form.

As one last example of how fashion trends come about, let us take the case of blue jeans. The trend of wearing this article of clothing has swept the entire Western world in the last few decades. Why has this happened, a semiotician would ask? After all, jeans have traditionally been identified as blue-collar work clothes, being cheap and strong. High fashion articles, on the other hand, have always been expensive and manufactured with fancy materials and fabrics. Moreover, blue jeans are mass-produced items, whereas high fashion clothes are aimed at those with discriminating tastes.

The answer is, of course, that the cultural *meaning* of blue jeans has changed dramatically. Blue jeans have been transformed into fashion items and, therefore, reclassified and perceived as such. This is why they are now much more expensive than they used to be, much more exclusive, often personalized, and available even at chic boutiques. Jeans no longer symbolize a blue-collar work force. Rather, they now symbolize the diffusion of fashion trends across all socioeconomic classes, and a blurring of the demarcation line between work and play. Social gradations are still, however, maintained by fashion details (brand of jeans, quality of fabric, etc.), but not by the item itself *vis-à-vis* other types of clothes.

Concluding Remarks

In this chapter I have looked at the semiotics of dress, focusing on how clothing constitutes a source of social meaning- and message-making. As a closing word, it is interesting to note that fashion, until relatively recently, was the prerogative of aristocrats and monarchs. But in this "postmodern" world of ours (see Chapter 13), steeped in the power of the image, virtually everyone has come under the influence of dress codes, even if these are designed to be "counter-codes" (i.e. signifiers of antisocial or antiestablishment philosophies and sentiments).

Just think of what you do routinely every day after you get up in the morning. Typically, after preparing your body semiotically (e.g. showering, brushing your teeth, putting on make-up or shaving, etc.), the next thing you do is to clothe it appropriately, selecting your clothes on the basis of what you are going to do that day (work, go out for recreation, go on a vacation, etc.). In other words, you synchronize your dress code to your lifestyle and social options on a routine daily basis. You will also have undoubtedly noticed that your general behavior "reflects your dress code," so to speak. If you dress formally, you will notice that your language code, your gestural and bodily codes, etc. also tend to become more formal. If you dress informally, your other codes likewise seem to follow suit. What this shows, in my view, is that we are semiotic animals, i.e. that we are constantly involved in making messages and meanings, consciously and unconsciously, every minute of our lives.

SUGGESTIONS FOR FURTHER READING

Barthes, R. (1967). *Système de la mode.* Paris: Seuil.

Enninger, W. (1992). Clothing. In: R. Bauman (ed.), *Folklore, Cultural Performances, and Popular Entertainments*, pp. 123-145. Oxford: Oxford University Press.

Fisher, H. E. (1992). *Anatomy of Love.* New York: Norton.

Hollander, A. (1978). *Seeing through Clothes.* Harmondsworth: Penguin.

Solomon, J. (1988). *The Signs of Our Time.* Los Angeles: Jeremy P. Tarcher.

Chapter 9

YOU ARE WHAT YOU EAT!

Preliminary Remarks

Imagine the following situation. Let's say that you have lived in the city of Toronto all your life. At home, you have adopted a furry little bunny a few years back. You have become rather fond of the animal. You hardly perceive it to be a potential source of food. On the contrary, you think of the rabbit as you would an "intimate friend" or any other family member. I use words such as "furry," "bunny," etc. to reflect the connotations that pets have in our culture. A "domestic" animal means literally an animal that has been brought into the house to share the same space with humans. The word *domestic* comes from Latin *domus* "house."

Now, let's say that you work for an Italian company that has opened up a branch in Toronto. You have been invited over to dinner one evening by your boss. This is your chance to "impress the boss," as the saying goes. For your first dish, you are served a delicious plate of ravioli, your favorite pasta. After eating the savory ravioli, you commend your gracious host on the exquisiteness of Italian cuisine. Next, a plate is brought out and you are served a portion of the cooked meat on the plate. It looks appetizing. You are ready to taste it. But before you put the fork in your mouth, you ask your host what kind of meat it is. "Rabbit," is the answer you receive.

Almost instinctively you take the fork away from your mouth and place it gently on your plate. Your stomach simply will not allow you to swallow the meat. Your thoughts turn sentimentally to your pet bunny, and you feel "disgusted," which literally means "without taste." What are you going to do? Do you give back the meat and thus risk offending your boss? Chances are that you will contrive some excuse for not eating it, aimed at not insulting your host: "I'm really too full to eat anything else after that marvelous dish of pasta!" "I really must make room for dessert!" and so on.

What this vignette reveals is that food is much more than just food. Like clothing, food belongs simultaneously to the factual and artifactual orders of the human world. At the level of biology, we eat to survive. At the level of culture, we are symbolically what we eat. This is the theme of this chapter. Specifically, I will look at the semiotic transformation of food into cuisine, at the edibility versus non-edibility paradigm, at food as a message-making code, and finally at the phenomenon of fast food restaurants.

From Food to Cuisine

As in the case of clothing, at a factual level, food has an obvious survival function.   At this level of existence, all animals seek out, by instinct, appropriate flora and fauna to satisfy hunger and for nutrition. This is what *food* implies in the strictly denotative sense. It is only when we prepare *food* in ways that have become culturally routinized that what we eat is transformed into *cuisine*. The latter is both *what* we eat and *how we make* it, as well as *how* we actually go about eating it.   Moreover, in the artifactual realm of culture, various prepared foods become signifiers that are associated, by connotation and various metaphorical and metonymic processes, with a whole range of signifieds. At this level, food codes crystallize that are tied into culture-specific realities. These transformational processes and codes largely determine what is classified (and perceived) as edible or inedible:

World 3 = Artifactual World

The food item takes on signifying power.
***Food* is transformed into *cuisine* and various food codes.**

World 2 =
Signifying Processes

Connotation, metaphor, me-tonymy, etc. These convert World 1 food items into World 3 signifying codes.

World 1 = Factural World

***Food* = flora and fauna that are sought out for survival (to satisfy hunger, for nutrition, etc.)**

The anthropologist Claude Lévi-Strauss (1964) referred to these two dimensions of food as "the raw" and "the cooked." The latter reflects the human ability to transform nature. According to Lévi-Strauss this transformation is accomplished by two processes—roasting and boiling—both of which are tied into the first technological advances made by civilization. Roasting implies a direct contact between the food and a fire, and so is technologically primitive. It is associated with "the raw." But boiling reveals an advanced form of technological thinking, since the cooking process in this case is mediated by a pot and a cooking medium. Boiling is thus associated with "the cooked." This dichotomy manifests itself frequently across cultures. In the Hindu caste system (Goode 1992: 235-236), for instance, the higher castes may receive only raw food from the lower castes; whereas the lower castes are allowed to accept any kind of cooked food from any caste.

To get a sense of the difference between these two dimensions associated with food, imagine being in a "Robinson Crusoe" situation. Let's suppose that you have somehow been abandoned alone on an isolated island in the middle of nowhere to fend for yourself. Without the support and security of culture, your first instincts are to survive in any way that you can. In this situation, your need for food and water takes precedence over all else. In a basic sense, your mind "descends" to the factual level of existence. When your hunger becomes extreme, your search for food will certainly not be guided by cultural perceptions of edibility! You will eat any flora or hunt any fauna that will satisfy your hunger. The eating of food in such a drastic situation has only one function—to ensure survivability.

Now, let's suppose that you discover other similarly-abandoned people on a remote part of the island. Since there is strength in numbers, you all decide to stay together as a group. To reduce the risk of not finding food and of not eating, the group decides to assign specific roles to each person for the hunting of food and for its preparation. After a period of time, what will emerge from these agreements is a "proto-culture," based on a shared survival strategy. As time passes, other "social contracts" and arrangements are made, and the cooking of food will become more and more routinized and subject to communal taste preferences. It is at this point that cooking is transformed within your newly-formed culture into a new artifactual reality with a new constellation of meanings assigned to it.

The purpose of this vignette has been to exemplify how food is tied, first and foremost, to survival and only subsequently to culture. Indeed, it might even be claimed, as do some anthropologists, that the preparation of food was the event that led to the "creation" of culture. The aim of semiotics is, of course, to unravel the signifying characteristics of all cultural artifacts, and food is, clearly, one of the most important. It should come as no surprise to find that food, like clothing, is associated with ritual behaviors in all the world's cultures. Most, if not all, of the world's religious ceremonies are centered on food. The *raison d'être* of the Catholic Mass, for instance, is to partake symbolically of the consecrated body and blood of Christ. Specific types of food are served and eaten traditionally at Thanksgiving, Easter, Christmas and so on. Food invariably is a primary constituent of common house parties, feasts (weddings, Bar Mitzvahs, etc.), get-togethers and the like. We schedule "breakfast," "lunch" and "dinner" events on a daily basis. Indeed, we plan our days around meals. Even going out on a common date would be virtually unthinkable without some eating component associated with this event (from the popcorn eaten at movie theaters to the elaborate restaurant meal after a concert).

The act of eating in a public setting always has something of a ritualistic quality to it. The predictable routines leading up to the "eating performance" at a high class restaurant, for instance, are suggestive of a rite emphasizing the continuity between body, mind and culture. There is no motive for eating at such places, really, other than to engage with our eating partner or partners in an act of symbolic acknowledgment that eating is basic to our existence— at both the factual and artifactual levels.

The symbolic value of food can be seen in most of the world's mythic and religious accounts of our origins. The story of Adam and Eve in the Christian Bible revolves around the eating of an apple. In the Garden of Eden, the apple is a "forbidden" fruit. In the Koran, on the other hand, the forbidden fruit is a banana. Think of the many religious connotations that these fruits have in many of the world's cultures. This is why the "Apple" computer company has chosen the logo of this fruit to symbolize its quest for "forbidden" knowledge. Eating and knowing are mythically intertwined.

The discovery and cultivation of the apple dates back to 6,500 BC to Asia Minor (Panati 1984: 98-100). Ramses II of Egypt cultivated apples in orchards along the Nile in the thirteenth century BC. The Ancient Greeks also cultivated apple trees from the seventh century BC onwards. They designated the apple "the golden fruit," since Greek mythology, like Christian doctrine, assigned to the apple a primordial significance. The apple was given to Hera from the Garden of the Hesperides as a wedding present when she married Zeus. Actually, the mention of the apple in the Bible is of unknown origin. In its original version, there is no mention of an "apple" as such in the Book of Genesis, just of a "forbidden fruit." It was only much later when painters and sculptors became interested in the story artistically that they assigned to the forbidden fruit an identity—namely, that of the apple.

The point of this mythic excursus on the apple is to underscore that food items are imbued with mythic-symbolic meaning across all cultures. Foods like bread and lamb, for instance, invariably evoke latent symbolism in our culture. This is why we talk of the "bread of life," of "earning your bread," of "sacrificial lambs" and the like. As Margaret Visser (1992: 2-3) aptly points out, in many western European languages words for *bread* are often synonymous with life:

> This is true even in our own day, when people eat far less bread than they used to, and when bread comes to us from a factory, bleached, squishy, ready-cut (so much for "breaking bread"), wrapped in plastic or cellophane. Yet we still expect to have bread on hand at every meal, as background, as completion, as dependable comforter and recompense for any stress or disappointment the rest of the meal might occasion. Bread is for us a kind of successor to the motherly breast, and it has been over the centuries responsible for billions of sighs of satisfaction.

It is interesting to note that the word *companion* comes from Latin and means literally the person "with whom we share bread." Bread is, evidently, as much symbol as it is food. So, too, with many other of our so-called "basic" foods.

Edible versus Inedible

Let us return to the unpleasant and difficult situation with which I started off this chapter of finding yourself in the situation of being served rabbit meat. The fact that your mind associated the meat with your bunny at home is based on your acquired mental classification of the rabbit as a "domestic animal." This forces you to perceive rabbit meat as "inedible." Unless you are a vegetarian, you would certainly not put into the same category the other "meats" that are served routinely in our culture: bovine meat (beef steaks, hamburgers, etc.), lamb meat, poultry meat, etc. This is because the animals from which we make meat dishes in such cases are not classified by our culture as "domestic." So the meats made from them are perceived to be "edible" food items. However, such classificatory decisions are not universal. In India, a cow is classified as "sacred" and, therefore, as "inedible." Incidentally, this is the basis of our expression *sacred cow* to refer to something unassailable and revered. Anglo-American culture does not eat foxes or dogs; but the former is reckoned a delicacy in Russia, and the latter a delicacy in China. Need it be mentioned that some people even eat human meat (known technically as anthropophagitism or cannibalism)?

Historically, the Romans were the ones who had domesticated the rabbit, which flourished throughout their empire as a source of food. In sixteenth-century England, rabbits were prized instead for their fur. For the first time they were bred selectively in order to enhance their rich coats. By the nineteenth century, England passed strict game laws prohibiting rabbit killing and theft. From that period onwards, rabbits have been classified as domestic animals in most of Anglo-American culture. In the remainder of the previous Roman empire, however, they continue to be perceived as food sources. This cultural discrepancy is what made your situation ambiguous and difficult vis-à-vis your boss. Perhaps the only truly "honest" thing to tell your boss in such a situation would be the truth—that you have a pet rabbit at home or, to show off your newly-gained semiotic expertise, that in your culture rabbits are classified as inedible.

Outside of those which have a demonstrably harmful effect on the human organism, the species of flora and fauna are considered to be edible or inedible is very much an arbitrary matter. We cannot get nourishment from eating tree bark, grass or straw. But we certainly could get it from eating frogs, ants, earthworms, silkworms, lizards and snails. Most people in our culture would, of course, respond with disgust and revulsion at the thought of eating such potential food items. However, there are cultures where they are not only eaten for nourishment, but also considered to be delicacies. Our expression "to develop a taste" for some "strange" food reveals how closely tied edibility is to cultural perception. Left alone on that hypothetical island described above, the question would certainly not be one of "taste," but of "survival" at any taste.

Once the classificatory system for food has been set up at the level of culture, what happens next is something that is rather revealing about human nature. We start to perceive differences in cuisine as fundamental differences in worldview and lifestyle. We perceive them, in other words, as differences between "us" and "them." We tend to feel that other people's "tastes" are "unnatural." Let us take a concrete example. We eat fish willingly, but we do not eat the fish's eyes. But this is exactly what many other cultures do. To see others eat the eyes generally causes discomfort or queasiness within us. It is a small step from this unpleasant sensation to a conception of the eaters as "barbaric" or "unnatural," for we regularly equate cuisine with ethnicity and ethnic lifestyle. It is interesting to note that when we do come to "accept" the food of "others" as appetizing—just think of how delicious we now perceive spaghetti (Italian), tacos and enchiladas (Mexican), and stir-fry (Oriental) to be—the food is reclassified as an "exotic" delicacy. Indeed, such reclassifications manifest themselves routinely in the desire we often have nowadays to eat "Italian," "Mexican," "Japanese," etc.

Food as Message-Making

Consider the following facts (Goode 1992: 236-245):

- In North America men tend to eat red meat and potatoes and to avoid white meat and quiches.

- Adult !Kung Bushmen of the Kalahari Desert in southern Africa never eat the scavenged contents of a bird's nest, but will use it to make soup for their children.

- Hindus rank beef eaters lower than other meat eaters.

- In traditional Chinese households, the eldest eat first, followed by the next generation, on down to the youngest.

- At certain intervals, the richest members of the Kwakiutl society of the Pacific Northwest put on a lavish feast during which they give away material gifts as a sign of bonding with all the members of the society.

Facts such as these show rather conspicuously that food tied to all kinds of codes and systems at the level of culture. Food is a primary component of gender-, age-, ethnicity- and status-coded behaviors. The complex rules of how to prepare food and when to eat it, the meanings that specific dishes (artifactually-transformed food items) have *vis-à-vis* group membership, the subtle distinctions that are constantly made in the ways food is cut and cleaned, etc. are all powerful signifiers of some sort or other. Food, social bonding and religiosity are intrinsically intertwined: many Christians say grace before starting a meal together; many Jews say special prayers before partaking of wine and bread; etc. It would seem that the entire social order is sewn together with the fabric of food-centered rituals.

Perhaps the most culturally pivotal aspect of cuisine has to do with eating events—the activities related to organizing meals for special occasions and the actual "performance" of the meals. The performance entails specific rules of presentation, arrangement, and interpersonal etiquette:

- In what order are the dishes to be presented?

- What combinations can be served *in tandem?*

- How are the foods to be placed on the table?

- Who has preference in being served?

- Who must show deference?

- Who does the speaking and who the listening?

- Who sits where?

- What topics of conversation are appropriate?

And the list could go on and on. There is indeed a lot of meaning- and message-making during the performance of such eating *texts*. To see how eating texts are carriers of meaning and social messages consider the following scenario, which I will call the "boss-over-to-dinner" scenario. The crucial questions related to this eating text are centered around the kind of message you want communicated through it. The subtle list of rules involved in carrying out the eating performance successfully requires much energy and mental astuteness. Here are just some of the vital questions and features that go into the make-up of this text:

- What kinds of foods and beverages are appropriate?

- What time is appropriate for the eating event to start? How does one find this out?

- What will the seating arrangement be like?

- What will the serving order be like?

- What will the topic of conversation be? Or, more appropriately, who is to be assigned the role of determining the topic?

- What events must be organized before and after the meal?

Intuitively, you feel that your success within your boss's company will be influenced by the success of your eating text as a social event. You will be judged—intellectually, socially, etc.—on the basis of how successfully you pull off the eating event. You know all too well that when your guests (your boss and his or her companion) leave your home, the first comment they will make will be directed towards the quality and degree of success of your eating text. It will be judged in the same way as, say, a professor will judge a written text such as an essay. The "grade" you receive will be translated into a work-related "grade." The whole event is indeed a socially dramatic one. As Visser (1991: 107) remarks, "dinner invitations can be fraught with hope and danger, and dinner parties are dramatic events at which decisions can be made and important relationships initiated, tested, or broken."

Eating events are so crucial to the establishment and maintenance of social relations and social harmony that there exists virtually no culture that does not assign an area of the domestic abode to eating functions and ceremonies. All cultures, moreover, have a discrete set of table rituals and manners which are inculcated into the members of the culture from birth. If you do not know the "table-manner code" of a certain culture, then you will have to learn it in order to continue living in that culture without censure and disapprobation. Let's take a concrete example. If you have never eaten spaghetti before, then you will have to learn what the "correct" way is to eat it, which today involves the use of a fork. Incidentally, in nineteenth-century Naples, where the modern-day version of this dish comes from (Visser 1991: 17-18), people ate spaghetti with their hands by raising each string of pasta in the hand, throwing back the head, and lowering the string into the mouth without slurping. Today, the correct manner of eating spaghetti is to twirl it around the fork, in small doses, and then to insert the fork into the mouth as one does with any other fork-negotiated intake of food.

Cultures also seem to vary widely as to the degree of sociability associated with the eating event: at the extreme ends of this sociability continuum some cultures see the act of eating as a private act similar to the sex act; others see it necessarily as a social act, never to be performed in private. Many cultures, as well, have a kind of "pecking order" which is designed to indicate the social class or position of the eaters. In our culture, eating in a high-class restaurant entails the activation and deployment of a whole set of complementary social codes and texts, from dress to language, that are meant to create a whole range of subtle and not-so-subtle messages about oneself.

Other features of the eating scene which vary across cultures and, in some cases within cultures, include:

- standing or sitting while eating;

- sitting at a table or on the floor;

- using the hands or eating utensils;

- speaking or maintaining silence during the eating event;

- whether or not, and what kinds of, liquids can accompany the event; and

- what sequence of subevents (who speaks first, who eats what, etc.) is operative and in what contexts.

It is obvious that eating constitutes a socio-semiotic text of great significance to World 3 life. There is no culture that does not ascribe great significance to its eating events. While the details of these may vary widely across cultures, the fact that they exist at all throughout the world is a rather revealing clue to the nature of humanity.

Fast Food Culture

Expressions such as "fast living," "the fast lane" and the like tell us an awful lot about the way we perceive life in modern technological cultures. There is hardly any time in such cultures to do anything "meaningful." Everything seems to be "moving too fast," as the saying goes. Even the way we eat has become a victim of the "fastness" of technological/consumeristic life. Since the sixties, the "fast food" business has become a multi-billion dollar industry. Why has this happened? The sociologist or the psychologist would look for an answer in some social or behavioral pattern. The semiotician would look for it in the *meaning* of the fast food event.

Ask yourself the following questions. These are "semiotic probes" into the nature of fast food eating: Why do I go to fast food restaurants? Is it because of the food? Is it to be with friends and family? Is it because the food is affordable and the service fast? Is it because the atmosphere is congenial? Your would probably answer most of these in the affirmative. Indeed, most people feel that the food at fast food restaurants is passable. In addition, most would say that the fast food restaurant provides an opportunity to stay a while with family and/or friends. Most people would also admit that the food at McDonald's or Wendy's is affordable and that the service is fast and polite. Indeed, many people today probably feel "more at home" at a McDonald's restaurant than in their own households. This is, in fact, the "semiotic key" to understanding the establishment and institutionalization of fast food restaurants as "family" and "socialization" restaurants throughout North America.

Consider the case of McDonald's:

- As of 1973 one new McDonald's outlet was being opened per day.

- Over one billion McDonald's hamburgers are sold every three to four months.

- Ronald McDonald is as much a cultural icon and childhood-related mythological figure as is Santa Claus.

- The McDonald's "golden arches" logo is now one of the more recognized ones in the world.

The message underlying the McDonald's iconography and commercial ads is one basically of Puritan values: law and order, cleanliness, friendliness, hospitality, hard work, self-discipline and family values. In a society that is on the verge of shedding its traditional Puritanical heritage and value systems, McDonald's comes forward as a savior that claims to "do it all for you." And like any religious institution, eating at McDonald's is imbued with ritual and symbolism. The "golden arches," like all the ancient arches in great cities, herald a "new age," one of traditional family values. By satisfying a "Big Mac attack," you are, in effect, satisfying a deep metaphorical need to eat symbolically. From the menu—which is McDonald's "Bible"—to the uniforms, McDonald's exacts and imposes standardization, just as do the world's "organized" religions. And as any ritualistic experience, the eating event at McDonald's is designed to be cathartic and redeeming.

The success of McDonald's, and its institutionalization as a bearer of symbolic meaning beyond the "fastness" with which it dispenses its menu offerings, reveals something rather fundamental about modern technological cultures. A fast food eatery would be inconceivable in a non-industrialized culture; and one would have been unimaginable just a few decades ago even in ours. So what has happened? In my opinion, and that of others, the popularity of fast food restaurants from the sixties onwards symbolizes a new reality in the make-up and organization of the North American household. Throughout the first half of this century, household roles were gender-coded: the husband went out to work and the wife stayed home basically to cook. Meals were structured and carried out by the wife/mother. This reality changed drastically in the sixties and continued to change throughout the seventies and eighties. The new socioeconomic need to have a two-person working household, bolstered by the feminist movement emphasizing the "liberation" of the woman from the household context, has led to an unprecedented number of women entering the work force in the last three decades. As a consequence, the "traditional" family structure has undergone irreversible changes.

Out of these changes, there has emerged the reality that fewer and fewer North Americans have the time to eat meals together within the household, let alone the energy to prepare elaborate dinners. And even when they do, it is highly unlikely that they will perceive the eating event as a structured one aimed at preserving family harmony and traditional moral values. In modern-day households, meals are routinely consumed in front of television sets, and given the increasing number of such sets in the house, family members may not even watch the same shows at dinner. The home, ironically, has become a place where people now tend to eat apart. Enter McDonald's (or Wendy's, or Burger King, or whatever) to the rescue! Eating out at such fast food places—which are affordable, quick, and cheery—is perceived to bring the family together, at the same table, under the same roof. As parents center their lives more and more on the place of work than on the home, the fast-food meal has become virtually a necessity to carry out our daily existence harmoniously. Note that, on occasion, the family is "treated out" to a more posh restaurant, just to add a little more class to the ritual of eating together.

This brings me to the last topic of this chapter—the phenomenon of "junk food." When fast food eateries first came onto the scene in the fifties—as burger and milkshake "joints"—they were perceived to be exclusively for adolescents out on a date. The food eaten at such "joints" was perceived, correctly, to be "junk" injurious to one's health and only to be consumed by young people because their metabolism could break it down more quickly and because they could eventually "recover" from its negative health effects. But in no time whatsoever junk food, nurtured by effective ad campaigns, became an indulgence permissible to anyone of any age, from very young children to seniors. Indeed, the compulsion to consume junk food has even led to descriptions such as "junk food addict," "junk food mania" and the like, which are all indicative of the "insanity" of eating such food. Yet, we continue to do so and with great gusto. It is rather obvious that consumption, at any risk, is tied to self-gratification. No one would ever contemplate eating junk food for anything but self-gratification. "I'm going to give myself a treat" is the expression we use, in fact, to rationalize our self-indulgences into the "junk heap" of food items which are replete with a concoction of chemicals that would kill most other species over a very short period of time.

Junk food is the paradigmatic opposite of social eating events. It is normally consumed alone, not in the company of others. Many, in fact, try to hide their "addiction" to junk food. Only teenagers in specific clique situations have adopted junk food as a kind of food sharing ritual. But it is a ritual of limited and ephemeral value. You can "throw out" the friends you eat junk food with, just as thoughtlessly as you throw out the wrappers that contain the food. At no other time in history (can you imagine someone in the Renaissance eating the equivalent of a box of potato chips?) have we developed such a knack for consuming anything so worthless and injurious as junk food. Sheer consumption is literally taking over traditional value systems and replacing them with a *Weltanschauung* (worldview) based on immediate self-gratification. The real message of what is happening to our social order is literally to be found in the food we eat.

Concluding Remarks

This chapter has focused on the semiotics of food, focusing on how food constitutes a source of social meaning- and message-making. While at the level of biological survival (World 1) we are prepared to eat anything that will sustain life, at the level of culture (World 3) we develop "tastes" only for certain kinds of foods. Moreover, eating in the world of culture is a signifying event that entails the activation of complex codes of behavior. Food is also intertwined with mythologies of ethnicity. When you think of pasta, you think of Italians. When you think of bagels, you think of Israeli culture. And the list could go on and on.

Finally, the complex codes and texts associated with eating do not exist in a vacuum. They are synchronized with other lifestyle and social options on a routine daily basis.

We cook our food to show that we are civilized animals. We discriminate among types of cooking and food preparations as signifiers of social occasions. We invariably associate food with events of great spiritual or ceremonial value. We use the consumption of different kinds of food and drink as markers of social occasions. The advent of fast food and junk food on the contemporary scene has signaled a radical change in value systems, beliefs and in the behaviors associated with them. Clearly, there is much more to food than mere eating for survival. The digestive system and the cultural system are entangled in a complex interplay of body/mind/culture semiosis.

SUGGESTIONS FOR FURTHER READING

Goode, J. (1992). Food. In: R. Bauman (ed.), *Folklore, Cultural Performances, and Popular Entertainments*, pp. 233-245. Oxford: Oxford University Press.

Goody, J. (1982). *Cooking, Cuisine and Class.* Cambridge, MA: Cambridge University Press.

Lévi-Strauss, C. (1964). *The Raw and the Cooked.* London: Cape.

Panati, C. (1984). *Browser's Book of Beginnings.* Boston: Houghton Mifflin.

Visser, M. (1991). *The Rituals of Dinner.* New York: Harper Collins.

Chapter 10

KEEP YOUR DISTANCE!

Preliminary Remarks

Imagine the following two common scenarios. Let's suppose that you have just entered an elevator on the fifth floor of a typical multi-floor skyscraper. There are two people already in the elevator—one in one corner and the other in the other corner. They are both facing the front of the elevator. Where will you stand? Near one or the other? Or will you stand in one of the two remaining corners? In what direction will you orient your body? Will you face the other two passengers or will you face the door? Without going into a detailed analysis of this situation, there is no doubt in my mind that you know exactly the answer to all these questions. You will probably stand in one of the remaining corners facing the front of the elevator. What you have done is, literally, "kept your distance" in what is really a socially-structured space known as the "elevator."

Now, imagine the next common situation. Let's suppose you are being introduced to a stranger of the opposite sex. As part of this social contact ritual, you know enough to extend your hand for a typical greeting handshake. Now, here are the relevant questions connected to this scenario. How close do you stand to your interlocutor, a couple of inches away or a couple of feet away? Do you hold on to the person's hand delicately or with force, for a relatively short or for a protracted period of time? Do you touch any other parts of his or her body to execute the greeting text? Once again, without going into a detailed analysis of this situation, there's no doubt that you know exactly the answer to all these questions. You certainly would not stand very close to your interlocutor as you shake his or her hand, for that would constitute a breach of "personal space" and it would be interpreted as a transgression of an imaginary boundary-line around the person that can only be traversed by those with whom that person is intimate (usually sexually). You would also not touch any other body parts—arms, face, etc.—in the perform-ance of this greeting text. Once again this action would be interpreted in sexual, not social, terms.

One might think that the dimensions of the spaces that people seem to maintain between themselves and others are unconditioned and instinctive. But, as it turns out, they are largely determined by *convention*. In other cultures, people routinely face each other in "crowds" and in enclosed spaces (like elevators): e.g. at sporting events or theaters, North Americans usually slide into a crowded aisle while facing forward with their backsides to the people already seated; in Russia one enters an aisle facing the people already seated. People in other cultures also touch much more upon meeting one another and stand closer to each than we do in our culture. The moral to this story is that "space" is imbued with semiotic meaning—both the space that we keep *vis-à-vis* other people (interpersonal space) and the spaces that we inhabit or frequent, such as the home and the public places we go to on a regular basis.

The semiotics of space constitutes the topic of this chapter. This area of inquiry falls more properly under the category of *proxemics*—the branch of semiotics that studies the symbolic structure of the physical space maintained between bodies in social contexts and of the physical space associated with buildings and places. Actually, this term was not coined by a semiotician but by the anthropologist Edward T. Hall (1966: 1): "Proxemics is the term I have coined for the interrelated observations and theories of man's use of space as a specialized elaboration of culture." I will start off with a discussion of the semiotic transformation of territoriality tendencies and shelter fabrications into signifying spaces and architectural constructions. Then, I will look at the semiotic organization of interpersonal space, at space (within buildings and in places) as a signifying phenomenon, and, finally, at *architecture*—the art of symbolic space management and organization.

From Territory and Shelter to Space and Architecture

As was the case for clothing and food, at the level of biological factuality, we need to have space around us to ensure our survival. Intrusions into the territory that we claim as ours will be perceived instinctively as signals of aggression by some intruder. Cats, for example, mark the boundaries of their proclaimed territory by urination. We do essentially the same thing by marking off our own appropriated territory (home or other living space) by various props (fences, landmarks, etc.). At the level of cultural groups, enclosed or marked-off territories constitute political entities (nations, states, etc.). Like all other animals, we are willing to fight and to die to protect our declared territories, personal and political.

Related to this "territorial imperative," as Ardrey (1966) calls it, is our need for shelter to protect us from the elements and to safeguard us against enemies. Any material "covering" that can be deployed to provide protection from weather changes and safeguard us from enemies constitutes a shelter. All animals seek, and many build, shelters within their natural habitats.

So far the story is a biological one. *Territory* and *shelter* belong to the world of biological instincts and needs. They increase our chances at survival. It is when these are transformed by signifying processes into artifactual realities that they take on signifying power respectively as *space* (interpersonal, social, etc.) and as *architecture:*

World 3 = Artifactual World

A *territory* becomes a signifying space. A *shelter* is transformed into an *architectural structure* with its signifying spaces.

World 2 = Signifying Processes

Connotation, metaphor, metonymy, etc. These convert World 1 territorial and shelter tendencies into World 3 signifying codes.

World 1 = Factural World

Territory = the demarcation of a specific area for personal safety.

Shelter = any covering employed for protection from the weather and as safeguard agains potential aggressors and enemies.

The cross-species need for territoriality and space was "demonstrated," so to speak, by psychological experiments a few years back that received much media attention because of the implications they seemed to have at the time for life in modern crowded urban centers. The gist of these experiments can be outlined as follows. When two laboratory rats were enclosed in the same cage, the researchers found that each one would instinctively appropriate an area of approximately equal dimensions *vis-à-vis* the other. When a third rat would be introduced into the same space, then a "tripartite" arrangement of equally-subdivided areas would seem to be negotiated among the three rats. However, there always seemed to be some initial "reluctance" to do so, as signaled by minor altercations among the three rats at the beginning of the "negotiations." As each extra rat would be introduced progressively into the same environment, more reluctance and aggression would ensue until a "critical mass" would apparently be reached whereby the rats in the cage would either fight aggressively and relentlessly or demonstrate some form of "aberrant" behavior. The implications for "urban overcrowding" that these experiments apparently had were not missed by journalists and reporters. It would seem that we all have an inborn territorial "critical mass" which determines how many "others" we can accept into a "shared territoriality" arrangement. Some people "snap," as the expression goes, when this critical mass is surpassed; others seek rational solutions such as escaping into the suburbs, moving away into the country, etc.

Interpersonal Space

Edward T. Hall (1966) may have been the first to investigate the dimensions of the invisible boundaries people establish and maintain when interacting. He noted that these could be measured very accurately, allowing for predictable statistical variation, and that the boundary dimensions varied from culture to culture. In North American culture, he found that a distance of under six inches between two people was perceived as an "intimate" distance; he measured the acceptable "social" distance at from four to 12 feet. Intruding upon the limits set by a boundary causes considerable discomfort. For example, if a stranger were to talk at a distance of only several centimeters away from someone, he or she would be considered rude or even aggressive. If the "safe" distance is breached by some acquaintance, on the other hand, it would be interpreted as a sexual advance.

More specifically, Hall identified four types of culturally-elaborated distances: intimate, personal, social and public. He was able to further subdivide these into "far" and "close" phases:

- *Intimate Distance* (up to 18 in.)

At intimate distance, all the senses are activated and the presence of the other person or persons is unmistakable. The close phase (up to 6 in.) is an emotionally-charged zone reserved for love-making, comforting, and protecting; the far phase (6 in. to 18 in.) is the distance of interaction with family members and close friends. Touch is frequent at both phases of intimate distance.

- *Personal Distance* (1.5 ft. - 4 ft.)

This is the minimum comfortable distance between non-touching individuals. In the close phase (1.5 ft. to 2.5 ft.), one can grasp the other by extending the arms. The far phase (2.5 ft. to 4 ft.) is defined as anywhere from one arm's length to the distance required for both individuals to touch hands. Beyond this distance the two must move to make contact (e.g. to shake hands). In essence, this zone is reserved for informal contact between friends. It constitutes a small protective space that separates the Self from the Other.

- *Social Distance* (4 ft. to 12 ft.)

This distance is considered non-involving and non-threatening by most individuals. The close phase (4 ft. to 7 ft.) is typical of impersonal transactions and casual social gatherings. Formal social discourse and transactions are characteristic of the far phase (7 ft. to 12 ft.). This is the minimum distance at which one could go about one's business without seeming rude to others.

- *Public Distance* (12 ft. and beyond)

At this distance, one can take either evasive or defensive action if physically threatened. Hall notes that people tend to keep at this distance from important public figures or from anyone participating at a public function. Discourse at this distance will be highly structured and formalized (lectures, speeches, etc.).

The proxemic organization of interpersonal distance is reflected as well in our language. Metaphorical expressions such as "Keep your distance," "They're very close," "We've drifted far apart," "You're trespassing into my personal space," "I can't quite get to him," "Please keep in touch," etc. are all verbal indicators that our conceptualization of interpersonal relationships is constrained by our perceptions of interpersonal distances.

Proxemic structures are culturally-conditioned. Observance of interaction zones is critical to the maintenance of social harmony. Research has demonstrated consistently that the distances characterizing interpersonal space increase between the ages of three and 20 at which time they reach the expected norms. Relative age, gender, familiarity and social status of the individuals involved in an interaction are also factors that influence interpersonal distances. In addition to such sociological variables, it would appear that culturally-shaped perceptions also enter into the picture: attitudes, likes and dislikes, attractiveness, odor, etc. are all factors that subliminally influence the distances people keep *vis-à-vis* each other in interactive settings.

It is interesting to note that proxemics plays a vital role in adolescent body presentation schemas. Conscious of bodily odors, facial imperfections, and the like, teens are more likely to stay well beyond the boundary limits set by North American culture generally. Intrusions occur primarily in the context of clique gatherings and intimate settings such as the party scene. But even in the latter context, the lighting is kept low and the music is played loudly as means of deflecting attention away from bodily imperfections. The use of bodily enhancers, such as perfumes, is common at parties for the same reason.

Needless to say, the signifying organization of interpersonal space extends into all kinds of structured settings. If someone is standing up at the front of an audience, he or she is perceived as more important than those sitting down. Speeches, lectures, classes, musical performances, etc. are organized in this way. On the other hand, officials, managers, directors, etc. sit behind a desk to convey importance and superiority. Only their superiors can walk behind them to talk to them. To show "friendliness," the person behind the desk will have to come out and sit with his or her interlocutor in a different part of the room.

As a final commentary on interpersonal space, consider touch. In modern urban centers, and in Western culture generally, people do not touch each other very much. Some clinical psychologists have even attributed most of our "social ills" and "psychological complexes" to this fear and abhorrence of touch. "Touch therapy" clinics are springing up all over North America. What does touching mean? Whom would you touch and whom would you not touch? And where is it permissible to touch another person?

Research on these questions has found some rather intriguing things.

- In public places the amount of touching varies enormously from culture to culture: e.g. in San Juan (Puerto Rico) the rate of couples touching is 180 times per hour, in Paris it is 110, and in London it is 0 (Argyle 1975).

- In North American culture, mothers tend to touch their daughters more than their sons on their arms and on their hair. On the other hand, they tend to touch their sons more than their daughters on their chests.

- In North American culture, fathers tend to touch their daughters more than their sons on their hair, faces, neck and shoulders.

- In North American culture, male friends touch each other more than female friends on the shoulders, chest, and legs. Female friends, on the other hand, touch each other more than male friends on the hair, face, neck and forearms.

- In North American culture, men touch women more on the knee than women touch men. However, women touch men more on the chest and hips than men touch women.

- Although touch is relatively unimportant in North American culture, it is still much more important than it is in Japan (Barnlund 1975). During infancy and childhood the Japanese encourage a much closer tactile relationship among family members than do North Americans. But at adolescence and beyond the situation changes dramatically. There is very little tactile communication among adults in traditional Japanese culture.

Let's look rapidly at the various types of touching that convey specific kinds of meanings. Actually, the study of tactile communication is known more technically as *haptics*. The most common form of haptic communication is hand-shaking. Intimate friends do not shake hands, unless they haven't seen each other for a protracted period of time or unless they want to congratulate one another. Cross-culturally, the form that hand-shaking assumes varies considerably. People can give a handshake by squeezing the hand (as we do), shaking the other's hand with both hands, shaking the other's hand and then patting the other's back or hugging him or her, leaning forward or standing straight while shaking and so on. But hand-shaking is not universal. Southeast Asians, for instance, press their palms together in a praying motion. Other forms of haptic communication include: patting someone on the arm, shoulder or back to indicate agreement or to compliment; linking arms to indicate companionship; putting one's arm around the shoulder to indicate friendship or intimacy; holding hands with family members or lovers; hugging to indicate happiness at seeing a friend or a family member; and kissing on the cheeks among friends to execute the greeting ritual.

Anthropologists are unclear as to why touching patterns and interpersonal zones vary so much across cultures. What is for certain is that all cultures have such patterns and zones, no matter how divergent they seem to be. In my opinion, the differences are no more than the culturally-conditioned reflexes of the factual tendencies associated with territoriality. The differences result, in semiotic terms, from different kinds of transformational signifying processes applied to these tendencies. This is why many people seem to think of themselves as literally "contained" in their skin. The zones of privacy that define "Self-space" in many cultures, therefore, include the clothes that cover the skin. This is because, as discussed in the eighth chapter, clothes are semiotic extenders of the body. On the other hand, in Arabic cultures the Self is located down within the body shell. This results in a totally different patterning and perception of proxemic relations. As a consequence, Arabs are in general more tolerant of crowds, of noise levels, of the touching of hands, of eye contact and of body odors than most North Americans are (Hall 1966).

Signifying Space

The built environment is a cultural reflex of "shelter-for-survival." As such, therefore, it is imbued with signification. A building is not simply a pile of bricks and cement. It constitutes a signifying system with a broad range of meanings. The rules which govern private and public spaces and buildings constitute signifying codes: e.g. you must knock on the door of a friend's house to announce your presence, but you do not knock on the door of a retail store; you may sit and wait for someone in a foyer, atrium or lobby, but you cannot wait for someone in a toilet; you can walk on a public sidewalk, but you cannot walk on someone's porch without permission; and the list could go on and on.

Rooms in a building all have a symbolic quality to them. When you enter a "sacred space" like a church or chapel, you feel differently than when you enter a crowded theater. In church you tend to speak with a lower voice, to be more careful with the walking noises you make, and so on. The space within rooms is, clearly, imbued with specific kinds of meaning.

Consider how you feel about your home. Your home is, at a factual level, a shelter. But at the level of signification, there's much more to a home than its function to provide protection against the weather and to act as a safeguard against enemies. If you live in a detached house, then the lines that demarcate your property also identify the territory you define as your own. Such a territory is a privately-bounded space that is designed to preserve our biological sanity (Ardrey 1966). When personalized property boundaries do not exist, as in public housing projects, prisons, etc., it should come as no surprise to find that people tend to lose respect for boundary codes. "De-territorialized" spaces such as these seem constantly to induce some residents to engage in defacement and vandalism. Even in posh high-rise apartment buildings, the residents seem to be constantly seeking "spaces" to satisfy an inborn need for personalized territory. This is why many apartment dwellers own cottages, gardens, etc. Incidentally, the marker of territoriality within an apartment is the doorway to the apartment itself. When one steps inside, one feels vastly different about the space than when one is in the corridor or in the lobby. This is because the "inside" of the apartment is a personal space.

Inside the home—be it a detached home, an apartment or some other kind of dwelling structure—each room is bound to elicit a specific type of feeling and to generate its own kind of semiosis. An adolescent venturing into his or her parent's bedroom is bound to feel uneasy about it. Indeed, bedrooms seem to be particularly meaningful places. Concealing a bedroom has a biological basis—we are extremely vulnerable when we are sleeping, and so it is judicious to keep sleeping areas concealed or secret. The Ancient Egyptians concealed their bedrooms at the back or the sides of their homes. North American families also prefer to keep their bedrooms away from the line of sight. North American teenagers are especially protective of their bedrooms. Adolescents are concerned about their appearance and behavior, believing that everyone is constantly observing them. In this persistent and dominant state of mind, the adolescent will go to great lengths to protect his or her vulnerable identity. This is why he or she transforms his or her bedroom into a haven for protecting and sheltering the Self. In fact, a teenager will guard the entry into his or her bedroom with the zeal of a religious fanatic. In this private space, the adolescent unwinds, relaxes and defines his or her symbolic universe through decoration (posters, photos), sound (stereo equipment with appropriate tapes, compact disks, etc.) and tokens of peer friendships (gifts, memorabilia, letters, etc.). This is a sacred space for the adolescent, a refuge and asylum from the world. Here no one is looking at his or her imperfections. Only "intimates" are allowed to share that space symbolically. All other habitations are considered to be intrusions (including when parents enter the room to clean it themselves or to instruct their adolescent to clean it).

Of course, not all teens have a private bedroom. In many households the bedroom is shared, by necessity, with others. But it is accurate to say that most teens at least desire a private space, whether or not one is obtainable.

When the contemporary teen is at home, generally within the confines of his or her bedroom, the telephone often becomes a crucial "pipeline" to other peers. Given the increasing economic feasibility of owning a personal phone, the contemporary teen will use it as the primary means for contacting peers, for recounting events of importance to their social life and for organizing social events. The phone is not a simple tool for relating information; it is a vital means for maintaining contacts with peers.

Our homes are further partitioned into spaces with specific functions— preparing food, eating, entertaining, etc. Spaces defined in such ways are determined by our conceptions of "clean" and "dirty." Dirt is really no more than displaced matter. An object out of place must be put back or reallocated; otherwise it might be perceived as litter or debris. Definitions of rooms along this paradigmatic axis vary from culture to culture. We define a kitchen as a kind of "dirt-free" or "dirt-removal" space. We find "dirty" kitchens repellent. We cook our food there, we will eat it there, but we always feel that the kitchen must be cleaned after our eating events have taken place. We can tolerate "dirty" bedrooms much more because they do not involve food and because they are out of the line of sight. Incidentally, the teenager's "messy" room is a matter of opinion. Parents might cringe at the look of their adolescent son's or daughter's bedroom. But, if they try to remove anything from the room or rearrange something, the teenager will react with hostility. The teenager will feel that his or her personal space has been violated and defiled.

Indeed, all personal objects acquire meaning within room settings. If something we own is stolen or somehow lost, we feel a sense of personal loss.

Objects are extensions or projections of ourselves. They are imbued with meaning in the context in which they are placed. A framed photograph that has been placed on, say, a living room table has meaning in that context. When we change its place, we somehow feel that something more fundamental has also changed. We commonly believe that some objects are "lucky." And we feel great comfort in seeing the objects in our home complete the details of its spatial configuration. No wonder, then, that people feel personally violated when their homes have been robbed or defaced.

Public spaces as well are imbued with signification. Specific areas in churches, synagogues, temples, mosques, etc. are all signifying spaces. In a Catholic church, for example, the altar is more sacred and therefore less traversable than the area containing the pews.

As examples of signifying public spaces consider the adolescent party scene and the modern shopping mall. The teenage party scene is an intriguing example of a signifying public space meshing with the privacy associated with the home space. There are, of course, many ways in which teens can socialize for reasons of entertainment. But the desire to be involved in a party scene stands out in all surveys of teen leisure time activities. Since the fifties, the Saturday night party has become a social space within which the symbolism of coolness can unfold in its most appropriate context. Here, smoking, consuming alcohol and (in some cases) drugs, telling jokes and making sexual advances are the specific behaviors that enact coolness rituals.

Perhaps the main reason why the party space has become such a common locus for symbolic socialization is that it involves the enactment of three affective states—sexual relations, peer pressure and the need to carve out a proper identity in the peer context. Above all else the teen party constitutes a kind of tribal mating ritual whose symbolic manifestations have been captured in movies such as *Animal House* (1978) which feature teen "party animals," i.e. young males who live for the party scene in order to "make out" with female peers. The party is a structured performance. Acting silly and rude is expected of males, whose roles are perceived to be similar to those of clowns or *pagliacci*. Females, on the other hand, are expected to provide the sexual flirtation signals that produce the comical and exaggerated behaviors in the males—the "party animals."

Being a participant at a Saturday night party space, especially during the pre-teen and early teen years, is felt strongly to be a prerequisite for the development of coolness. Teens will often go to extremes of deception, on the Monday after, to hide the fact that they were not part of a Saturday night social event. Those who are forced to admit that they were not invited to a party, or that they preferred not to go to one, are often ostracized, derided and even confronted physically.   In later adolescence, this need is gradually attenuated as older male and female teens form sexual bonds between each other.

The shopping mall has become a popular "hang out" not only for teens, but for virtually everyone living in an urban or suburban setting. The mall is hardly just a locus for shopping. The mall satisfies several symbolic needs at once: it provides a space for human socialization and is thus a cure for loneliness and boredom; it provides a theatrical atmosphere proclaiming the virtues of a consumeristic utopia; it imparts a feeling of security and protection; it protects against the world of cars, mechanical noises and exhaust pollution; it provides protection against rain, snow, heat, cold; it conveys a feeling of control and organization. The mall is placeless and timeless—there is no appearance of aging or of time passing in its ambiance.

More and more, cinemas, high-class restaurants and even amusement parks are being built within malls. Malls are fast becoming self-contained cities, veritable "fantasylands" where one can leave the problems, dirt and hassles of ordinary urban and suburban life literally "outside."   In the controlled environment of the mall everything is clean, shiny, cheery and ever so optimistic. The mall is a nirvana of endless shopping. When you enter a mall, you are venturing into a "television-designed" world, cosmeticized and simplified to keep grisly reality out of sight and out of mind. And as with a remote-controlled television set, you can "switch" from scene to scene—from clothing store, to coffee stand, to pinball parlor, to lottery outlet and so on. Such is the nature of contemporary life—a life centered on media-generated illusion and artifice, not on a confrontation or spiritual struggle with reality. But unlike the fruits of all spiritual conflicts—understanding and wisdom—there are no fruits to be gleaned from the illusory world created by our media-influenced existence whose message is essentially *shopping = paradise on earth*. Very few people will claim that their experiences at shopping malls are rewarding or meaningful. Indeed, they won't even remember them for very long past the last time they were there.

Architecture

Architecture is the cultural elaboration of shelter. It is, therefore, the art of imbuing living spaces with symbolic meaning.

Consider, as an example, how the height of a building conveys specific kinds of meanings. Cities are semiotic texts. European cities built during the medieval period, for instance, had an "outstanding" feature or signifier: the tallest buildings noticeable along their landscape were churches. The spires on medieval churches rose majestically upwards to the sky. There is something overpowering about looking up at tall buildings. It makes us feel small and insignificant in the global "scheme of things." There was no doubt as to which group had political and social power in medieval Europe. The churches were, literally and symbolically, repositories of power and wealth. But, as the churches lost their clout and wealth after the Renaissance, cities were gradually redesigned architecturally to reflect the new cultural order.

Today, the tallest buildings in sprawling urban centers are certainly not churches. The tallest structures in cities like Toronto, Montreal, New York, Chicago, etc. are large corporations and banks. Wealth and power now resides in these institutions. Inside these monolithic structures hierarchical symbolism also follows an "up-down" arrangement: the jobs and positions with the lowest value are at the bottom of the building; the more important ones are at the top. The company's executives reside, like the gods on Mount Olympus, on the top floor. The atmosphere on this level is perceived to be rarefied and other-worldly. Prestige is up. This why we use such expression as "to work one's way up, "to make it to the top," "to climb the ladder of success," "to set one's goals high," etc. These metaphors reflect the architectural conceptualization of power as a tall building, which produces a "looking up to heaven" effect.

Modern architectural trends can be traced to the post World War I period with the founding of the Bauhaus School in 1919 in Chicago by Walter Gropius. Gropius wanted to rebuild the landscape by stripping it of its past symbolism with a geometrically pure style which intentionally excluded references to the past. The Bauhaus School envisioned a proletarian architectural landscape with no ornamentation (cornices, pillars, gables, etc.). Buildings were to be fashioned as box-like forms which eliminated all the symbols of power. Out of this movement, modern office towers, housing projects, hotels and other public buildings were built with the same basic box-like blueprint.

But the landscape started to change a few decades ago. Today's world does not emphasize industry or doldrum factories, but high-tech communications and glamorous professions. The new office towers are beginning to reflect this new mindset. As the modern period seems to be coming to an end, modernist Bauhaus architecture is giving way to "postmodern" design and style. More will be said about postmodernism in Chapter 13. Suffice it to say here that postmodernist architecture rejects the severe pragmatism of Bauhaus modernism, emphasizing consumeristic values instead. The shopping mall is an example of the postmodern mindset. Its architectural symbolism emphasizes consumerism and entertainment, the only values that truly seem to count in this kind of world.

Concluding Remarks

This chapter brings the theme of culture—the world made by humans—to an end. Cultures are social territories as well as ideological entities. At the level of culture, biological territoriality and the need for shelter are elaborated respectively as meaningfully-structured spaces (interpersonal and social) and architectural structures.

As a final word, I wish to emphasize that space symbolism is not isolated from other kinds of cultural symbol systems and codes. Clothing codes, for example, are routinely synchronized with spatial codes. The clothes one wears around the house differ from the clothes one wears to the office. Indeed, when one comes home from the office, one will tend to change clothes to reflect the change in ambiance. Only in cases where this is not economically possible, or where the workplace is an extension of the home, is the same clothing system deployed at work and at home.

The human-made world is an intriguing and constantly-changing one. In medieval Europe the tallest buildings were churches because religiously-constructed texts determined and controlled the life of society. In the modern period, industrial-shaped texts became the dominant ones. This was reflected architecturally by the fact that the tallest buildings built in modern societies were companies and banks. In this postmodern world, the landscape is changing once again. The appearance of shopping malls on the landscape is a testament to this radical change in cultural outlook.

SUGGESTIONS FOR FURTHER READING

Ardrey, R. (1966). *The Territorial Imperative*. New York: Atheneum.

Barnlund, D. (1975). *Public and Private Self in Japan and the United States: Communicative Styles of Two Cultures*. Tokyo: Simul Press.

Douglas, M. (1992). *Objects and Objections*. Toronto: Toronto Semiotic Circle.

Greenbie, B. (1981). *Spaces: Dimensions of the Human Landscape*. New Haven: Yale University Press.

Hall, E. T. (1966). *The Hidden Dimension*. New York: Doubleday.

Preziosi, D. (1979). *The Semiotics of the Built Environment: An Introduction to Architectonic Analysis*. Bloomington: Indiana University Press.

Wolfe, T. (1981). *From Bauhaus to Our House*. New York: Farrar, Strauss & Giroux.

Part 3

The Medium Makes the Message

Chapter 11

I'TS "ALL IN THE FAMILY"!

Preliminary Remarks

Throughout the seventies, households across North America tuned in with unswerving fidelity to watch the CBS sitcom *All in the Family*. The continent was divided, ideologically and emotionally, into two camps—those who supported the so-called "bigoted" views and attitudes of the father, Archie Bunker, a staunch defender of the Vietnam War, and those who despised him and the War. What was happening in the Bunker family was apparently happening in families across the continent. North American culture had entered into a period of emotional turmoil and bitter debate over such controversial issues as the Vietnam War, racism, the role of women in society and so on. But, as the popularity of *All in the Family* suggests, within their family habitat people seemed to prefer to have their own debates fought for them through the medium of a television program.

Clearly, by the early seventies television had become much more than just a technologically-advanced *medium* of entertainment. Psychological research papers on the effects television purportedly had on society started to proliferate, and continue to fill pages of scientific journals and popular magazines to this day. Typically, psychologists started to collect data and to speculate on the effects television was having on society. Today, television is blamed for causing virtually everything, from obesity to street violence.

Are the media the shapers of behavior that so many would claim they are today? Has television spawned the contemporary world? Are the victims of media, as Key (1989: 13) suggests, people who "scream and shout hysterically at rock concerts and later in life at religious revival meetings?" Key and psychologists generally are, in part, correct in emphasizing the role that media play in shaping some behaviors in some individuals. The highly inflated amount of consumption of fast foods, tobacco, alcohol and other media-hyped substances is probably related to the slick promotion ploys utilized by magazine ads and television commercials. But, in my view, the supposed influence of behaviors by the media is more reflective of a conscious mimetic type, making it, therefore, not as powerful a shaper of behavior as the unconscious osmotic type. Even though viewers mindlessly absorb the messages promulgated constantly by television advertisements, and although these may have some subliminal effects on behavior, we accept media images only if they suit our already-established preferences. It is more accurate to say that television produces programs and images that reinforce already-forged lifestyle models. Media moguls are more intent on extracting the models already inherent in our behaviors and on reinforcing them, than in spreading commercially-risky innovations. Even programs like MTV are not in themselves disruptive of the value systems of the cultural mainstream; rather, they reflect "shifts" already present in popular culture.

In the fifties, teens watched *American Bandstand* with the same kind of fanaticism and loyalty that was reminiscent of religious zealotry at its most intense. As a consequence, they modeled their musical and dress codes, in large part, on the basis of that program. But *American Bandstand* did no more than reflect what the teens were already predisposed to model. It is my view that child and adolescent behaviors are influenced primarily by peer and family osmosis. It is within the peer context that the teen, for instance, chooses which programs to watch, which rock videos to buy and so on. Peer osmosis is a much more powerful shaper of the teenage *persona* than is media mimesis.

The theme of this chapter is television, perhaps the most significant contributor to social semiosis ever in the history of human culture. In this chapter the term *medium* is used not only in its primary sense as the technical or physical means *through which* a message is transmitted, but also as the actual "substance" *with which* the message is constructed. Thus, for example, clay is the medium *through which* and *with which* an artist makes his or her sculptures. Similarly, television is a physical and technical means *through which* messages are transmitted and *with which* these are constructed. The main semiotic issues related to television are its power as a social text and its role as a primary source of social mimesis.

Television

Radio waves were first used to carry visual information in 1926 when the Scottish scientist, John Logie Baird (1888-1946), invented a method by which an image could be scanned mechanically into lines of dots of light. In 1931 the Russian-born engineer Vladimir Zworykin (1889-1982) built the first electronic scanning system which became the prototype of the modern TV camera. By the late thirties, television service was in place in several Western countries. The British BBC, for example, started a regular service in 1936. By the early forties there were 23 television stations operating in the United States. But it was not until the early fifties that technology had advanced to the point so as to make it possible for virtually every North American household to afford a television set. Almost immediately, television person-alities became household names, mythologized into "deities" who loomed larger than life. Actors and announcers became society's lifestyle leaders. People began more and more to plan their lives around television programs, waiting anxiously for their favorite shows to come on the air. I can still remember the enthusiasm with which the *Ed Sullivan Show* on Sunday evenings was anticipated in the fifties and early sixties. Performers like Elvis Presley and the Beatles became instant mythic heroes after only one appearance on the show.

Throughout the fifties and sixties television programming developed rapidly into what it is today—a *social text* geared to the daily viewing habits of an increasingly larger segment of society. Today, 98% of North American households own a television set, and a large portion of these have more than one. Through advances in satellite communications, we can now even perceive ourselves as "participants" in wars, conflicts, etc. going on in some other part of the world. Indeed, today most of our information, intellectual stimulation, entertainment and lifestyle models come from, or are related to, the television. People have become as dependent upon television as a drug addict to some chemical substance. Psychological studies are constantly pointing out that people who are deprived of their daily dose of television display the same "withdrawal-like symptoms" as do addicts.

As mentioned at the start of this chapter, it is obvious that television has developed into much more than just a medium for recreation. It has become one of the primary and most powerful message-making media ever built by humans. As the great Canadian communications theorist Marshall McLuhan (e.g. 1962, 1964) pointed out, the *medium* in this case has become the *message*.

Whatever the behavioral effects of television—and there is no reason to believe that psychologists have any particular claim to knowing what these effects are—from a semiotic standpoint there are three kinds of message- and meaning-making effects whose manifestations are easily detectable in the population at large. I will refer to these as the *mythologizing effect*, the *event fabrication effect* and the *information compression effect*.

By *mythologizing effect* I am referring to the fact that television imbues its personages with a mythological aura. Like any type of privileged space—a platform, a pulpit, or any other specially-constructed locus that is designed to impart focus and significance to someone—television creates mythic heroes by simply "containing" them. To see what I mean, just think of how you would react to your favorite television personality coming to visit you in your own home. You certainly would not treat the presence in your house of, say, someone like Geraldo Rivera of the *Geraldo* talk show as casually as you would that of any other stranger. His presence would be "felt" to constitute an event of momentous proportions, an almost unreal and other-worldly happening. Media personalities of all types are infused with this deified quality by virtue of the fact that they are "seen" inside the mythical space created by television. In general, the presence of famous actors, musical stars, etc. in our midst causes great enthusiasm and excitement. We are more affected by the presence among us of a Madonna or of a Tom Cruise than we are by scientists or thinkers who may have done something very significant for the benefit of the human race. Such is the power of the mythologizing effect of media. The celebrities of our own making are the contemporary equivalents of the graven images of the Bible.

By *event fabrication effect* I am referring to the common perceptual state that television induces in its viewers as it transforms some ordinary happening into a momentous *event*—an election campaign, an actor's love affair, a fashion trend, etc. People make up their minds about the guilt or innocence of people by watching *60 Minutes*; they see certain behaviors as laudable or damnable by tuning into *Oprah* or *Geraldo*; they experience the moral sentiments of rectitude and justice by viewing the capturing of some criminal on *Cops*; and the list could go on and on. Television programs literally create *events* by holding them up as significant and meaningful to society at large. A riot that gets airtime becomes a momentous event; one that does not is ignored. This is why terrorists are seemingly more interested in simply "getting on the air," than in having their demands satisfied. The mere fact of getting on television imbues their cause with event status and, therefore, with significance. Political and social protesters frequently inform the news media of their intentions, and then dramatically stage their demonstrations in front of the cameras. Sports events like the *World Series*, the *Super Bowl* or the *Stanley Cup Playoffs* are transformed on television into herculean struggles of mythic heroes. Events such as the John Kennedy and Lee Harvey Oswald assassinations, the Vietnam War, the Watergate hearings, the Rodney King beating and the like are transformed into portentous and prophetic historical events, similar to the import the great Classical dramas must have had on ancient civilization. It is probably no great exaggeration to suggest that television has become the *maker* of history and its *documenter* at the same time. In other words, television is how people now *experience* history. And, conversely, television is *shaping* history. The horrific scenes coming out of the Vietnam War that were transmitted into people's homes daily in the late sixties and early seventies brought about disastrous military and social consequences. More recently, just think of the incredible image of an MTV flag being hoisted by East German youths over the Berlin Wall as it was being torn down a few years back. And as Anderson (1990: 233) has remarked, it is truly incredible to contemplate that according to "trivia-keepers, more people watched the wedding of England's Prince Charles and Princess Diana than had ever before in human history observed such an event at the same time," and that many international events were postponed one year, at the height of the popularity of *Dallas*, simply because people "wanted to stay around and find out who shot J. R. Ewing!"

Anderson (1992: 125-130) calls events staged for the cameras "pseudoevents." These are events that are never spontaneous, but planned for the sole purpose of being put on television. Pseudoevents are usually intended to be self-fulfilling prophecies. The invasion of Grenada and the Gulf War were concomitantly real events and pseudoevents. The actual military operations and conflicts were real events. But the reporting of these wars was orchestrated by a massive public-relations operation. Reporters were censored and kept away from the action so that the news coverage could be stylized and managed more effectively. The idea was to give the viewing public a military and social victory and, therefore, to allow Americans to "feel good about themselves." Pseudoevents constitute theater at its best, because they mesh reality (the real killing and terrorizing of people) with acting, drama and social meaning (power conflict, intrigue, etc.). As Anderson (1990: 126-127) aptly puts it, the "media take the raw material of experience and fashion it into stories; they retell the stories to us, and we call them reality."

By *information compression effect* I am referring to the fact that the medium of television presents personages, events, information, etc. globally and instantly leaving little time for reflection on the topics, implications, words, etc. contained in a segment. This has created a new way in which we now tend to perceive messages and meanings. As a culture, we have developed short attention spans that require constant variety in information content. When we are without television for a period of time—say when we are away on vacation—we start to feel a kind of addictive need for TV-mediated information of all kinds (news, sports scores, etc.). It is as if we have become so habituated to large doses of information cut up, packaged and digested beforehand that we have developed a psychological dependency on information and visual stimulation in the same way that one develops an addiction to alcohol, smoking, or junk food. This effect is, in my view, the reason why television is vastly more popular than reading. After work or school in the evenings, it is an arduous task to read a book, since its form and contents must be decoded at various levels of cognition. The reading process thus causes a slowdown in the information taken in. TV viewing, on the other hand, is very easy to do. Just sit back and let the images do the thinking and decoding for you!

As an example, just think of how television news programs work. The amount of information presented in a short period of time on a news program is torrential. We are able to take it all in because the information is edited and stylized for effortless mass consumption. The camera moves in to select aspects of a situation, to show a face that cares, that is suffering, that is happy, that is angry, and then shifts to the cool handsome face of an anchorman or to the attractive one of an anchorwoman to tell us what it's all about. The news items, the film footage, the commentaries are all fast-paced and brief. They are designed to be visually dramatic snippets of easily digestible information. "Within such a stylistic environment," remarks Stuart Ewen (1988: 265), "the news is beyond comprehension." The facts of the news are subjected to the stylized signature of the specific news program—the same story will be interpreted differently according to whoever the television journalist is. Thus it is that as "nations and people are daily sorted out into boxes marked 'good guys,' 'villains,' 'victims,' and 'lucky ones,' style becomes the essence, reality becomes the appearance" (Ewen 1988: 265-266).

The technical innovation of the last decade that has entrenched the *information compression effect* into our cultural mindset even more deeply is the remote control. Actually, this device was invented in 1956 by a man named Robert Adler. But it wasn't until the eighties that it became a standard prop of virtually every television set. The remote control has had an enormous impact on how we view television. More significantly, it has made the further compression of information a reality. When we are bored with something on a specific channel, all we have to do from the comfort of our viewing seats is to flick through the panoply of viewing options at our disposal rapidly and with very little deliberation or reflection. We seek instant gratification and control with this versatile little device. Whoever holds the remote control during family viewing sessions is also the one who has implicit control over the others.

Television and Social Textuality

Perhaps the most important semiotic aspect related to television is its power as a *social text*. To see what I mean by this term, let us step back in time with our imaginations. Let us pretend that we are living in some village in medieval Europe. How would our daily routines be conceived and organized? To put it in semiotic terms, what social text would we likely be living by? Recall from Chapter 3 that the word *text* is used in this book with a specific meaning. It is used to designate a "putting together" of signifiers to produce a message, consciously or unconsciously. The text can be either verbal or nonverbal, written (as in legal codes) or unwritten (as in some moral codes).

Many of the social actions and routines that we commonly perform can also be thought of as texts. The connection between social actions and textuality is borne out by the fact that those actions that each culture deems to be particularly crucial to its existence are eventually textualized—in the form of laws, religious narratives, rules of conduct and etiquette, etc.

In medieval Europe the social text by which most people lived was a religious text. The routines of the day, the week, the month, the year centered around a Christian form of textuality. Some of the "contents" of the Christian text are still around today. This is why religious dates such as Christmas and Easter are regularly-planned yearly time frames within which we emphasize and organize significant social events and behaviors. In medieval Europe, the Christian text probably regulated one's entire day. People emphasized going to church regularly during the day and the week, lived by moral codes that were stated explicitly in the Bible and listened conscientiously to the dictates of clergymen. The underlying "theme" of the medieval text was that each day brought us closer and closer to our true destiny—salvation and an afterlife with God. Living according to this text imparted a feeling of security, emotional shelter and spiritual meaning to life. All human actions and natural events could be explained and understood in terms of this text.

With the scientific advances brought about by the Renaissance, the Enlightenment and the Industrial Revolution, the Christian social text came gradually to be replaced by a more secular form of textuality. Today, the social text by which people live—unless someone has joined a religious community or has chosen to live by the dictates of the Bible or some other religious text— is hardly a religious one. We organize our day around work commitments, social appointments, etc., and only at those traditional "points" in the calendar (Christmas, Easter, etc.) do we synchronize our secular text with the more traditional religious one. The need to partition the day into "time slots" is why we depend so heavily upon such devices and artifacts as clocks, watches, agendas, appointment books, calendars, etc. We would feel desperately lost without such things. In this regard, it is appropriate to note that in his great 1726 novel, *Gulliver's Travels*, Jonathan Swift (1667-1745) satirized the tendency of modern (post-Renaissance) culture to rely on the watch as the method by which we have come to organize our daily routines. The Lilliputians were intrigued and baffled to note that Gulliver did virtually nothing without consulting his watch! Today, most people would indeed deem it unthinkable to go out of the home without a watch. We need to know continually "what time it is" in order to carry on the normal conduct of our day. Such is the nature of rational culture—it is a world in which everything is planned, especially the temporal organization of the day's anticipated events.

Outside of special cases—such as in certain cloisters and monasteries—the textual organization of the day is hardly ever conscious. If we started to reflect upon the value and import of our daily routines, it is likely that we would soon start to question them and eventually to abandon them. This does indeed happen in the case of those individuals who have decided to "drop out" of society, i.e. to live their lives outside of the constraints of social textuality. Because they provide reassurance, social texts are crucial to the existence and cohesion of a culture. People not only follow social texts faithfully, but when a change has been triggered in textuality, they tend to resist it.

When television entered the scene in the fifties, it started a process of text construction that now has a powerful control over the entire North American cultural mindset. It is no exaggeration to claim, in fact, that television has become *the* social text by which our culture lives. This does not mean that it necessarily determines our daily behaviors. Rather, it implies that it is reflective of the needs for textuality that our culture has in lieu of its tendency to deconstruct traditional textuality. If you pick up the daily TV listings and start classifying the programs into morning, noon and evening slots, you will get an idea of what it means to say that television has become a social text. With cable television and satellite dishes, the range of programming offered would, at first, appear to be a broad and random one. But a closer critical look at the listings will reveal a different story.

Consider morning programming. Virtually all the networks start off their daily fare of offerings with several stock types of shows. These are, invariably, information programs (news, weather, sports), children's shows, exercise programs and (later in the morning) talk and quiz shows. There is remarkably little digression from this stock. One may, of course, subscribe to a movie channel or to some special interest channel to get a broader range of choice. But, as ratings research has shown, the morning time slot is not conducive towards attracting a significant audience for specialty programming. By and large, people start off the day before heading off to work, school, or to do house chores by watching the news and/or by exercising to the directions of television fitness instructors. Young children living in urban centers, and not yet allowed to go out, are offered an array of morning shows which range from educational *Sesame Street* type programs to cartoons. Men or women who are at home and are in need of some kind of stimulation, recreation or relaxation can tune in later in the morning to talk shows, quiz shows and early soap operas. The morning text is, clearly, reflective of how we perceive this time frame. This is why morning programming—and programming generally—changes on weekends, so as to reflect the new social requirements of Saturdays and Sundays. Sunday mornings in particular reveal how the Christian *subtext* continues to exert its influence on social semiosis and behavior. But on weekdays "Wake up America" is the underlying morning theme of the TV text. "Here's a selection of the things you need to know," blurt out the newscasters. "You're too fat and sluggish, so get into shape," exclaim the fitness instructors. "You're bored and need to gossip, so here are some very bizarre people and their grim or weird stories," bellow the talk show hosts. Switch back and forth and you'll know "what's going on." In the same way that the morning prayers which medieval people said probably comforted, reassured and provided them with a symbolic act of meaning-making to start off the day, so too the morning news, exercises programs, etc. provide parallel kinds of comforting meaning-making formats within which the day can be imbued with symbolic value.

A second glance at your *TV Guide* will reveal that the afternoon is the next significant time frame for television viewing. In the fifties, sixties and early seventies the primary viewing audience during the afternoon was made up of housewives who, after a grueling morning of housework, sat down in front of their television sets to relax. It was, in fact, in the fifties that the phenomenon of watching the afternoon soap opera crystallized, bearing witness to a new aspect of television textuality. Rather than go out and chitchat with other women of the surrounding area as did medieval women, female viewers in the fifties and sixties did virtually the same thing by participating daily in the complicated lives and plots of soap opera personages. Watching a soap today extends to both sexes and cuts across all classes—a fact which reflects the dramatic changes in social role-structure over the last few decades. As less and less women stay at home, soaps have become more and more geared to a general audience of viewers. They have become a fixed part of daily life, a narrative continuum which provides an outlet for participation in other people's lives, the traditional role of gossip. Gossip does indeed give us glimpses into other people's lives. But television has taken us one step further—it has put us on intimate terms with the private lives of make-believe lawyers, doctors, executives, etc. who populate the worlds of *The Young and the Restless* and other soaps.

The late afternoon has become *the* time slot for a second type of show which has, in my view, the same function that the morality plays and public confessions of medieval life had. Shows like *Oprah* and *Geraldo* now let people reveal and confess their "sins" in public and, consequently, allow a large viewing audience to participate cathartically in acts of self-revelation and of possible repentance. More significantly, viewers can peer into the private lives of others, compare these lives to their own, and, as a consequence, extract principles of morality daily with the help of the talk show hosts themselves who skillfully manipulate the flow of the show as would the orchestrators of medieval morality plays or as would a confessor in a confessional. As Stern and Stern (1992: 123) write, daytime talk shows "are a relief in the sense that it is always nice to see people whose problems are worse than yours." Some of the "problems" showcased on these shows are bizarre indeed. As I write, I have recently viewed shows whose themes have been "women in love with serial killers," "custody battle over frozen sperm," "men who live with several married women," "teenage strippers and their supportive mothers," to mention but a few. *Oprah* and *Geraldo* are high moral dramas, acted out upon a media stage that has replaced the pulpit and the altar as the platform from which moral issues are discussed and where sin is condemned publicly. The host, like the medieval priest, comments morally upon virtually every medical and psychological condition known to humanity. And, just to be sure that what he or she says is perceived to be "correct," there always seems to be some "expert" in the audience to give a "scientific" corroboration to what the host is preaching.

The third part of the television text inheres in the programs of so-called "prime time," the period in the evenings, from about 7 PM to 10 or 11 PM, when most people are home to watch TV. It is significant that the prelude to the evening text is, as it was for the morning time-slot, the "news hour" from around 6 to around 7 PM. After this, quiz shows like *Wheel of Fortune* and *Jeopardy* maintain curiosity and interest until family programming commences for a couple of hours, with sitcoms, adventure programs, documentaries, movies and the like. By the eighties, evening soaps like *Dallas*, *Dynasty*, and *Twin Peaks* were introduced into this time frame, a fact that bore witness to the emergence of a new social reality. The need for soaps as gossip formats was no longer restricted to housewives, but extended to everyone, as society continued to tear down traditional gender-role categories.

Prime time is particularly adept at meshing fiction with reality. Prime-time movies, situation comedies, crime dramas, specialty programs and evening news combine fictional scenarios with moral and social messages for the entire family. Shows like *America's Most Wanted*, *Cops* and *Unsolved Mysteries* have come up with the ideal combination of the fictionality/reality interface. These are documentary programs which showcase real-life events bolstered by dramatic portrayals of the events and subsequent moral commentaries.

As in medieval Europe, the evening hours are reserved for sober contemplation on the vicissitudes of life. But there is one main difference between the medieval social text and the modern television text. The latter extends into late-night programming. There was nothing for medieval people to do past the early evening hours, except sleep or meditate. But, in contemporary North America from 10 PM on, when the kids are safely in bed, shows like *Love Connection* and *Studs* allow viewers to indulge their "peeping Tom" sexual curiosities. And, a little later, talk shows à la "Johnny Carson," "David Letterman," "Arsenio," etc. provide an outlet for more gossip and a means for prying into the sex lives of media personalities (the guests on these talk shows). Under the cloak of darkness and with "innocent eyes and ears" fast asleep, one can fantasize and talk about virtually anything under the sun with social impunity.

Given the increasing eclecticism of society at large, with its many interests, groups and ideologies, it is no wonder that the mainstream television text has recently been rendered more complex by an increasing diversity of options. There are now specialty channels for sports, movies, and music enthusiasts. Of particular interest to the present discussion are the religious channels where "televangelists," in line with the tradition of the hucksterism of traveling medicine men, are willing to perform miracles and provide salvation for all— for the price of a small donation. Massive audiences of emotionally-charged believers are worked up into a state of frenzy for all to see as rhetorically-clever preachers exhort them, cajole them and incite them on to reject the devil and to seek salvation. Miracles are performed for the world to see, and in the same way that the potions concocted by traveling medicine men were purported to cure all maladies from rheumatism to baldness, people can now find a cure for whatever ails them by purchasing the preacher's spiritual guidebooks through a 1-800 number! A few years back, one of these apparent miracle workers was found to have contrived the healing scenarios in which he seemingly cured people of cancer, blindness and other dreadful maladies. As always happens when such hucksters are exposed, the preacher was immediately ostracized and banished into obscurity. But it seems that the faithful have not learned their lesson yet. As I write, a new cadre of miracle-workers are performing their magic nightly on the Total Christian Network. The show, it would seem, must go on!

The continuing popularity of televangelism makes several blatant comments about North American culture: it reveals the gullibility of that segment of America's populace which is poorly-educated for a "fast" anything, including a miracle; it is consistent with the tradition of oratorical evangelism of small-town America; and it provides reassuring, absolute moral guidelines to follow in a world characterized increasingly by a rampant relativistic outlook and spiritual nihilism. The televangelist text provides the same kind of emotional reassurance that all religious texts do with its clear-cut and unambiguous answers to the spiritual questions that human beings are bound to formulate during their lives, even if it changes absolutely nothing. Key (1989: 43) puts it appropriately in the following way:

> Show-business personalities such as Jimmy Bakker, Pat Robertson, Jimmy Swaggart, and Jerry Falwell promote themselves to massive audiences—who already agree with them—by attacks upon sin and disbelievers. They change nothing, except possibly their financial positions. Indeed, they ensure continued popularity for virtually anything they attack with stormy right-wing diatribes. Threats of eternal damnation mean little to those under attack; perhaps they even provide incentives to persist in what they are doing. This, of course, provides an inexhaustible resource for continued attacks against sin.... Fund-raising abilities would collapse if stated objectives were accomplished. The evangelists' failure to change the world is actually the basis for continued financial success.

The Mythology of Fatherhood: A TV Version

One of the complementary functions of social texts is to encode mythologies and to incorporate them into the *modus vivendi* of the population at large. To see how the television text has become instrumental in this regard, let us consider the mythology of fatherhood.

Between the years 1946 and 1964 a baby boom took place in North America. During that period, over 75 million babies were born. As a consequence, the fifties saw a juvenilization of culture and the emergence of a teenage subculture. There were no medieval or Renaissance "teenagers" as such! By 1957 the new teenage market was worth over 30 billion dollars a year. And the modern family became a primary target for the television industry.

Fifties television programs like *Father Knows Best* and *The Adventures of Ozzie and Harriet* sculpted the new teenage persona to fit the requirements of family values and traditions. As teenagers entered the sixties, they became "older" and more socially-committed in media portrayals. The mythology had changed somewhat to fit new realities. Today, the teen in programs like *90210* has reacquired some of the traits of fifties teen prototypes. But the contemporary postmodern world is not so simple. The rosy-colored family relations in *The Adventures of Ozzie and Harriet* —which went on the air in 1952—have degenerated into macabre, senseless actions parodied for the sake of parody in *Married...with Children*. The father on this program, Al Bundy, has been totally deconstructed, i.e. literally taken apart and reduced to basic physicality. He is a reprehensible character who is merely "married" and who just happens to have "children" just as shallow and despicable as he is. Al Bundy, who is a throwback to Ralph Kramden of the *Honeymooners* in the fifties and to Archie Bunker of *All in the Family*, is the end result of the evolution of the baby-boomer father mythology fabricated by television. He is the opposite of wise and judicious TV dads such as Jim Anderson of *Father Knows Best* and Bill Cosby. Al Bundy is a fifties ex-teenager who still yearns for his own particular brand of mindless adolescence.

Married...with Children is indeed a "deconstructive" parody—a scathing mimicry of traditional family values and roles. Its viewpoint is characterized above all else by an all-deriding, all-dissolving destructiveness. "Al Bundy is the father figure as he really is," the show blurts out. The television programs of the fifties and sixties had built up an idyllic mythology of fatherhood. Even the titles of the shows—*Father Knows Best*, *Life with Father*—clearly revealed a mythology based on patriarchy and paternal authority within the family. This patriarchal mythology started to be challenged in the late sixties and throughout the seventies by programs such as *The Mary Tyler Moore Show*, *Wonder Woman*, *Rhoda*, *Maude*, *The Days and Nights of Molly Dodd*, *Cagney and Lacey* and others which portrayed strong, independent women who were attempting to survive, socially and professionally, in a world that was deconstructing patriarchal structures. Women were achieving a new image and status, and men were being increasingly relegated to an Archie Bunker type status as anti-heroes.

It is interesting to note that in the midst of this mythological deconstruction, a show like *Bill Cosby* achieved unexpected success throughout the eighties. There were a number of reasons for the success of this apparent throwback to the patriarchal programs of the fifties and sixties. First and foremost is the fact that Bill Cosby himself is a true comedian who can easily endear himself to a large audience. But, more importantly, the *Bill Cosby Show* was appropriate for the eighties. Throughout the seventies, programs like *All in the Family* and *The Jeffersons* were products of an iconoclastic movement to tear down all kinds of authority models and figures. But during the eighties, with the ascendancy of a new right-wing moralism, as evidenced by the election of conservative governments in Canada and the United States (Mulroney, Reagan, Bush), the myth of patriarchal authority was making a kind of comeback. Once more, audiences were searching for TV father figures who were strong and understanding at the same time. Bill Cosby fit this image perfectly. Bill Cosby is our culture's idealization of what a father should be like. He is a success story. The only real difference between Bill Cosby and Jim Anderson of *Father Knows Best* is the fact that Cosby's wife, unlike Anderson's wife, played a different, more assertive role within the revamped mythology of patriarchy. The family scene on the *Cosby Show* reflected what a tightly-knit, successful family should look like. It provided a symbolism of reassurance and faith in traditional values in a world that was, and continues to be, in constant moral doubt and flux.

Like Archie Bunker and Al Bundy, Homer, the father on *The Simpsons* is portrayed as an anti-hero. He's a downtrodden boor who spends most of his time eating donuts. He loses his temper, has all the wrong answers to family problems and, like Al Bundy, always feels sorry for himself. His wife, who like Al Bundy's wife sports a moronic hairdo, struggles to make Homer more refined and more sexually interested in her. Both the Bundys and the Simpsons are crude and obnoxious. Bud Bundy is unappealing and boorish. His sister Kelly is ignorant and interested only in sex. There is no sugar-coating here. The Bundys and the Simpsons are caricatures of what is traditional in television family shows—warmth, moral rectitude, success and high ideals. These two families are boorish, inept, unsuccessful, vulgar and cynical. There are many social messages coming out of these programs. But above all else, they satirize parents who base their love on their children's accomplishments, they critique male chauvinism and child exploitation, and they satirize sex relations and the emphasis on female sexuality.

The purpose of such television programs is paradoxically to take apart the television text and along with it those structures—moral, social, and mental—that have been shaped by it. They offer a mirror on reality. Through the medium itself, they are attempting to counteract the effects of television textuality, which has brought about a cultural mindset that is no longer capable of distinguishing between what is original and what is imitation.

Al Bundy is a parody of those who still live in what can be called "the Elvis culture." People invariably recall with amazing detail their affectively-coded teen experiences (the first kiss, party incidents, etc.); they remain tenaciously attached to the songs and rock stars of their era; they continue to dress and groom themselves as they did when they were teens. The reverence for Elvis Presley that the fifties generation of "ex-teens" continues to have is a case in point. Presley died on August 16, 1977. Since then, there have been constant pilgrimages to his house; his records and movies (in video form) are being continually remade; and many fans even keep shrines to his memory and tokens from his life (vials of his sweat, scraps of carpet from his house, etc.) in their homes. Recently, Elvis was immortalized on a US stamp. It is both humorous and disconcerting to contemplate how powerful adolescence has become emotionally and how much of an indelible imprint it leaves on memory and personality.

Today, many middle-aged parents are experiencing a hard time accepting the new behavioral models of their teens. On the one hand, there is some substance to their dismay and apprehensions. Drug and alcohol consumption, partying, smoking, etc. have become fixtures of the cool lifestyle of contemporary adolescents. On the other hand, it seems to me that many contemporary adults find themselves in frequent confrontational situations with their teen sons or daughters because they do not see a discontinuity between themselves and their children. Many parents today do not see themselves, as do adults in primitive tribes, as elders preparing to become wise for the benefit of their culture and their youth. The boundary line between *young* and *old* is being effaced more and more and nurtured by vested economic interests. Al Bundy is the symbolization of this ultimately deleterious trend in our culture.

Media Mimesis

As mentioned at the beginning of this chapter, I believe that it is unlikely that young people are the primary victims of television, as many psychologists would claim. Children and teens are more influenced by their families and by their peers than they are by media images. In my opinion, there is no causal link between television violence, for instance, and violence in society in general. Did television engender the wars fought throughout history, including the two devastating world wars of this century? Did it spur Jack the Ripper to slash his victims to death? Of course it didn't. It makes no sense whatsoever to think of television as an instigator of an individual's behavior. If that were so, then this principle would apply to all media, codes and texts, including religious ones—more wars have been fought in the name of the latter than in the name of television! In their authoritative 1988 study of the effects of television on children and adolescents, Liebert and Sprafkin showed that there was a link between aggressiveness in children and watching violent television; but, they also showed that television is only a factor in this increased behavioral pattern, not *the* cause, and that its effects were extremely short-lasting. There is no one cause of aggressive behavior in children. What is more accurate to say is that the general *modus pensandi* and behavioral models of our culture are reflected in the television text. But, as programs like *Married...with Children* and *The Simpsons* reveal, this text is always subject to criticism and ultimately to change. Social texts are made by people and, therefore, they reflect what people think and want.

Semiotically, all that can be said about television is that it is a source of social mimesis and textuality. Even though viewers absorb the messages transmitted constantly by television advertisements, and although these may have some unconscious effects on behavior, we accept media images only if they suit our already-established preferences. Television offers a medium through which we can live our daily lives as routinely and as automatically as did other social texts of the past. If we complain about the shallowness of our television-dominated culture, we really have no one to blame but ourselves.

It is true, however, that television has contributed significantly to creating a desire for the lifestyles it portrays in other parts of the world. When asked about the stunning defeat of communism in eastern Europe, the Polish leader Lech Walesa was reported by the newspapers as saying that it all came from the television set, implying that television undermined the stability of the communist world's relatively poor and largely sheltered lifestyle with images of consumer delights seen in western programs and commercials. Different cultures have indeed been reshaped mimetically to television's textuality. Marshall McLuhan's phrase of the "global village" is an appropriate one—television has shrunk the world and diminished the interval between thought and action.

People under 40 today cannot remember a time without a television set in their homes. There are now more than 1 billion TV sets around the globe. Spending on television programming has reached nearly 70 billion dollars. As the automobile did at the turn of the century, television is set to change the general shape of world culture. Demographic surveys now show consistently that people spend more time in front of television sets than they do working, that watching TV is bringing about a gradual decline in reading, that television's textuality is leading to the demise of the nation state concept as ideas and images cross national boundaries daily through television channels. When the German printer Johann Gutenberg (1400?-1468) invented movable type to print the Bible, he initiated a veritable revolution in human mental evolution and culture by making ideas readily available to a larger population. Television has triggered the twentieth century's own "Gutenberg revolution." But rather than homogenizing the world, it is my view that human diversity and ingenuity will lead to a greater variety in television programming and, therefore, in social textuality. As Solomon (1988: 124-125) aptly puts it, our "craving for variety is nature's way of providing us with an evolutionary edge in the struggle for survival in a constantly changing world." The only thing for certain is that there is no turning back the clock. The world today can no longer exist without a television set, in the same way that it could no longer live without a car at mid century.

Concluding Remarks

The focus of this chapter has been the role that television plays in culture. Archie Bunker of *All in the Family* sat constantly in front of a television set, reacting mindlessly to what was being shown. How emblematic this was! By the seventies television had become a fixture inside the household, transforming North American culture into its present form. From morning to late at night, television now provides programs "to live by," in the same way that previous religious texts provided strict moral codes of behavior to live by.

Television has produced some dramatic effects on our culture. Among these are the mythologizing effect the event fabrication effect, and the information compression effect. The former has led to the situation whereby television personalities are viewed with much more significance than are, say, scientists and philosophers. The event fabrication effect has led to the situation that any event in the world will be viewed as significant if and only if it makes it on the tube. The information compression effect has induced a kind of insatiability for entertainment, variety and visual stimulation in society at large. With its constant changes of scene and with its cornucopia of images, television both satisfies and induces a constant craving for sensory stimulation and variety. We want to know and to do things quickly and without effort.

So in a semiotic sense television has indeed had far-reaching effects on message- and meaning-making in our culture. As Fiske (1987: 83) has observed, in order to remain popular with an increasingly diverse audience, television must provide the textual space for meaning-making all the time, since viewers "will only produce meanings from, and find pleasures in, a television program if it allows for this articulation of their interests." It is only if we understand the true semiosic nature of television that its effects can be recognized and subsequently controlled. This is the function of semiotic analysis. Nochimson (1992: 198) puts it appropriately in the following way:

> The only real counterforce to the oppressiveness of the commercial television emphasis on ratings and income from sponsors is *knowledge*. The quality of a form is most easily imagined by its practitioners and its audience through knowledge of and respect for the history of the form: what it has been and how it has grown. [italics mine]

SUGGESTIONS FOR FURTHER READING

Anderson, W. T. (1990). *Reality Isn't What It Used to Be.* San Francisco: Harper.

Crispin Miller, M. (1988). *Boxed In: The Culture of TV.* Evanston: Northwestern University Press.

Ewen, S. (1988). *All Consuming Images.* New York: Basic Books.

Fiske, J. (1987). *Television Culture.* London: Methuen.

Goodwin, A. (1992). *Dancing in the Distraction Factory: Music Television and Popular Culture.* Minneapolis: University of Minnesota Press.

Key, W. B. (1989). *The Age of Manipulation.* New York: Henry Holt.

Kubey, R. and Csikszentmihalyi, M. (1990). *Television and the Quality of Life.* Hillsdale: Lawrence Erlbaum.

Liebert, R. M. and Sprafkin, J. M. (1988). *The Early Window: Effects of Television on Children and Youth.* New York: Pergamon.

McLuhan, M. (1962). *The Gutenberg Galaxy.* Toronto: University of Toronto Press.

McLuhan, M. (1964). *Understanding Media.* London: Routledge & Kegan Paul.

Nochimson, M. (1992). *No End to Her: Soap Opera and the Female Subject.* Berkeley: University of California Press.

Schrag, R. (1990). *Taming the Wild Tube.* Chapel Hill: University of North Carolina Press.

Solomon, J. (1988). *The Signs of Our Time.* Los Angeles: J. P. Tarcher.

Spigel, L. and Mann, D. (eds.)(1992). *Private Screenings: Television and the Female Consumer.* Minneapolis: University of Minnesota Press.

Stern, J. and Stern, M. (1992). *Encyclopedia of Culture.* New York: Harper.

Umiker-Sebeok, J., ed. (1987). *Marketing Signs: New Directions in the Study of Signs for Sale.* Berlin: Mouton.

THERE'S MORE TO PERFUME THAN SMELL!

Preliminary Remarks

A few years ago, the following ad for a man's perfume, named resonantly *Drakkar noir*, filled the pages of magazines all over the world. This particular version of the ad is taken from an Italian magazine*:

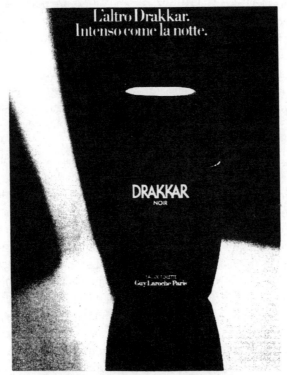

Drakkar Noir de Guy Laroche

l'Autre Ligne pour Homme de Guy Laroche.

At first, the ad seems intent simply on spotlighting a perfume bottle with very little else in the way of meaning-making. At this surface textual level, the ad seems to be saying: "Look at this great bottle of perfume. It's for you!" But a closer analysis will reveal that the ad is imbued with many subtle, hidden connotations and innuendoes that transform it, at an unconscious level, into a powerful meaning-making text. To start off, let's look at some of its iconic features. Note that the bottle is painted a ghastly, frightful black color and that it has been placed right in the center of the picture. Note as well the dark background whose foreboding dimness is interrupted dramatically by a beam of mystical white light that just misses the bottle but illuminates the platform on which it stands. This *chiaroscuro* effect is overwhelming, evocative of awe and veneration. Now, ask yourself, where have you seen this kind of picture? What is it reminiscent of? What feelings does it elicit?

Let's attempt a few guesses. Darkness in our culture connotes fear, evil, the unknown. Children are perpetually afraid of the dark; we stay away from dark forests; we talk of "black masses;" we expect our evil personages in movies and in fictional lore to be dressed in black (just think of how fictional evil characters like Dracula, Darth Vader and others are portrayed); we sense that forbidden, mysterious, happenings occur at night; etc. The placement of the bottle in the middle of what could be interpreted to be an "altar" setting is also suggestive of an evil, taboo ritual being performed in the darkness. The sepulchral name of the perfume, *Drakkar noir*, reinforces our feeling that something dark, mysterious, evil, forbidden but nevertheless *desirable*, is about to happen. The guttural sound of *Drakkar*—obviously suggestive of *Dracula*, the deadly vampire who would mesmerize his sexual prey with a mere glance—instills both a surreptitious fear and a feeling of lust in the viewer. It's as if the bottle were being worshipped on an altar of dark sexuality—recall that the complete name of the perfume is *Drakkar noir* ("black"). Perfume is, of course, worn with one specific goal in mind—to enhance one's sexual *attractiveness*. Sexual activity, moreover, is normally conducted in the dark. The verbal part of the text *Intenso come la notte* ("Intense like the night") reinforces this mode of interpretation.

To complete the picture, the piercing beam of light is evocative of several possible scenarios: the turning on of the light after sexual intercourse; a symbolic sign "from above" warning us about the unholy paganism of sexual urges; a "breakthrough" in satisfying our lustful desires; and the list could go on and on. Semiotically, light is the paradigmatic opposite of dark.

If you still have any doubts that the underlying meaning of this text is anchored in a web of sexual and macabre connotations—*darkness of the night = sexuality = forbidden pleasures = pagan rites = collusion with the*

devil = *fear* = *desire* = *mystery* = etc.—then take a closer look at the shape
of the bottle. The perfume is meant for men to wear. Now, ask yourself, what
sexual objective would men have in wearing the perfume? What is the specific
target of their desire? The vaginal shape of the bottle answers this question
rather bluntly.

There is obviously much more to perfume than smell, at least according
to the makers of ads. The *Drakkar noir* ad illustrates rather strikingly how
powerful visual texts are in making messages and how they enlist various levels
of interpretation. In a certain sense, this ad is a small "work of art," which has,
however, the specific commercial purpose of enhancing sales of a product.
Such ads put on display a vast range of sign-making techniques employed in
the process of message construction. For this reason, they are especially
significant for semiotics as signifying texts that go far beyond their apparent
surface simplicity. The iconic structure of the ad (recall the strategic placement
of the perfume bottle, the effective juxtaposition of light and darkness, the fear-
inducing sound of the perfume's name, etc.), the symbolic connotations that
this structure evokes (recall the meaning of black, the allusion of the name
Drakkar to sinister personages, etc.) and the accompanying verbal text
("Intense like the night") all intertwine thematically to create a *subtext* with
many *intertextual* ramifications. The term *subtext* is used here to mean any
message which a given text connotes that is not immediately accessible to
interpretation. A *subtext* is a text hidden within a text. In the case of the above
ad, the subtext inheres in the constellation of meanings derivable from the
name and shape of the bottle, as well as the iconic features of the text (the
placement of the bottle, the strategic use of darkness, etc.). *Intertextuality*
refers to the feature by which some texts allude to other culturally-defined or
culturally-institutionalized texts. The placement of the bottle in the center of
the scene with a dark background broken by a beam of light recalls sacrificial
texts and rituals.

The contemporary advertising industry originated as a psychologically-
designed marketing strategy at the threshold of the present century. The
premise which propels this industry is that an ad's consumption-inducing
effectiveness is proportional to its capacity to evoke appropriate subtexts and
intertexts in the consumer. This is, after all, the reason behind the use of so-
called "subliminal" techniques in advertising (e.g. Vestergaard and Schrøder
1985, Ewen 1988, Dyer 1988, Barthel 1988, Key 1989). Whether or not
the psychological effectiveness of such methods is demonstrable empirically
is beside the point of the present discussion. The fact is that ad creators
continue to employ them in a variety of ways for a wide array of products. The
study of ads as message- and meaning-making texts is of obvious relevance to

semioticians. The purpose of this chapter is therefore to look at ads from a semiotic standpoint, focusing especially on perfume ads because these provide salient examples of how advertisers attempt to tap into/create subtextual and intertextual structures in the unconscious mind.

Advertising

It may come as a shock to discover that advertising is over 3000 years old! A poster found in Thebes in 1,000 BC. is thought to be an archeological relic of one of the world's first ads. In large letters it offered a whole gold coin for the capture of a runaway slave. Similar kinds of posters have been found by archeologists scattered throughout ancient societies. It would seem that throughout history poster advertising in marketplaces and temples has constituted a popular means of disseminating information and of promoting the barter and sale of goods.

The dawn of the modern era of advertising occurred in the fifteenth century when Gutenberg made the printed word an accessible mode of communication. Fliers and posters could be printed easily and posted in public places or inserted in books, pamphlets, newspapers, etc. In the latter part of the seventeenth century, the *London Gazette* became the first newspaper to reserve a section exclusively for advertising. So successful was this venture that by the end of the century new agencies came into being for the specific purpose of creating newspaper ads for merchants, artisans, etc. Advertising spread rapidly throughout the eighteenth century and proliferated to the point that Samuel Johnson felt impelled to make the following statement in *The Idler*: "Advertisements are now so numerous that they are very negligently perused, and it is therefore become necessary to gain attention by magnificence of promise and by eloquence sometimes sublime and sometimes pathetic" (quoted in Panati 1984: 168).

By the turn of the present century, advertising had become a large business with a stock set of techniques and methods. The goal of advertising in consumerist cultures is to get people to think of themselves as "market units" rather than as individuals or as a public. Advertising promotes consumerism and constitutes an ideology that proposes marketplace solutions to all our social problems. We live in a culture that views shopping as much more than just acquiring the essentials required for daily living. No wonder, then, that the shopping malls are filled with thrill-seekers who would otherwise become stir crazy. We live in a world conjured up by lifestyle ads and TV commercials. Ewen (1988, p. 20) puts it eloquently in the following manner:

> If the "life-style" of style is not realizable in life, it is
> nevertheless the most constantly available lexicon from
> which many of us draw the visual grammar of our lives. It
> is a behavioral model that is closely interwoven with
> modern patterns of survival and desire. It is a hard to
> define but easy to recognize element in our current
> history.

The emergence of our advertisement-mediated world occurred in the decades between 1890 and the 1920s when industrial corporations grew into the mammoth structures that they are today, transforming the workplace into a mechanized, automatonic system of mass production. At that point in time advertising became a crucial medium not for informing people about the availability and qualities of goods, but for restructuring perceptions of lifestyle that could be associated with the goods. Business and aesthetics had obviously joined forces by the first decades of this century. From the twenties onwards, advertising agencies have continued to broaden their approaches, attempting more and more to build an unbroken, imagistic bridge between the product and the consumer's consciousness. Everything from product name, design and packaging to the creation of lifestyle moods now falls within the purview of the advertising business.

Advertisers know that the contemporary consumer has an insatiable desire for pleasure. Their technique, therefore, is to speak indirectly to the unconscious, factual level of mind where sensory stimulation and the Freudian *Id*—the unconscious part of the psyche actuated by fundamental impulses toward fulfilling instinctual needs—can be triggered artifactually. The senses of touch and smell, which are largely downplayed in our culture, can be evoked rather effectively by the ad subtext and used to induce an unconscious desire for the product by association. As Freudian psychoanalysis emphasized, any one of the factual sensory structures that a culture represses can be manipulated and actuated easily by suasion techniques into motivating forces and drives.

In this world of image and style, there is an incessant need for change, for new objects of consumption. Barthes (1967) referred to this new restlessness and madness for constant novelty as "neomania." Obsolescence is, in fact, regularly built into a product, so that the same product can be sold again and again under new guises. All the glitz and imagery of ads and commercials yells out one promise to all: "Buy this or that and you will not be bored, but you will be *happy!*" The sad truth is that what we call happiness cannot be bought.

We are living in a very unstable world which puts much more of a premium on satisfying consumerist urges than it does on spirituality and wisdom. This is why advertisers rely on a handful of hedonistic themes—happiness, youth, success, status, luxury, fashion, and beauty—to peddle their products. Their general message is that solutions to human problems can be found in buying and consuming. You can join the Pepsi Generation to be a part of the action, wear a Benetton sweater to help unify the world, save the environment by buying some recyclable garbage bag and so on.

It was probably Roland Barthes (1957) who first drew the attention of semioticians to the value of studying the field of advertising. Barthes inspired the first semiotic works analyzing signification in ads. Today there is considerable interest in the semiotics of marketing (e.g. Umiker-Sebeok 1987, Umiker-Sebeok, Cossette, Bachand 1988). If there is one theme that can be extracted from this new line of inquiry that is of specific relevance to the present discussion, it is that many ads are interpretable at two levels—a "surface" artifactual level and an "underlying" factual one. The surface level contains the actual iconic and verbal signs of the ad. These are both the "reflexes" of, and the "traces" to, the underlying level: i.e. the surface elements cohere into signifiers that conjure up an array of signifieds in the underlying level. More often than not, the signifieds inhere in mythic, or archetypal, subtextual and intertextual structures that work psychologically at a subthreshold level of mind.

The perfume ad discussed above, for instance, creates archetypal genital and taboo ritualistic symbolism at an unconscious level. Indeed, when the underlying subtext is decoded we tend to become alarmed and repulsed by the ad's hidden message. The makers and advertisers of *Drakkar noir* have obviously learned their Freudian and Jungian psychoanalysis rather well.

Advertisers refer to *positioning* and *brand image* as the key ingredients in marketing a product. *Positioning* is the placing or targeting of a product for the right people. *Drakkar noir* is positioned for a male audience, *Chanel* for a female audience. The marketing of *Audis* and *BMWs* is aimed at yuppie consumers, the marketing of *Dodge vans* is aimed at middle-class suburban dwellers. *Brand image* is the creation of a personality for the product. This implies that a product's name, packaging, price and advertising style creates a recognizable personality for the product that is meant to appeal to specific consumers. Take beer as an example. What kinds of people drink *Budweiser*? Your answer would probably include remarks about the educational level, class, gender, etc. of the targeted consumer. The personality of the one who drinks *Budweiser* is vastly different from that of the one who drinks *Heineken*. The former is a rough, vulgar, country-and-western type male; the latter a smooth, sophisticated, yuppie type. Note as well that *Budweiser* commercials are positioned next to a sports event on television, whereas *Heineken* ads are found primarily in "highbrow" magazines. The idea is to speak directly to the one who drinks a certain kind of brand. The *Bud* drinker is one who holds old-fashioned patriarchal views; he usually drives a Dodge or Plymouth (especially a truck or van); he also drinks Coke or Pepsi; he eats at McDonald's; he loves Jello-O; and so on. Advertisers have indeed reshaped the world. They have gotten consumers to see their own personalities in the style and substance of the products they consume or buy.

Decoding the Ad Text

The semiotic analysis of an ad constitutes an act of decoding, of unraveling the subtext(s) and intertext(s) that are hidden below the ad text. *Decoding* refers to the fact that there is a hidden *code* in the ad text that unfolds in subtextual, intertextual and metaphorical terms. The opposite of *decoding* is *encoding* which refers, of course, to the opposite process of creating codes. There are three relevant questions you must ask yourself when decoding an ad:

- For whom is the ad intended?

- What do the iconic and verbal features connote at subtextual and intertextual levels?

- What metaphorical structures make up the subtext?

As the analysis of the *Drakkar noir* ad reveals, it is helpful to know who the primary target of the product's and ad's subtext is. The vaginal shape of the bottle suggests that the target audience is primarily male. It is not always the case that a product intended for the consumption of males is advertised with male fantasies and psychological urges in mind. An ad for men's perfume can, and often is, aimed at female consumers, so that they can be induced to buy the product for their lovers. In the case of the *Drakkar noir* ad there is a seemingly hidden play on male fears and fantasies. The feeling of mystery and fear that females engender in males constitutes the source of many archetypal or mythic structures in the unconscious mind. The image of the "huntress," for instance, can be seen to have a sexual-erotic mythic structure in most Western cultures. The image of a fierce, powerful and sexually dangerous female surfaces in all kinds of popular narratives—from ancient myths such as that of Diana to contemporary movies such as *Fatal Attraction* and *Basic Instinct*. The figure of the "female-as-huntress" seems to form a kind of paradigmatic cultural counterpart to the figure of the "female-as-mother."

The iconic configuration of the ad's visual signifiers normally implies an "action." The scene in the *Drakkar noir* ad suggests a secluded, dark place where the vaginal bottle is to be worshipped and then conquered. This scene, with its erotic and macabre connotations, is reinforced at the surface verbally by the phrase "Intense like the night." But the ad does not stop there. It also plays, as mentioned above, on a mythic fear in potential male consumers—the fear of women. As Campbell (1969: 59-60) has observed, the fear of women has been "for the male no less an impressive imprinting force than the fears and mysteries of the world of nature itself." So, at the level of mythic unconsciousness this ad tells male customers that they will relentlessly seek and, at the same time, fear the erotic enchantments of women.

It is to be noted that the subtext of such lifestyle ads is generally structured metaphorically. In the case of the *Drakkar noir* ad, there is at least one metaphorical interpretation—*sex is a hidden or forbidden desire*. Indeed, the metaphorical open-endedness of the subtext's meaning and message gives the ad its semiosic richness. The more literal an ad, the less effective it is. Note that what is emphasized in the subtext is not the actual act of sexual intercourse, but the ritualistic feelings that accompany it at the "altar" of female sexuality.

Subtexts create symbolic associations between the product and what consumers covet. Recall the *Budweiser* versus *Heineken* discussion above. To my own taste buds, both beers taste about the same. But, as mentioned, *Budweiser* ads speak to a working class audience, while *Heineken* ones speak to an upscale one. So *Bud* ads and TV commercials are set in working-class bars which play hard rock or country and western music, where people wear cowboy-style clothes and boots, where the men look rugged and tough, and where the women appear to be very little more than sex objects. The subtext in these ads is: "You're one of the guys, bud," so "this *Bud's* for you!" *Heineken* ads, on the other hand, show a much more sophisticated scene—nightclubs, country clubs, etc.—where yuppie customers seemingly listen to soft rock, jazz or even classical music, where the men look country-clubbish, suave and debonair, and where the women are chic, sophisticated, charming.

As one decodes more and more ads, one eventually comes to the realization that advertisers perceive our culture to be an egomaniacal one. Almost without exception, ads speak to the Freudian ego. Diane Barthel

(1988: 18) puts it appropriately as follows:

> Would-be advertising men are advised that the one word
> consumers never tire of is *me*. Advertisers simply tell
> them who that "me" is, and how to make it ever more
> attractive, comfortable, exciting, appealing. To do this,
> advertisers must do more than communicate information
> on a product. They must communicate *image*. Their task
> is somehow to position a product within a market of
> competing goods and to aim it toward an identifiable
> population. They must give it a personality.

The Perfume Ad: A Case in Point

I started off this chapter by decoding a perfume ad aimed at men. The ad constitutes a case in point of how to decode an ad's subtextual, intertextual and metaphorical levels. Perfume can be defined as an artifactual extension of the olfactory system. At the factual level humans, like other animals, are responsive to odors and scents that they receive from the environment. The sense of smell is especially functional as a sexual stimulant in all animal species. Although the sense of sight has largely replaced the sense of smell for sexual arousal in humans—we are more inclined to respond to erotic images than we are to bodily smells—the need for activating the olfactory sensory system at the more basic factual level does not go away.

So perfume is definable semiotically as an artifactual surrogate for sexually-meaningful scent. Perfume works on the sexual emotions and is therefore quite apt to make a long-lasting impression. Odors generally are mnemonically evocative. Years after our first infatuation we seldom fail to recognize a perfume fragrance that was worn by our loved one. This is because odor is often associated with a meaningful situation. A perfume fragrance can bring back vividly to mind a past situation and reawaken the corresponding feelings associated with it rather easily (Engen 1982: 13). It has even been found that adults in a T-shirt experiment would value the body odor of their sexual partner as more pleasant and fragrant than the corresponding odor of a stranger (Schleidt 1980). Odors are also associated with meaningful spaces and places. We prefer the familiar "smell of home" to that of other abodes. We react negatively to the smell of places such as elementary schools, dental offices, etc. where we might have had unpleasant experiences.

Since bodily odors are stigmatized in contemporary industrialized societies, perfumes and deodorants have taken over the biological functions associated with olfaction. Our culture also makes categorical paradigmatic distinctions between "healthy" versus "unhealthy," "sexy" versus "unsexy," etc. in terms of specific kinds of scents. The perfume ad plays precisely on such paradigmatic dichotomies, defining sexuality in an artifactual way. Indeed, most perfume ads implicitly present their products as improvements on nature. As Vestergaard and Schrøder (1985: 159) remark, such ads present their product as "somehow superior to their natural source," offering, in effect, "to lend nature a hand." The overall message transmitted by such ads is: "You too can be sexually attractive by simply wearing the fragrance of perfume X." As in the case of beer, perfume also assumes a personality in advertising. Some perfumes are portrayed as "rugged" and "virile," like *Brut*; others as "smooth" and "refined," like *Blue Velvet*. *Drakkar noir* obviously appeals to the dark, macabre, sinister side of masculine sexual fantasies. And it is evocative of mythic portrayals like Don Juan, Dracula, and even Mephistopheles, the darkest of all. Is *Drakkar noir* alluding to the intertext of Faust selling his soul to the devil so that he could satisfy all his desires? Does wearing *Drakkar noir* constitute a pact with the devil to achieve erotic power? There is certainly much more to perfume than smell in this image-mediated world!

Other Kinds of Ads

Dyer (1982) and others provide useful typologies of ads according to target audience. Clearly, an ad meant for a specialist in ophthalmology is going to be conceptualized and designed differently than a perfume ad meant for today's upscale office worker. But there is general consensus among semioticians that lifestyle ads are the ones which generate the most meaning-intensive subtextual and intertextual structures.

As another case in point consider the following ad for *Marilyn Peach**, a sparkling wine, which was found in many European magazines a few years ago:

The first thing to note is that the background in the ad is in a peach color, apparently to match both the color and the taste of the wine. But a closer look reveals that the background is highly suggestive of the dawn. In fact, by reflecting on the mythical meaning of the dawn in expressions such as the "dawn of creation," the "dawn of life" and so on, we can start gaining access to the subtextual and intertextual domains of meaning.

So at this point let us assume the hypothesis that the subtextual and intertextual levels allude to the creation theme of the Bible. Are there any other indications that this is a plausible hunch? Look at the woman's hand which is holding out a glass of the bubbly drink in an obvious toasting gesture. Could this be an offering, or a temptation, just like the one of Eve in the Book of Genesis? Just look at the woman's wrist and there you will see a bracelet in the form of a snake. Recall that the devil came to Eve in the body of a snake to prod her on to tempt Adam. It would seem that our working hypothesis is being corroborated iconically. Adam, of course, is the one who will have to pick up the other glass. Will he do it? Well, if you offer him a glass of *Marilyn Peach*, how can he resist? If you still have doubts about this analysis, just read the accompanying French verbal text—*La pêche, le nouveau fruit de la tentation* "Peach, the new fruit of temptation"—and you will be left with little doubt as to the presence of a "Garden of Eden" intertext in this ad and all its sexual-erotic connotations. Note as well that the peach is a cultural metaphor for female genitalia, given its isomorphic shape to the vagina.

In my opinion the hidden code is aimed at female consumers. The subtextual message is: "If you want to ensnare your man, offer him a drink of *Marilyn Peach*; and he, like Adam, will not be able to resist your charm." Metaphorically, the offer of the drink is equivalent to the offer of the vaginal "peach." So, like the *Drakkar noir* ad, this one too taps mythic subtextual structures that apparently reverberate effectively in the realm of the subconscious *Id*. Note, finally, that the color, design and "feel" of the two ads are in paradigmatic opposition. This clearly reflects cultural models and perceptions of sexuality that are differentiated along gender lines.

Concluding Remarks

It has been said that the best "art" of the late twentieth century has been produced by advertisers. In a sense, this is a correct statement. As we have seen in this chapter, ads generate a truly interesting and rich array of meanings, and thus can be compared to the great paintings and sculptures of all time. The main techniques employed in decoding an ad—the search for a subtext, the search for intertextuality, the identification of any metaphorical themes, etc.—are, more or less, the stock methodological tools used by art critics.

But there is something about advertising that is illusory and, in my view, ultimately destructive. The art of a Michelangelo or a Renoir was not conceptualized to entice someone to buy a manufactured product. At the risk of sounding élitist, I believe that the traditional forms of visual representation document humanity's search for meaning: advertising, on the other hand, exploits our need for meaning to enhance sales of a product. In the end, advertising may be reshaping the world in more ways than we might think. As I look at people shopping, at parties, driving down the road, sitting at an outdoor café sipping coffee, etc. I cannot help but see in their bodily movements, in the way they wear their clothes, in the discourse they generate, etc. a reenactment of the images created by advertisers. People are seeing themselves more and more in terms of those images. I witnessed a striking example of this a few years ago when I attended a party of young upscale professionals. At a certain point during the evening, I saw an interactional scene that reminded me of a beer commercial that was popular on television at the time. The young men and women were posturing towards each other in ways that were almost identical to those of the actors in the television commercial. A culture mediated so pervasively by advertising images is asking for trouble. What Kubey and Csikszentmihalyi (1990: 199) have to say about the psychosocial effects of television applies, in my view, as well to advertising:

> Because consciousness is necessarily formed by exposure to information, media fare helps define what our most important and salient goals should be. Being an intimate part of the consumer society, television tells us that a worthwhile life is measured in terms of how many desirable material objects we get to own, and how many pleasures we get to feel. To achieve such goals complex skills are unnecessary. Even though some people spend a great deal of attention in trying to find bargains, in monitoring prices and sales, in developing culinary taste and fashion sense, in keeping abreast of new models and new gadgets, for the most part consumption does not require much disciplined effort and therefore does not produce psychological growth.

The answer to the dilemma of advertising is not to be found in censorship or in any form of state control of media and information. Even if it were possible in a consumerist culture to control the contents of advertising, this would invariably prove to be counterproductive. The answer is, in my view, to become aware of the signifying effects of ads and commercials with the help of semiotic analyses such as the ones illustrated in this chapter. When the human mind is aware of the hidden codes in texts, it will be better able to fend off the undesirable effects that such texts may cause.

NOTE

* The Drakkar Noir and the Marilyn Peach advertisements were taken from an Italian magazine *PM: Panorama Messe*, Arnoldo Mondadori (ed.). Milano: PMPress.

SUGGESTIONS FOR FURTHER READING

Bachand, D. (1992). The Art of (in) Advertising: From Poetry to Prophecy. *Marketing Signs* 13: 1-7.

Barthel, D. (1988). *Putting on Appearances: Gender and Advertising.* Philadelphia: Temple University Press.

Barthes, R. (1957). *Mythologies.* Paris: Seuil.

Barthes, R. (1967). *Système de la mode.* Paris: Seuil.

Bell, S. (1990). Semiotics and Advertising Research: A Case Study. *Marketing Signs* 8: 1-6.

Campbell, J. (1969). *Primitive Mythology.* Harmondsworth: Penguin.

Drummond, G. (1991). An Irresistible Force: Semiotics in Advertising Practice. *Marketing Signs* 10: 1-7.

Dyer, G. (1982). *Advertising as Communication.* London: Routledge.

Engen, T. (1982). *The Perception of Odors.* New York: Academic.

Ewen, S. (1988). *All Consuming Images.* New York: Basic.

Key, W. B. (1989). *The Age of Manipulation.* New York: Holt.

Kubey, R. and Csikszentmihalyi, M. (1990). *Television and the Quality of Life.* Hillsdale, N.J.: Lawrence Erlbaum Associates.

Leiss, W., Kline, S. and Jhally, S. (1990). *Social Communication in Advertising,* 2nd ed. Toronto: Nelson

McCracken, G. (1988). *Culture and Consumption.* Bloomington: Indiana University Press.

Panati, C. (1984). *Browser's Book of Beginnings.* Boston Houghton Mifflin.

Schleidt, M. (1980). Personal Odor and Nonverbal Communication. *Ethology and Sociobiology* 1: 225-231.

Umiker-Sebeok, J. (1987) (ed.). *Marketing Signs: New Directions in the Study of Signs for Sale.* Berlin: Mouton.

Umiker-Sebeok, J., Cossette, C. and Bachand, D. (1988). Selected Bibliography on the Semiotics of Marketing. *Semiotic Inquiry* 8: 415-423.

Vestergaard, T. and Schrøder, K. (1985). *The Language of Advertising.* London: Blackwell.

Wernick, A. (1991). *Promotional Culture: Advertising, Ideology, and Symbolic Expression.* London: Gage.

Williamson, J. (1985). *Decoding Advertisements: Ideology and Meaning in Advertising.* London: Marion Boyars.

Chapter 13

STILL WAITING FOR GODOT!

Preliminary Remarks

Samuel Beckett's late forties play (published in 1952), *Waiting for Godot*, is a remarkable work of dramatic art in more ways than one. Above all else, it came forward at the time to reflect, in the theatrical medium, an emerging state of mind which we now commonly call *postmodern*. Postmodernism has become *the* defining feature of the contemporary psyche. Like the two tramps in the play, late twentieth-century humans have literally "lost faith." We appear, by and large, to be skeptical and cynical about the "meaning" of human existence. We feel that there really is nothing "out there," that everything is a human-made illusion, and that life is a momentary state of consciousness on its way to extinction. But on a deeper intuitive level we seem to be constantly and desperately hoping that there is a "plan" to existence, and that our otherwise senseless actions can be tied together in a teleologically meaningful way. The tramps in Beckett's masterpiece are perpetually waiting for a character named Godot—an obvious sarcastic allusion to God. Godot never comes in the play. But deep inside us, as audience members, we yearningly hope that Beckett is wrong, and that on some other stage, in some other play, the design of things will become known to us—that Godot will indeed come.

This is the dilemma, the contingent emotional plight that is nowadays commonly called *postmodern*. The purpose of this chapter is to take a brief look at this vast topic as it relates to the study of the contemporary human psyche, using Beckett's play and a movie made in the early eighties, *Blade Runner*, to reflect upon the implications of this new form of mentality. It is typical of modern-day urbanized individuals to be able to "step outside" traditions and value systems and see them as concoctions of human beings, rather than as the results of inevitable historical processes. To the postmodern mind, nothing is universal; everything is relative. As the philosopher John Searle has recently remarked (1992: 5-6), this mindset has brought about many of the currently fashionable, but implausible, materialistic views in philosophy: e.g. the idea that the mind does not exist at all; the notion that mental states are no more than causal relations between inputs and outputs of the system (organic or inorganic) of which they are a part; the view that a computer has a mind; the view that consciousness as inner reality does not exist. Contemporary intellectual culture seems to be afflicted by a kind of "ironic" imagination—a state of mind that has led to perverse philosophies such as those listed by Searle as we continue, *ironically*, to search for meaning to life. It is indeed ironic to find modern humans reducing themselves to mere automatons, millennia after having striven to distinguish themselves from all other systems. Such is the state of mind in this postmodern age.

Postmodernism

What is the postmodern mind like? As we did in chapter 11, let us use our imaginations to answer this question by stepping back in time to the medieval period. How did the medieval mind view the meaning of existence? Well, if the historical record coming out of that period is accurate, it is obvious that the medieval mind had very few doubts. The medieval individual probably saw his or her life as being put on earth by God on a historical journey—a journey that started with the creation of the world and the fall from grace of humanity because of original sin, that was subsequently recharted by the coming of Christ, and that will end when Christ will come again. The medieval individual saw himself or herself as being on a journey towards the afterlife. The journey metaphor, in fact, imbues Dante's great medieval work, the *Divine Comedy* of 1307. Written as an imaginary journey through hell, purgatory and heaven, Dante's epic masterpiece constitutes an allegorical "search for meaning" that both captures the essence of the medieval worldview and transcends it at the same time.

Whether or not there was any substance to the beliefs of medieval people, it would seem that because they believed themselves to be part of a "larger picture," and because they perceived themselves as "characters" in God's narrative, they possessed a sense of purpose and reassurance. With the advent of the Renaissance and the Age of Reason, the modern secular mind started to take shape. Although this mind put more faith into human reason and its products—science and logic—it was nevertheless convinced, by and large, that the world had a design and a meaning. Unlike the medieval mind, it did not seek for the design in the words of God, but in the discoveries of science and in the theoretical creations of the logical mind. The modern mind believes that the world is self-contained and can be perfectly well understood by the methods of science without reference to supernatural explanations. But like the medieval mind, the modern mind believes that God is at the "center" of this design, that God is ultimately the "author" of the human story.

In the eighteenth century, the dizzying growth of technology and the constantly-increasing certainty that science could eventually solve all human problems—perhaps even prolong life indefinitely by discovering the "life principle" and thus conquering death—brought into existence a new form of mentality. By the end of this century, the now famous assertion that "God is dead" by the great German philosopher Friedrich Nietzsche (1844-1900) both acknowledged that the modern mind had run its course and that a new worldview had crystallized—a worldview that had lost its belief in anything beyond the immediate material form of existence.

As pointed out in chapter 10, the term post*modernism* comes out of the field of architecture to describe the eclectic, colorful variety of building styles designed by urban architects in the seventies. Immediately after it was coined, the term caught on like wildfire, and is now used to describe everything from contemporary paintings to the methods of computer-influenced cognitive science. *Postmodernity* can be defined simply as the worldview of late twentieth century urban culture that everything "out there" is a creation of the human mind. It is, therefore, a term that has come forward to nicely capture the widely-held view that all knowledge and history are concoctions of the human mind. The term *postmodernism* is now used to refer to trends in society, art and science that reflect this worldview.

In my view there is no doubt that the contemporary version of the postmodern mind has been in large part fostered by our TV-mediated culture. Viewing the world through a television camera or through advertisements leads to a perspective that Solomon (1988: 212) aptly characterizes as "perceptual montage." We gaze upon the world as if it were a TV program or a scene in an ad. Day in and day out these fragmented images of life influence our overall view that reality is illusory. Ultimately, we are led to form the view that human actions are a montage of nonsensical skits, docudramas, commercials, etc.

Language in the postmodern mind takes on a new modality of representation. Postmodern language is either imbued with irony or else it is reduced to mere formulas, stock phrases and the kind of babble that an Al Bundy or a Homer on TV constantly blurt out. The music that the postmodern ear hears is the senseless sounds strung together randomly by a John Cage. The art that defines the postmodern eye is that of an Andy Warhol. The postmodern mind sees no meaning in the world beyond the satisfaction of immediate survival urges and drives, and therefore finds any search for meaning as itself *meaningless* . The postmodern mind is ahistorical and nihilistic. As the sociologist Zygmunt Bauman (1992: vii-viii) has perceptively remarked, postmodernism is "a state of mind marked above all by its all-deriding, all-eroding, all-dissolving *destructiveness."*

How did this all come about? Nietzsche's nihilistic prediction that "God was dead" meant, of course, that everything in human belief systems, including religious beliefs, was a construction of the human mind. By the early part of the twentieth century the view that history had a purpose which was "narrated," so to speak, by a divine source (as, for example, in the Western Bible) was coming increasingly under attack. At mid-century, Western society was starting to become increasingly "deconstructive," i.e. more inclined to take apart the structures—moral, social, and mental—that had been shaped by this narrative. By the sixties, Western society had become fully entangled in a postmodern frame of mind. The results have been quite noticeable in the contemporary teenager. He or she does not aspire necessarily to the traditional moral structures and value systems of the culture; he or she tends to live his or her life without a sense of purpose above and beyond the immediacy of the moment. The music of Guns N' Roses, for instance, glorifies drug addiction, suicide and hate mongering. Demonic imagery is becoming more and more typical, as rock bands like Motley Crüe and Death Metal attract a small, but not insignificant, group of followers.

Now not everyone in our culture thinks and behaves in this way. There are many who, as a matter of fact, react against this kind of outlook. But it is becoming symptomatic of increasingly large sectors of the culture. Image-making has now become fully externalized in the form of products manipulated by media specialists. Television in particular has become the postmodern mind's imagination. This is an imagination that is no longer capable of distinguishing between what is original and what is imitation. It is an imagination that fails to distinguish between information and knowledge.

An example of a classic movie that violently rejects the emerging postmodern world order is Stanley Kubrick's cinematic masterpiece of 1971, *A Clockwork Orange*. The setting for the movie is Britain in the near future. A teenage thug, Alex De Large, perpetrates a daily routine of crime and sex in a wanton and reckless fashion. Caught and imprisoned for murder, he volunteers to undergo an experimental shock treatment therapy which brainwashes him to become nauseated by his previous lifestyle. Mr. Alexander, an author and one of Alex's victims, traps him with the aim of avenging himself. He hopes to drive Alex to commit suicide to the strains of Beethoven's Ninth Symphony. But Alex is supported by the press and soon after he is released and restored to health.

The movie ends in typical postmodern fashion with no true conclusion. But the scenario of senseless, aimless violence that a teenager is capable of perpetrating has a profound warning in it. Alex is a portrait of a goalless and ruthless late twentieth-century human trapped in a weary, decaying environment. His only way out is through intimidation and physicality. He is a "ticking timebomb" ready to explode at any instant. Alex feels an acute and urgent need to change—indeed to "save"—the world. And he aims to do it in a physically destructive manner. The rage in Alex's eyes is the rage shown by contemporary street youths.

What has gone wrong? Are we living in the world depicted by *A Clockwork Orange?* As novelist Douglas Coupland has so persuasively demonstrated in his 1991 novel *Generation X*, many of today's identity-less, obscure, unmotivated young adults have nowhere to go and nothing to conquer. They are in a society without goals, a society facing the constant threat of AIDS, child abuse, wife abuse, rape, cancer, divorce, unemployment and dissatisfaction with one's job. Coupland (1991: 105-106) calls the X-generation a community of "Global Teens:"

> I muse all the while about Tyler and his clique—Global Teens, as he labels them, though most are in their twenties. It seems amusing and confusing —unnatural— to me the way Global Teens...live their lives so *together* with each other: shopping, traveling, squabbling, thinking, and breathing.

Another classic movie portrayal of the contemporary postmodern world and mind is Godfrey Reggio's brilliant 1983 film *Koyaanisqatsi* which is both an example of postmodern technique in cinema art and a scathing critique of the postmodern world. It is a film without words which, like the world manufactured by TV images, unfolds in the form of a series of discontinuous, narrativeless images. On the one hand, this shows us how narrativeless, disjunctive and distracted the contemporary world has become; on the other hand, it is an example of what postmodern art is like, a parody of documentary-style films and TV programs. The film has no characters, plot, dialogue, commentary; in a word, nothing recognizable as a narrative. The camera simply juxtaposes contrasting images from the natural and industrialized worlds—cars on freeways, atomic blasts, litter on urban streets, people shopping in malls, housing complexes, buildings being demolished, etc. We see unfolding before our eyes the world as the TV camera sees it. It is a turgid, gloomy world with no purpose or meaning whatsoever. People appear to be mindless creatures. The world of culture is reduced to cars, decaying buildings, crowds bustling aimlessly about. To emphasize the insanity and absurdity of the world Reggio incorporates the mesmerizing music of Philip Glass into his technique. The music acts as a guide to understanding the images, interpreting them presentationally, to use Langer's concept once again (see Chapter 1). We can "feel" the senselessness of human actions and the ugliness of our postmodern world in the contrasting melodies and rhythms of Glass's music. His slow rhythms drag us into a state of *ennui*, and his *prestissimi*—which accompany a demented chorus of singers chanting in the background— assault our senses. When this musico-imagistic frenzy finally ends, we feel an enormous sense of relief.

In a certain sense, the whole film can be conceived to be a musical *sonata* with an opening part, or exposition, a middle developmental section and a final recapitulation with coda. The film, in fact, starts off with a glimpse into a vastly different world—the world of the Hopi Indians of Arizona. This is a world firmly implanted in a mythical and meaningful view of existence, a view that does not extricate the cultural dimension of human life from the natural one, a view that sees a sacred continuum linking human beings, nature and the world made by humans. Glass's choral music in this exposition is spiritual, sacred, prayer-like. It inspires reverence for the human, the natural and the cultural all at once. This stands in dark contrast to the development of the filmic sonata—a cornucopia of dissonant images of a decaying, senseless, industri- alized world. Then, we are taken back, at the end, to the Hopi world. As in any recapitulation, the opening profound strains of the choir come back, hauntingly, awesomely and with a warning this time (the coda) which is projected onto the screen:

> koyaanisqatsi (from the Hopi language) 1. crazy life, 2. life
> in turmoil, 3. life out of balance, 4. life disintegrating, 5.
> a state of life that calls for another way of living.

This Hopi word not only makes sense at this point, but is "felt" to be particularly applicable to the plight of our contemporary culture because of the way in which the movie *makes* its own message. The medium of the movie has become the message, providing a truly deep insight into the postmodern world.

Waiting for Godot

Perhaps the most recognizable aspect of the postmodern worldview is its rejection of the traditional narratives and the traditional narrative techniques which have always aimed to imbue universal human experience with meaning and sense of purpose. The great works of art, the great dramas, the great music of *all* cultures, not just the Western one, are meant to transform the experience of human events into memorable works that transcend time and culture.

The meaning-making narrative that has been the most critical one in forming our culture is, of course, the Judeo-Christian Bible. For several millennia, Western culture has lived with the idea that this world was created to help us go back to our real world in heaven which we lost because of original sin. This world has a divine Author who put us on a "journey" leading to a reunification with Him. Within the framework of this narrative, human actions are centered around God's plan and desires. The narrative has been our guarantee that death is not extinction.

Waiting for Godot is a dramatic, disturbing parody of this narrative. Written in the late forties, before the term *postmodern* became a fashionable one, Beckett's play is a striking precocious example of a work of art that dramatizes what it means to live in a "decentered" world, a world that has lost its belief in the Judeo-Christian narrative and in the human spirit. There is only a void out there, no heaven or hell. Human history has no beginning or end. Human beings fulfill no particular purpose in being alive. Life is a meaningless collage of actions on a relentless course leading to death and to the return to nothingness.

The play shows two tramps stranded in an empty landscape attempting to pass the time with a series of banal activities reminiscent of slapstick comedians or circus clowns. The two tramps, Vladimir and Estragon, seem doomed forever to repeating their senseless actions and words. They call each other names, they ponder whether or not to commit suicide, they reminisce about the senseless past, they threaten to leave each other but can't, they perform silly exercises, and they are constantly waiting for a mysterious character named Godot who never comes. A strange couple, named Lucky and Pozzo, appears, disappears, reappears and finally vanishes in the second act, which is virtually a mimesis of the incongruous actions of the first. Pozzo whips Lucky, as if he were a cart horse. Lucky kicks Estragon. The two tramps tackle Lucky to the ground to stop him from shrieking out a deranged parody of a lecture in philosophy. Vladimir and Estragon go back to talking about nothing in particular, and wait with no purpose whatsoever for Godot. Their dialogue is meaningless, a chain of silly clichés. Intertextuality with the Bible narrative and scenery is sardonic and acrimonious—there is a bare tree on stage in parody of the Biblical tree of life, the tramps constantly engage in meaningless theological discourse which satirizes the questions raised by the Bible, etc. The play ends with the two tramps still waiting. "In the beginning was the word," announces Genesis; "the word is hollow," Beckett's play retorts. There is no meaning here, nor will there ever be! Life is meaningless, a veritable circus farce! The God we are supposed to meet will not come.

But Beckett's bleak portrait is somehow not totally convincing. Like the six characters in Luigi Pirandello's 1921 play, Six *Characters in Search of an Author*, we seem to urgently need to continue our search for an author to write us into existence. The search may lead errantly to televangelism, cults, pseudo-meditation sects and the like, but more often than not it is leading to a profound reevaluation of the meaning of consciousness and particularly of the concept which we have labeled the human "spirit." The greatness of Beckett's play in my view rests not in its parody of our search for meaning, but in stimulating in us a reexamination of who we are. We may be condemned to waiting for Godot, and the rational part of our mind might tell us that existence is absurd, but at a more profound level we sense that there is a spiritual reality that can only be felt, not understood.

Blade Runner

As will be discussed in the final chapter, postmodern humans are fascinated by the idea of bringing machines to life. Indeed, a distinguishing feature of the postmodern mind is that it rejects the age-old contention that human beings are unique in the scheme of things. Humans are not perceived anymore to be "the measure of all things." More and more, in this Age of the Computer, human beings are seeing themselves as no more than special kinds of biological "machines."

What if we could really bring machines to life? What would happen? That is the question pursued by a truly remarkable postmodern movie, Ridley Scott's 1982 B*lade Runner*, based on a story titled *Do Androids Dream of Electric Sheep?* by Philip K. Dick. This is a detective-type story played out against the depressing backdrop of the choking, urban, postmodern landscape. Rick Deckard is one of a select few of futuristic law-enforcement officers, nicknamed "blade runners," who have been trained to detect and track down "replicants," powerful humanoid robots who had been engineered to do the work of humans in space. But the replicants have gone amok. They have somehow taken on the mental characteristics of humans and have started to ask fundamental philosophical questions about their own existence made urgent by the limited lifespan programmed into them. A desperate band of these killer replicants has made its way back to earth seeking to have their programs reversed. They are looking desperately to find and get the sinister corporate tycoon responsible for their creation to give them new life (another example of Pirandello's characters in search of an author?). Deckard's assignment is to track down these runaway replicants and terminate them.

The movie is not about genetic engineering and the dream of artificial intelligence workers of bringing machines to life. It is about the nature of humanity. The movie asks if "humanity" is itself a human concept. It is relevant to note that the method used by Deckard to detect whether a suspect is "human" or "replicant" is reminiscent of the classic "Turing test" used by artificial intelligence theorists. The work of the British mathematician Alan Turing (1936, 1963) shortly before his untimely death in his early 40s suggested that one could program a computer in such a way that it would be virtually impossible to discriminate between its answers and those contrived by a human being. This notion has become immortalized as the "Turing test." Suppose you are an observer in a room which hides on one side a programmed computer and, on the other, a human being. The computer and the human being can only respond to your questions in writing, say, on pieces of paper which both pass on to you through slits in the wall. If you cannot identify, on the basis of the written responses, who is the computer and who the human being, then you must conclude that the machine is "intelligent." It has passed the "Turing test." Deckard's detection technique is a kind of Turing test that he hopes will allow him to distinguish between "human" and "replicant." His task is, metaphorically, to seek out the true essence of what "humanness" is.

Deckard's search unfolds in a postmodern urban wasteland where punk mutants control the streets while the pathetic inhabitants of endless blocks of gloomy high-rises remain glued to their TV sets. Deckard relies on—what else in a postmodern world?—a futuristic VCR, complete with stop action and precision image-enhancers, to find the replicants through dark alleys abandoned to the forces of anarchy.

In this scenario the replicants, paradoxically, are more "human" than the human characters. Deckard even falls in love with one of them, Rachel, whose name has obvious intertextual connections with the Biblical character of the same name. She helps him track down his prey, falling in love with him in the meanwhile. Deckard is saved at the end by a replicant who shows him mercy, one of the quintessential of all human qualities. The implications of the movie are rather obvious. We have made a dehumanized world. Only the machines we make, which are icons of our best qualities, seem capable of being "human," in the idealistic sense of the word.

The search for what it means to be human is the theme of the film. Not only the replicants, but the mannequins in the movie as well are all icons of the human form. Indeed, one of the replicants is killed sardonically by a mannequin. Human-like toys are seen from time to time. But there is one feature that differentiates human anatomy from artificially-made anatomies—the eye. Deckard's version of the Turing test discussed above unfolds through a specific type of procedure that involves the particular kinds of responses that only the human eye manifests. Replicants use their "eyes" exclusively to see; humans use them as well to show "feeling." Aware of the mysterious power of the human eye, the replicants kill their maker by poking out his eyes.

The film also asks basic questions about the nature of so-called human emotions like love and mercy, and above all else about the nature of human memory—the generator and container of what we call the Self. Awareness of who we are is largely autobiographical. Anyone afflicted by amnesia will have to redefine his or her identity and thus construct, in effect, a new "Self." Rachel's quest to become human involves the construction of a signifying autobiographical past—family photos, mementos from childhood, etc.

Intertextually, the film makes many ironic references to the Biblical narrative. Near the end, a naked replicant with only a white cloth around his waist, in obvious parody of the Crucifixion scene, saves Deckard's life at the cost of his own. The whole scene is suggestive of the saving of "humanity" at the cost of Jesus's life. The white dove that appears when the replicant dies is reminiscent of the dove that was sent to Noah's ark in the midst of torrential rain to help the ark find a safe place away from the deluge—a symbolic quest for a safer future. Finally, when Deckard and Rachel escape the gruesome city scene to fly off into the countryside, the dark, gloomy atmosphere suddenly clears up, the sun comes out, and a "new dawn" rises. These are images that call to mind the Garden of Eden scene. But in typical postmodern style, we are left with a parody of this scene—the new world order will be in the hands of a human about to mate with a robot!

But all is not parody in this movie. Blade Runner asks the fundamental questions of philosophy in a new way: What is a human being? What is real? Is there any meaning to existence? By making the replicants the iconic mirrors of human beings, and by transforming their struggle to survive and to know who they are into a reflection of our own struggle, the movie is about the nature and meaning of humanity. We cannot help but feel a need, after viewing the movie, to examine ourselves and the world we live in with more scrutiny.

Whither Postmodern Culture?

The postmodern perspective came forward originally to destabilize the rational, logocentric and patriarchal worldviews of Western culture. As Jean-François Lyotard (1984: xxiv) states, postmodernism implies that the "narrative function is losing its functors, its great heroes, its great dangers, its great voyages, its great goal." Some, especially radical deconstruction critics, see this new awareness as a welcome relief, a liberation from the "great male story" that has guided the course of Western civilization since its inception. In one sense, such critics are absolutely correct. The idea that language and narrative texts have latent meanings that are biased ideologically in favor of a male perspective of the world is a justifiable assertion. In deconstructing language and narrative, postmodern criticism has done *all* humanity, not just one gender, a service. However, it may be turning out to be a two-edged sword. In making Western cultures more aware of their own logocentrism, it has concomitantly engendered a kind of ahistoricity and nihilism that is of little value to the progress of the human species. The postmodern perspective is itself a product of the kind of thinking that has crystallized from minds that have long ago severed their link to their experiential, sensorial origins, of minds that have become self-deprecatingly ironic. As Kearney (1991: 213) similarly observes, postmodern criticism and art is nothing if it is not ironic, a parody of life. Symbols, relations, human actions are all parodied for the sake of parody.

But, then, as Vico would advise us, there really is no need to despair. Rational cultures will eventually end and be replaced by something much more "humane"—either by a "recourse" to a previous age, or by a new, more imaginative form of cultural cognition. Radical deconstruction is a "symptom" of moribund rationality.

Vico proposed a cyclical theory of human cultural evolution, according to which human societies progressed from barbarism to civilization and then back to barbarism. The term "barbarism" in Vico refers simply to a primitive stage of civilization. In the first stage—which he called the "age of the gods"—religion, burial rites, the family, and other basic institutions emerge to lay the foundations of human culture. He called this primordial phase of humanity the age of the "gods," because he saw the first reflective humans as being filled with an intense fear of natural phenomena such as thunder and lightning. Not possessing the knowledge to understand or "explain" such environmental events, the first humans ascribed them to awesome and frightful "gods" or "divine" creatures—hence the designation "age of the gods." In the succeeding "age of heroes," a dominant class of humans—the "heroes" of the evolving culture—emerges typically to subjugate the common people. These are men with great physical prowess who inspire fear and admiration in the common people. The latter typically ascribe divine powers to these "nobles." After a period of domination, a third stage—the "age of men or equals"—invariably takes shape in which the common people rise up and win equality; but in the process society begins to disintegrate as it returns to a more vile and violent form of barbarism (rational or reflective barbarism). This, according to Vico, is the natural "course" of human civilized cultures—a course that is not linear and endlessly progressive, but cyclical and finite. Cultures are born and cultures die. They do not go on forever; they are "killed" by their barbarism of reflection, so to speak. But in their "death" they are going to be "reborn" with a more ethical form of humanity.

During the first divine age, humans spoke a mute, iconic language. The second heroic age saw the emergence of a concrete, metaphorical language based on perceptual modalities. During this age there is a middle ground, a balance between "ancient" gods and "modern" humans. The Vichian "hero" is a half-formed thought, a way of mentally encoding a virtue such as valor or civil wisdom. The third age is one in which humans speak a vernacular, literal language. It is an age of decline. It is a period in a culture's development in which language has lost its power to express the basic meanings within it, when any memory of the gods and the heroes has dimmed. It is an age of solitude, of subtle irony and wit. Education in such an age is technical and specialized. Language is shallow and does not reflect the passions; it is a language of concepts, method, and scientific research devoid of the poetic.

Vico argued for this three-stage historical progression primarily on the basis of the etymology of our common word-concepts. He persuasively demonstrated that words start out as concrete, iconic Gestalts based on our perceptions of the referents. Then metaphor transforms this sensorially-based meaning-universe into a conceptual one: i.e. one in which the referents of iconically-formed words are connected into generalized ideas. Finally, as cognition becomes increasingly conceptual through the workings of the metaphorical capacity, the referents of the word-concepts also become increasingly abstract and removed from their perceptual origins. At this point we tend to think more communally than individually. It is an age when "cultural cognition" replaces *fantasia*.

Our postmodern age is an age of "reflective barbarism," as Vico would surely characterize our contemporary culture. It is no coincidence that the naive belief that machines can take over the work of humans has surfaced at a time when a belief in Divine Providence, which in the primordial age of "sensory barbarism" was motivated by a universal instinctive feeling that Vico labeled "poetic religion," has crumbled under the weight of materialism and mechanistic rationalism. Whereas Jove was the god of poetic barbarism, the Machine has become the god of reflective barbarism. The central idea espoused by a sector of cognitive science, namely that human beings are protoplasmic automatons in the service of their genes, rather than "individuals" in the traditional humanistic sense of the word, is gradually and surreptitiously permeating our entire social fabric. As the great psychoanalyst Carl Gustav Jung (1957: 19-20) warned several decades ago, there is an intrinsic danger in viewing a human being as "a recurrent unit" rather than "as something unique and singular which in the last analysis can neither be known nor compared with anything else."

I am nevertheless optimistic about where our culture is ultimately heading. My optimism is not completely unmotivated either. The recent demise of the most powerful form of political postmodernism to ever emerge, communism, demonstrates that the human spirit is alive and well. Like Rollo May (1991), I believe that our culture is "crying out" for myth once again. Myths are not told by males alone, nor do they show biases in favor of one particular group or other. They are simple stories that we create to make sense of the world. The rejection of myth is typical of rational culture, where science and logic alone are utilized as tools for conceptualizing the world. Our culture is in a search mode, a search for new ways of making meaning and, more importantly, of finding meaning to existence.

Concluding Remarks

This chapter has dealt with the complex theme of postmodernism in art and society. Born as an architectural term to describe the eclectic building styles that emerged in the seventies, it has become a term to describe a new psychic awareness of ourselves as makers of meaning. Above all else, it has shaken the foundations of both the Judeo-Christian worldview and the modern worldview brought about by the scientific revolution that started in the Renaissance, a worldview that naively believes that everything can be eventually understood by the logical methods of science.

The characteristics of postmodern art are especially interesting from a semiotic perspective. Postmodern plays, compositions, paintings, buildings, etc. reject the symbols and structures of the past while at the same time evoking them intertextually. The heart of postmodernism is parody and the belief that there is nothing beneath the parodies. But ultimately the postmodern movement itself is bound to fall victim to the very thing it attacks, the making of meaning. Because it so severely minimizes the world outside language and artistic fabrications, it may not realize that the views of chic, fashionable postmodern critics are themselves fabrications and presuppositions. By parodying and deconstructing symbols, images and texts, these new "sooth-sayers" have forgotten our hunger for them. The have forgotten, in other words, that human beings are *semiosic* beings. They have completely overlooked the fact that the products of the imagination—poetry, myths, paintings, scientific theories, musical compositions, etc.—are the only windows we have into the landscape of consciousness.

SUGGESTIONS FOR FURTHER READING

Bauman, Z. (1992). *Intimations of Postmodernity*. London: Routledge.

Coupland, D. (1990). *Generation X*. New York: St. Martin's.

Jameson, F. (1991). *Postmodernism or the Cultural Logic of Late Capitalism*. Durham: Duke University Press.

Kearney, R. (1991). *Poetics of Imagining: From Husserl to Lyotard*. New York: Harper Collins.

Lyotard, J.-F. (1984). *The Postmodern Condition: A Report on Knowledge*. Minneapolis: University of Minnesota Press.

May, R. (1991). *The Cry for Myth*. New York: Norton.

Norris, C. (1991). *Deconstruction: Theory and Practice*. London: Routledge.

Searle, J. R. (1992). *The Rediscovery of the Mind*. Cambridge, Mass.: MIT Press.

Solomon, J. (1988). *The Signs of Our Time*. Los Angeles: Jeremy P. Tarcher.

Turing, A. (1936). On Computable Numbers with an Application to the Entscheidungs Problem. *Proceedings of the London Mathematical Society* 41: 230-265.

Turing, A. (1963). Computing Machinery and Intelligence. In: E. A. Feigenbaum and J. Feldman (eds.), *Computers and Thought*, pp. 123-134. New York: McGraw-Hill.

Chapter 14

DO BEES REALLY DANCE?

Preliminary Remarks

If by chance you happen to be around a beehive, you will eventually get a close-up look at a truly remarkable event in nature. You will witness the fact that worker bees returning to the hive from foraging trips have the extraordinary capacity to inform the other bees in the hive about the direction, distance and quality of the food with amazing accuracy through movement sequences which biologists call a "dance," in obvious metaphorical analogy to human dancing as a sequence of preset, repeatable bodily movements. The remarkable thing about bee dancing is that it is representational, thus sharing with human communication codes the feature of conveying information in the absence of the referential domain to which it pertains.

Several kinds of dance patterns have been documented by entomologists. In the "round" dance, the bee moves in circles alternately to the left and to the right. This dance is apparently deployed when the cache of food is nearby:

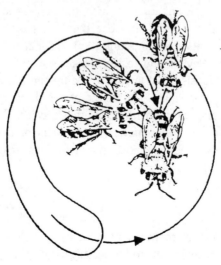

When the food source is further away, then the bee is said to dance in a "wagging" fashion, moving in a straight line while wagging her abdomen from side to side and then returning to her starting point.

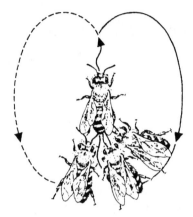

The straight line in this dance points in the direction of the food source, the energy level of the dance indicates how rich the food source is and the tempo provides information about its distance. As an example, Frisch (1962) reports on one experimental study in which a feeding dish placed 330 meters from the hive was represented by 15 complete rounds in 30 seconds, whereas a dish located 700 meters away was communicated by only 11 runs carried out in the same period of time.

Do bees really *dance*? What does this anthropomorphic metaphor mean? Even though it constitutes a rigid code which is narrowly restricted in its representational range, in contrast with the infinite range that human communication systems entail, the bee dance raises several fundamental questions about the nature of communication and animal consciousness. But perhaps the most relevant one to the subject matter of this course is the implication that semiosis is not limited to the human species, but that it is a feature of all living organisms. The theme of this chapter is, in fact, to look briefly at semiosis and communication in other species. Thomas A. Sebeok (e.g. 1990) uses the term *zoosemiotics* to refer to the branch of semiotics that aims to study and document semiosis in and across species.

Zoosemiotics

The study of animal communication traces its roots to Darwinian evolutionary biology (Darwin 1859), and especially to Darwin's (1872) contention that animal behavior constituted a viable analogue for human mental functioning. So, by the end of the nineteenth century, Darwininan-inspired work led to the establishment of comparative animal psychology (e.g. Morgan 1895, Thorndike 1898). Some of the early animal experiments led to the theory of classical conditioning *in humans*. Ivan Pavlov (1902), for instance, rang a bell while he presented meat to a dog. Initially, only the meat stimulus, not the ringing of the bell, evoked an instinctive salivation response in the dog. However, after repeated bell ringings, Pavlov found that the bell alone would evoke salivation. The dog had obviously "learned" to associate the sound of the bell to the presence of meat. It was then claimed that humans too learned in a similar way. Spurred by such findings, work on animal intelligence was pursued with great fervor during the first quarter of this century. Robert Yerkes (1916), for instance, succeeded in showing that monkeys and apes had the capacity to transfer their conditioned responses to novel tasks. And in 1925 Wolfgang Köhler showed that apes could achieve spontaneous solutions to problems without previous training.

The goal of early comparative psychology was to generalize the findings from the animal experiments to human learning. The assumption was that the same laws of learning applied across all species and, therefore, that universal principles of learning and problem-solving could be deduced from animal behavior. Some psychologists continue to work under this very assumption. However, already before mid-century, the use of animals as convenient substitutes for people in the laboratory came under attack. The *ethological* movement stressed that animals and people lived in separate worlds, and that animals should be studied within their natural habitats. The work of Lorenz (e.g. 1952), Thorpe (e.g. 1961), Tinbergen (e.g. 1963) and Frisch (e.g. 1967), for instance, came forward to establish the basic research categories for studying animal behavior in its own right.

By mid-century, linguists too came to regard the study of animal communication as particularly relevant to their own field of inquiry. In 1960 Charles Hockett proposed a series of points of contact between animal and human communication systems which he claimed would be useful for understanding the origin of language. Since the sixties we have also witnessed a slew of widely-popularized, and still ongoing, primate language experiments (e.g. Gardner and Gardner 1969, Premack 1976, Rumbaugh 1977, Patterson 1978, Terrace 1979, etc.). These have been motivated by the proposition that interspecies communication is a realizable goal (Linden 1986). Although there have been reports of some symbolic activity (e.g. Savage-Rumbaugh, Rumbaugh and Boysen 1978), of some comprehension of humor (Patterson and Linden 1981), and of some control of sentence structure (Gardner and

Gardner 1975), the ape experiments have not really established the learning of symbolic language by the higher primates. It is perhaps more appropriate to say that ape language is analogous to the kind of iconic language that the early hominids probably developed in several respects, but that it does not have the same structure and origin (Reynolds 1983).

It is obvious that the whole area of animal communication bears directly upon what semioticians study. So, it should come as no surprise to find that in the early sixties one of this century's greatest semioticians, Thomas A. Sebeok, coined the term *zoosemiotics* (1963) to refer to the branch of semiotics intersecting with ethology aiming to study semiosic behavior in and across species. The systematic study of animal communication allows semioticians to view human semiosis and communication in relation to the properties displayed by the animal systems. Sebeok, incidentally, was among the first, as Linden (1986: 14) aptly points out, to detect flaws in the ape language experiments which purported to show that our simian relatives were capable of human verbal symbolism.

Human versus Animal Communication

The opinions of Sebeok (e.g., 1990) are particularly germane to the whole issue of human versus animal communication. Taking inspiration from the work of the biologist Jacob von Uexküll (1909), Sebeok suggests that every organism has different inward models of representation that reflect its species-specific outward experiences. The key to understanding this duality is in the anatomical structure of the organism itself. Animals with widely divergent anatomies do not experience the same kind of reality. There exists, therefore, no common world of representation and consciousness shared by humans and animals equally. When we study animal behavior with our own rational minds we are dissecting it in terms of our own anthropomorphic categories. What we are really describing are these categories.

This does not mean that we cannot envisage studying animal semiosic and communication systems. It simply means that we will have to be very careful about what "we" have to say about how animals produce and comprehend signs. Perhaps the more appropriate word to use in the case of animals, in general, is not signs but *signals*. A *signal* is an unconditioned (unlearned) response to some stimulus. It is an automatic corporeal emission or movement prompted by some environmental, physiological or affective stimulus. Like the instincts, signals are part of the animal's biological heritage. Signals communicate something about specific stimuli, urges or physiological needs.

Animal semiosis is characterizable in general as unconditioned and unreflective signaling behavior, at least from the human perspective.

The specific aim of zoosemiotics is to identify the various properties that differentiate human from animal systems. One the earliest attempts to identify the main differences was the work of the American linguist Charles Hockett (1960). He proposed a set of 13 design features to describe oral language. These categories have come to constitute an early zoosemiotic matrix for understanding communication systems in general:

Design Feature	**Mode of Communication**
1. Auditory-vocal channel	Linguistic communication unfolds between mouth and ear, as opposed to visual, tactile or other modes of communication.
2. Broadcast transmission and directional reception	A verbal signal can be heard by any auditory system within ear rance, and the source can be located using the ears' direction-finding capacity.
3. Rapid fading	Auditory signals are transitory and do not await the hearer's convenience.
4. Interchangeability	Speakers of a language can reproduce any linguistic message they can understand.
5. Total feedback	Speakers of a language hear and can reflect upon eveything that they say (unlike the visual displays often used in animal courtship signaling).
6. Specialization	The sound waves of sppech have no function other than to signal meaning.

Design Feature	Mode of Communication
7. Semanticity	The elements of the linguistic signal convey meaning through their stable reference to real-world situations.
8. Arbitrariness	There is no necessary dependence of the element of a verbal signal on the nature of the referent.
9. Discreteness	Speech uses a small set of sound elements that form meaningful oppositions with each other. This is Hockett's term for paradigmatic structure.
10. Displacement	This is Hockett's term for *representation* or the capacity of language to refer to situations remote in space and time from their occurrence.
11. Productivity	This is the infinite capacity to express and understand meaning by using old elements to produce new ones.
12. Traditional transmission	Language is transmitted from one generation to the next primarily by a process of teaching and learning (not only by genetic inheritance).
13. Duality of patterning	Verbal sounds have no intrinsic meaning in themselves but combine in different ways to form elements (e.g. words) that do convey meanings.

Hockett applied his typology to various animal systems of communication, showing how only language possesses all of these features simultaneously. A part of his chart (1960: 10-11) is worth reproducing here. It compares bee dancing to human language:

Communication Feature	Bee Dancing	Language
1. Auditory-vocal channel	no	yes
2. Broadcast transmission and directional reception	yes	yes
3. Rapid fading	?	yes
4. Interchangeability	limited	yes
5. Total feedback	?	yes
6. Specialization	?	yes
7. Semanticity	yes	yes
8. Arbitrariness	no	yes
9. Discreteness	no	yes
10. Displacement	yes	yes
11. Productivity	yes	yes
12. Traditional transmission	probably not	yes
13. Duality of patterning	no	yes

What Hockett's typology made possible, perhaps for the first time, was a concrete comparison of different communication systems on the basis of categories derived from human language. But there are many more differences between animal and human semiosis than just those pertaining to language. What keeps humans and animals cognitively separate is the fact that humans alone have the ability to create the World 3 domain of symbols, language and culture. There is no other animal that can paint, sculpt, put on plays, compose music, make humorous remarks and so on. This in no way implies that animals do not have some form of consciousness (a World 2 trait), or that they are incapable of communicating their feelings, drives, and urges in some form or other. What it does mean is that they lack the ability to go from signaling behavior and rudimentary representation to full abstract symbolism. There is no evidence to even hint that an animal can understand the connotations that we extract from a painting, feel the moods evoked by a Beethoven piano sonata, understand the intent of a narrative and so on.

Interspecies Communication

The so-called ape experiments of the last three decades were designed to see if simian primates were capable of human language and concepts. These experiments were examples of "interspecies" communication, i.e. of communication between two different species.

Aware that gorillas and chimpanzees were incapable of audio-oral language because they lacked the requisite vocal organs, the first experimenters chose American Sign Language (ASL) as the human code for teaching the animals to speak. The first widely-known "subject" was a female chimpanzee named Washoe whose training by the Gardners (Gardner and Gardner 1969, 1975) began in 1966 when she was almost one year of age. Remarkably, Washoe learned to use 132 ASL signs in just over four years. What appeared to be even more remarkable was that Washoe began to put signs together to express a small set of relations. These resembled the early holophrastic sentences of children (see Chapter 5).

Inspired by the results obtained by the Gardners, others entered upon an intensive research program throughout the seventies and most of the eighties aimed at expanding upon their teaching procedures. The Premacks (e.g. Premack and Premack 1983), for example, whose work actually began as far back as 1954 with a five-year-old chimpanzee called Sarah, taught their subject a form of written language. They instructed Sarah to arrange and respond to vertical sequences of plastic tokens on a magnetic board which represented individual words: e.g. a small pink square = "banana"; a small blue triangle = "apple"; etc. Sarah eventually developed the ability to respond to combinations of such symbols which included references to abstract notions.

Although there was an initial wave of enthusiasm over such results, with the media reporting on them on a regular basis, there really has emerged no solid evidence to suggest that chimpanzees and gorillas are capable of symbolic and verbal behavior *in the same way* that humans are. Like the comparative and behaviorist psychologists of a previous era, who were able to get animals to respond to stimuli such as the ringing of a bell through a program of "conditioning," it is highly likely that these experimenters too simply conditioned their apes to respond to the signs to which they continually exposed them, triggering in them only a very small range of human-like creativity (e.g. combining the signs into sequences and using them in different contexts).

As mentioned above (and in previous chapters), the work of the biologist Jakob von Uexküll (1909) at the turn of the present century is instructive in this regard. Von Uexküll claimed that an organism does not perceive an object in itself, but according to its own particular kind of innate mental modeling system that allows it to interpret the world of beings, objects and events in a biologically-determined way. For von Uexküll, this inner system is grounded in the organism's body, which routinely converts the external world of experience into one of mental representation in terms of the particular features of the organism's anatomical system. An animal perceives an object according to its species-specific mental "blueprint." It is highly unlikely that any other animal, other than the human one, is capable of making connections among percepts. This is because it would seem that humans alone are endowed with the metaphorical capacity as part of their biological "blueprint." This allows them to connect and subsequently to "narrativize" world events. Washoe and Sarah were indeed "communicating" with their human experimenters, but only in the same way that there is an empathy among all species at the factual level of signal detection. It is, however, highly unlikely that Washoe and Sarah were capable of grasping conceptual domains such as *love is a sweetness, time is money,* etc. (see Chapter 6) which reveal something rather unique about human semiosic and communication systems. In my view, the difference between animal and human communication is to be sought in the transformational power of metaphor to generate the artifactual order. The "making" of artifacts—physical and mental—seems to be unique to the human species. When archeologists look for the "signs" of extinct human cultures, they do not look only for bones and skulls, but, more importantly, for artifacts. These are the clues to the previous existence of a World 3 symbolic order. This is why Ernst Cassirer (1946, 1979) aptly defined the human being as the *symbolic animal,* in contradistinction to all other living creatures.

What Is Communication?

The ape experiments raise the question of what is *communication?* It is clear that while we may not be able to *communicate* with other species in the same ways that we do with each other, there is a level at which we do indeed "make contact" with them. There is no doubt in my mind that my cat and I enter into a rudimentary form of *communication* on a daily basis. Sharing the same territory and living space, and being codependent on each other for affective exchanges, we do indeed communicate our feeling-states to each other. We do this by sending out signals and by utilizing modes of communication other than those that depend exclusively on abstract symbolism. Tones of voice, the postures assumed, the movements made, etc. are all aspects of our mutually-developed "interspecies communication code." This code taps basic factual structures that cut across my human and her feline communication system, emerging "adaptively" from our shared territoriality context.

From a zoosemiotic perspective, human communication entails various *modes* (ways) and *media* for sending out signals and signs to make our feeling-states, as well as our concepts, known to other humans and to other species. Communication within our own species enfolds the whole range of verbal and nonverbal semiosis; interspecies communication is constrained to fundamental signaling subsystems that develop adaptively from shared territoriality contexts. Communication modes include the auditory-vocal, visual, tactile, olfactory and the gustatory (see also Crystal 1987: 399-403):

Communication Mode and/or Medium	**Features**
Auditory-vocal	This mode is the basis for speech, physiological vocal signals and symptoms (e.g. coughing and snoring), musical effects (e.g. whistling) and voice qualities (to communicate identity and feeling-states).
Visual	This includes sign languages, writing, artisitic representation

Visual, continued	and all forms of kinetic communication (see Chapter 3).
Tactile	This includes all forms of proxemic communication (see Chapter 10) as well as deafblind languages and various kinds of speacialized body codes.
Olfactory	The odors that organisms are capable of picking up are anchored in signaling behavior. In human communication systems, olfactory signaling is transformed connotatively to involve social semiosis, as evidenced by our use of perfumes (see Chapter 12).
Gustatory	This involves the sense of taste to signal various feeling and drive states. In human communication systems the gustatory mode is often transformed to generate social semiosis, as evidenced by our cuisine and eating events (see Chapter 9).

Communication is definable as any act of conveyance of signals or signs, unconditioned or learned, that actualizes species-specific transmission modes and media for the purpose of relaying feeling-states, drives, urges and (especially in the case of humans) *intentions*. The message inherent in any transmission can be received successfully by another organism only if that organism has biological access to the same kind of modal and medial subsystems that the message subsumes. If the organism receiving an audio-oral message, for instance, is not endowed with an internal modeling system based, in whole or in part, on the auditory-vocal modality, the message transmission will turn out to be unsuccessful.

It is obvious that the tactile mode cuts across human and feline communication systems. I touch my cat often to send out messages of affection to her, and she rubs against me when she is "happy" or wants something. We have reached this interspecies "compromise," so to speak, instinctively and intuitively. However, even within the confines of this versatile communicative mode, there is no way for me to communicate a broader range of tactile feeling-states to my cat that are implied by words such as *embrace, guide, hold, kiss, spank, tickle,* etc. Interspecies communication is realizable, but only in a very restricted sense. It can occur in some modes, partially or totally, to various degrees according to species. If the anatomical structures of the two species are vastly different, however, then virtually no communication is possible.

A good typology of communicative modes intersecting with semiosic capacities is the one put forward by Sebeok (e.g. 1990: 49-75). His typology is organized according to the paradigmatic structure of the features:

Communication Mode and/or Medium	**Features**
Vocal/Nonvocal	This dichotomy alludes to the fact that semiosis and communilist either or both of these two channels. Vocalization is not restricted to humans. Birds, for instance, possess the capacity to change their songs subtly, in a "dialectal" fashion.
Verbal/Nonverbal	This alludes to the basic distinction between verbal codes and all aother ones. Note that *language* is verbal, but not vocal; *speech* is both vocal and verbal.
Witting/Unwitting	This is practically equivalent to saying that certain messages

Communication Mode and/or Medium	Features
Witting/Unwitting	are unconditioned (e.g.signals such as pupil responses) and others are cognitively controlled or intentional.
Left/Right	This refers to the semiosic and communicative capacities associated with the LH and RH of the brain (see Chapters 4 and 6). It would seem that LH characteristics are virtually unique to the human species.
Formation/Dissolution	This refers to the fact that sign systems need to be formed within the organism, and that they are subject to change or even dissolution over time (diachronic semiosis). Semiosicn in all organisms other than the human one is inherited biologically. The human being receives his or her semiosic capacities both from biology and from culture through learning.

Sebeok's typology is clearly very useful in pinpointing essential differences between human and all other semiosic/communicative systems. The human system would seem to be unique in several respects: e.g. only humans are capable of verbal communication; only human systems are subject to diachronic forces; etc.

Concluding Remarks

This chapter has dealt with communication from a zoosemiotic perspective. I conclude by returning to the question with which I started off the chapter; namely, what does it mean to say that bees *dance*? What this expression reveals, once again, is that we are constantly searching for meaning. This time the search has led us to *labeling* in understandable human terms the movements that an insect species in the physical world makes. Our use of the expression *bee dancing* to describe what we see bees as doing reveals, in other words, the specific way in which we conduct our quest to understand the world around us. Since we do not know *really* what the bees are doing, we use our metaphorical capacity to compare their actions to human dancing. How typical this act of *naming* is! But, even more significant, after we have *named* that act as *dancing*, then we start to understand it in terms of human dancing. We should therefore be very careful when we say that animals are capable of such things as "dancing," "concept-formation," "consciousness" and the like. These are all human notions. We have no idea what animal concepts are like, nor do we know what animal consciousness involves. We can only understand these things in metaphorical terms. Such is the nature of our minds!

A well-known example of how easily duped we are by our own perceptions of animal behavior is the case of Clever Hans. Clever Hans was a world-famous German "talking horse" in 1904 who appeared to understand human language and communicate human answers to questions by tapping the alphabet with his front hoof—one tap for A, two taps for B, and so on. A panel of scientists ruled out deception and unintentional communication by the horse's owner. The horse, it was claimed, could talk! Clever Hans was awarded honors and proclaimed an important scientific discovery. Eventually, however, an astute member of the scientific committee which had examined the horse, the Dutch psychologist Oskar Pfungst, discovered that Clever Hans could not talk without *observing* his questioners. The horse decoded—as most horses can—*signals* that humans constantly transmit and over which they have no conscious control. Clever Hans sensed when to tap his hoof and when not to tap it in response to inadvertent cues from his human handlers, who would visibly relax when the horse had tapped the proper number of times. To show this, Pfungst simply blindfolded Clever Hans who, consequently, ceased to be so clever. The "Clever Hans phenomenon," as it has come to be known, has been demonstrated with other animals as well (e.g. a dog will bark in lieu of the horse's taps).

The subliminal power of signals cannot be underestimated. Signals are what Sebeok (1990: 66-67) calls unwitting signs in communication. It has been shown, for example, that men are sexually attracted to women with large pupils *unwittingly*. Large pupils signal a strong and sexually-tinged interest, as well as making a female look younger. This signaling subsystem, incidentally, explains the vogue in central Europe between the two world wars of women using a crystalline alkaloid *eye* drop liquid derived from *belladonna* (literally "beautiful woman" in Italian). It was felt that this drug would enhance facial appearance by dilating the pupils.

Communication is the transmission of species-specific feeling-states, urges, drives, etc. All species have this capacity. Most of the transmissions in the animal realm involve signaling. In the human world, however, not only is communication multimodal and multimedial, but it is also open-ended. Moreover, human communication is text-based: i.e. it inheres in combinations, juxtapositions, etc. of signs that are to be decoded not discretely but holistically. A sentence, for instance, is much more than the sum of its words— just think of the meaning of the individual words and of the entire sentence in *He was born with a silver spoon in his mouth.* Phenomena such as irony, metaphor, narrativity, textuality, aesthetic representation (painting, music, etc.), language and the whole domain of World 3 culture (institutions, technology, science, etc.) are unique to the human species, at least until proven otherwise.

All this does not mean that animals are incapable of what we call *thought.* They may even have what we call *consciousness.* But we have no access whatsoever either to the nature of their thinking or to the nature of their consciousness states. All we can do is compare them metaphorically to ours. Animals do indeed manifest qualities that we recognize as "intelligent;" they do indeed evince what appears to us as "love," "hate," "hope," "fear," etc. But do we really *know* how animals think, love, hate, etc.? Or are we really seeing in their behaviors what we want to see, as did the Clever Hans researchers? Are we *narrating* the story of animal intelligence and communication in the same way that the TV producers of the program *The Wild Kingdom* did (see Chapter 7)?

The zoosemiotic perspective is an instructive one. It has shown that only humans have the capacity to create and change the modes and means they use to communicate. Yet, by investigating how human semiosis and communication is unique, zoosemiotics has also forced us to be more sensitive to the vital role that animals play in the natural order. It has led us, in effect, to a better understanding of what an "animal" is—a word, incidentally, deriving from Latin *anima* "breath, soul, life"—and to a deeper respect for *all* life.

SUGGESTIONS FOR FURTHER READING

Cassirer, E. (1946). *Language and Myth.* New York: Harper & Brothers.

Cassirer, E. (1979). *Symbol, Myth, and Culture: Essays and Lectures of Ernst Cassirer 1935-1945,* D. P. Verene (ed.). New Haven: Yale University Press.

Crystal, D. (1987). *The Cambridge Encyclopedia of Language.* Cambridge: Cambridge University Press.

Darwin, C. (1859). *The Origin of Species.* New York: Collier.

Darwin, C. (1871). *The Descent of Man.* New York: Modern Library.

Darwin, C. (1872). *The Expression of the Emotions in Man and Animals.* London: Murray.

Frisch, K. von (1962). Dialects in the Language of Bees. *Scientific American* 207: 79-87.

Frisch, K. von (1967). *The Dance Language and Orientation of Bees.* Cambridge, Mass.: Harvard University Press.

Gardner, B. T. and Gardner, R. A. (1975). Evidence for Sentence Constituents in the Early Utterances of Child and Chimpanzee. *Journal of Experimental Psychology* 104: 244-262.

Gardner, R. A. and Gardner, B. T. (1969). Teaching Sign Language to Chimpanzees. *Science* 165: 664-672.

Griffin, D. R. (1981). *The Question of Animal Consciousness.* New York: Rockefeller University Press.

Griffin, D. R. (1992). *Animal Minds.* Chicago: University of Chicago Press.

Haraway, D. (1989). *Primate Visions: Gender, Race and Nature in the World of Modern Science.* London: Routledge.

Hockett, C. F. (1960). The Origin of Speech. *Scientific American* 203: 88-96.

Köhler, W. (1925). *The Mentality of Apes.* London: Routledge and Kegan Paul.

Linden, E. (1986). *Silent Partners: The Legacy of the Ape Language Experiments.* New York: Signet.

Lorenz, K. (1952), *King Solomon's Ring.* New York: Crowell.

Morgan, C. L. (1895). *Introduction to Comparative Psychology.* London: Scott.

Patterson, F. G. (1978). The Gestures of a Gorilla: Language Acquisition in Another Pongid. *Brain and Language* 5: 72-97.

Patterson, F. G. and Linden, E. (1981). *The Education of Koko.* New York: Holt, Rinehart and Winston.

Pavlov, I. (1902). *The Work of Digestive Glands.* London: Griffin.

Premack, A. (1976). *Why Chimps Can Read.* New York: Harper and Row.

Premack, D. and Premack, A. J. (1983). *The Mind of an Ape.* New York: Norton.

Reynolds, P. (1983). Ape Constructional Ability and the Origins of Linguistic

Structure. In: E. de Grolier (ed.), *The Origin and Evolution of Language*, pp. 185-200. Amsterdam: Harwood Academic Publishers.

Rumbaugh, D. M. (1977). *Language Learning by Chimpanzees: The Lana Project*. New York: Academic.

Savage-Rumbaugh, E. S., Rumbaugh, D. M. and Boysen, S. L. (1978). Symbolic Communication between Two Chimpanzees. *Science* 201: 641-644.

Sebeok, T. A. (1963). Communication in Animals and Men. *Language* 39: 448-466.

Sebeok, T. A. (1990). *Essays in Zoosemiotics*. Toronto: Toronto Semiotic Circle.

Stamp Dawkins, M. (1993). *The Search for Animal Consciousness*. Oxford: Freeman.

Terrace, H. S. (1979). *Nim*. New York: Knopf.

Thorndyke, E. L. (1898/1911). *Animal Intelligence*. New York: Macmillan.

Thorpe, W. H. (1961). *Bird-song*. Cambridge: Cambridge University Press.

Tinbergen, N. (1963). On Aims and Methods of Ethology. *Zeitschrift für Tierpsychologie* 20: 410-433.

Uexküll, J. von (1909). *Umwelt und Innenwelt der Tierre*. Berlin: Springer.

Yerkes, R. (1916). *The Mental Life of Monkeys and Apes*. New Haven: Yale University Press.

ARE OUR GENES REALLY SELFISH?

Preliminary Remarks

Recently, an interesting theory has come forward to claim that all ideas and styles (dress, musical, etc.) develop a kind of mimetic "life of their own." The sociobiologist Richard Dawkins (1976, 1987) has argued rather persuasively that mimesis is, in fact, responsible for the transmission and entrenchment of concepts within specific cultures. He designates these "transmitted ideas" as *memes*, in direct imitation of the word *genes*. Dawkins defines *memes* simply as replicating patterns of information (tunes, ideas, clothes fashions, etc.).

Dawkins' term captures rather nicely how the forms of behavior we pick up from mediated messages tend to develop "a life of their own." Through media and commercial products such as TV, movies, videos, ads, etc. we are constantly influenced by general "mimetically-shaped" models of social behavior. For example, the rock music channel MTV, which is now seen in many countries, has become a primary source for the spread of North American teen models or memes of behavior abroad.

But Dawkins does not stop there. His claim is that ultimately humans are no more than the sum total of their genetic propensities. Everything we *make*, including artifacts, are reflexes of basic genetic survival tendencies. Dawkins' perspective of human beings poses an obvious challenge to virtually everything that I have said in this book. If Dawkins is right, the search for meaning is really over!

Dawkins' approach to the study of humanity is reflective of two new trends. One has come to be known as *cognitive science* and the other as *sociobiology*. Remarkably, both have many features in common with semiotics. They are interdisciplinary, based on a nature-to-culture (factuality-to-artifactuality) conception of human mentality, and critical of the traditional methods of Western science. But, in my opinion, they have come forward typically in a postmodern culture to deconstruct the traditional idea of *human*. Many cognitive scientists and sociobiologists see humans as no more than "genetically-based replicants," so to speak. The challenge that both cognitive science and sociobiology pose for traditional humanistic enterprises like semiotics is hardly an academic one. It is a very serious one, especially within a postmodern culture that is in the process of deconstructing its entire World 3 artifactual order. My aim in this chapter is to look critically at these two new "sciences." Specifically, I will examine the view that the mind is a computing device; I will revisit the Turing test (see Chapter 13) and John Searle's "Chinese Room" retort; and finally I will critique the aims and objectives of sociobiology.

Computers and the Mind

The underlying conception that has driven the whole discourse in this book is that semiosis is ultimately a reflex of sensory, factual tendencies. But this conception is not accepted universally. Historically, among the first to discredit the senses as potential sources of thought, and to lay the foundation for the development of the science of logic, was Zeno of Elea (fifth century BC). Although the universe may appear diversified to the senses, Zeno argued, it exists as a single, undifferentiated substance. With a series of brilliant arguments, which have come to be known appropriately enough as "Zeno's paradoxes," he sought to show how the senses can betray and mislead us. One of his famous paradoxes asserts that a runner cannot reach a finish-line because, as our sense of sight would have it, the runner must first traverse half the distance to the line; then half of *that* distance; then half of *that* new distance; and so on *ad infinitum*. Because of the infinite number of bisections that exist in such linear paths, Zeno concluded that one could never travel any linear distance in a finite period of time. With arguments such as this one, Zeno wanted to demonstrate the logical impossibility of motion as perceived by the senses. Shortly after, Democritus (c. 460-c. 370 BC), who formulated the first atomic theory of matter, reduced the sensory qualities of things, such as warmth, cold, taste and odor, to quantitative differences among their atomic properties. For Democritus, even the mind could be explained in such purely physical terms. He thus formulated the first comprehensive statement of deterministic materialism by which all aspects of existence can be reduced to the operation of physical laws. In contrast, the Sophists—a group of traveling teachers who became famous throughout Greece towards the end of the fifth century BC—denied the existence of objective knowledge. They were, in a certain sense, the forerunners of modern-day *postmodernists*.

It can be said that the proper systematic inquiry into mentality started with Socrates (c. 470-399 BC), who taught that only individuals had full knowledge of truth, and that this knowledge could be accessed through conscious reflection. Socrates was, therefore, the first "innatist." He demonstrated that even an untutored slave could be led to grasp the Pythagorean theorem (the square on the hypotenuse of a right-angled triangle is equal to the sum of the squares on the other two sides). This, he claimed, showed rather conspicuously that such knowledge was innate, rather than acquired from experience. Socrates also laid the foundations of the rationalistic tradition in philosophy by stressing the need to analyze beliefs, to formulate clear definitions of basic concepts, and to approach ethical problems rationally and critically.

Like Socrates, Plato (c. 428-c. 347 BC) stressed the rational basis of intellect. His most influential contribution to the study of mind was his *Theory of Ideas*, also known as the *Doctrine of Forms*, which divided reality into two realms, one inhabited by invisible *ideas* or *forms*, and another by concrete familiar objects. The latter are imperfect copies of the ideas because they are always in a state of flux. Thus, Plato rejected any philosophy that claimed to explain knowledge on the basis of sensory experience—true knowledge is the offspring of innate ideas or forms. In his *Republic*, Plato portrayed humanity as imprisoned in a cave where it mistook shadows on the wall for reality. Only the person with the opportunity to escape from the cave—the true philosopher—had the perspicacity to see the real world outside. The shadowy environment of the cave symbolizes the realm of physical appearances. This contrasts with the perfect world of ideas outside. Plato's ideas or forms can be best understood as geometrical figures or models. A circle, for instance, is a perfect form which no one has ever seen. What people actually see are approximations of the ideal circle. When geometers define a circle as a series of points equidistant from a given point, they are referring, in effect, to logical ideas, not actual points. "Circularity" is an innate mental notion which has greater reality than circular objects because it is a perfect model of them. An object existing in the physical world may be called a "circle" insofar as it resembles the form "circularity."

Plato's most illustrious pupil, Aristotle (384-322 BC), has come to have perhaps the greatest influence on subsequent Western thinking about mentality. He laid the foundations for modern logical approaches by developing the theory of deductive inference, represented by the *syllogism*—a formula of argument consisting of two premises ("All humans are mortal"/"Kings are human") and a conclusion logically derived from them ("Kings are mortal").

Aristotle criticized Plato's separation of form from matter, maintaining that forms are contained within the concrete objects that exemplify them. The aim of science is to define the essential forms of reality and to arrange them in terms of a natural hierarchy. Aristotle's hierarchical organization of nature contin-ues, to this day, to be the predominant model of how the mind is purported to sort things.

The Platonic and Aristotelian views on the innateness of forms and on the power of logic to explain reality remained as cornerstones of Roman philosophy and, later, of the emerging Christian world. By the third century AD Christian scholars were, in fact, attempting to combine the religious teachings of the Gospels with the philosophical concepts of the Greek and Roman schools. The first great Medieval thinker, who reconciled the Greek emphasis on reason with Christian beliefs, was St. Augustine (354-430 AD). Like Plato, he viewed the soul as a higher form of existence than the body and stressed the need to contemplate ideal forms. By the eleventh century, interest in the mind-body problem was kindled further by Arab scholars who translated the works of Plato, Aristotle and other Greek thinkers. The result was the movement known as Scholasticism. Through dialectical reasoning, the Medieval Scholastics wanted to demonstrate the truth of existing religious beliefs. Their methods thus helped to entrench even further the Western tradition of rational logic.

No doubt the greatest intellectual figure of the Medieval era was St. Thomas Aquinas (1225-1274), who combined Aristotelian logic with Augus-tinian theology into a comprehensive system of thought that came to be *the* acclaimed philosophy of Roman Catholicism. In his *Summa theologiae*, he constructed a theoretical structure that integrated Classical logic with religious experience. For Aquinas, the truths of science and philosophy were discovered by reasoning from the facts of experience, whereas the tenets of religion were beyond rational comprehension and, therefore, had to be accepted on faith.

The legacy of Classical rationalism continued well into the fifteenth and sixteenth centuries when the revolutionary discovery of heliocentricity by Copernicus (1473-1543), the explorations of the unknown world, and the rise of commercial urban societies gave this persuasive form of conceptualization a more mechanistic and materialistic quality. The Medieval view of the universe as hierarchically designed by God was supplanted by a picture of the world as a vast machine whose separate parts worked according to physical laws without purpose or will. In the new intellectual climate known as the Renaissance, reason and experience became the sole standards of truth.

It was the English philosopher and statesman Francis Bacon (1561-1626) who persuasively criticized Aristotelian logic on the grounds that it was futile for the discovery of physical laws. He called for a scientific method based on inductive observation and experimentation. Paradoxically, both Bacon's and Galileo's (1564-1642) emphasis on induction as a method of discovery led, by the late Renaissance, to the entrenchment of Aristotle's idea that a meaningful understanding of reality could be gained only by exact observation and logical thinking. By the seventeenth and eighteenth centuries this very same idea was extended to the study of mind. Philosophers like Thomas Hobbes (1588-1679), René Descartes (1596-1650), Benedict Spinoza (1632-1677), Gottfried Wilhelm Leibniz (1646-1716), and David Hume (1711-1776) assumed that the mind could, and should, be studied as objectively and as mechanistically as nature.

In contrast to Bacon and Galileo, these thinkers put philosophical and scientific inquiry back on a deductive course. Descartes, for instance, refused to accept any belief, even the belief in his own existence, unless he could "prove" it to be necessarily true. And it was Descartes who gave the Platonic mind-body problem its modern formulation, known as "dualism." Descartes was, however, unable to solve the fact that two different entities, the mind and the body, can so affect each other. The English philosopher Thomas Hobbes provided his own solution to the mind-body problem by reducing the mind to the internal activities of the body. For Hobbes, sensation, reason, value and justice could be explained simply in terms of matter and motion. The British philosopher and historian David Hume went somewhat against this deductive grain. But, in other ways, he had an even greater impact on transforming the study of mind into a mechanistic methodology by stressing the need to use mathematical techniques to investigate all forms of existence.

The modern era in the scientific study of mind was ushered in by Cartesian dualism, and specifically by the belief that the mind was an entity that could be studied separately from the body. Among his contemporaries who renounced this view were the British philosopher John Locke (1632-1704) and the Irish philosopher George Berkeley (1685-1753). In line with the inductive empiricism begun by Bacon, Locke also attacked the prevailing belief of his times that knowledge was independent of experience, although, paradoxically, he accepted the mechanistic approach of the physical sciences to study the mind. For Locke, all information about the physical world came through the senses and all thoughts could be traced to the sensory information on which they were based. Berkeley went even further by casting doubts on our ability to know the world outside the mind. He maintained that no evidence for such a world existed because the only observable things are sensations which are within the mind.

Ever since the Enlightenment, science and philosophy have developed a split personality. Immanuel Kant (1724-1804) claimed to have solved Cartesian dualism by suggesting that the mind imposed form and order on all its experiences, and that this could be discovered *a priori* by reflection. He did not, however, see the intrinsic developmental link between these two cognitive modes. Georg Wilhelm Friedrich Hegel (1770-1831) argued that reality was subject to mental processes, although there existed a rational logic that governed human actions. Karl Marx (1818-1883) developed Hegel's philosophy into the theory of dialectical materialism by which it was claimed that matter, not the mind, was the ultimate reality. For Marx history unfolded according to laws that were more concretely real than the mind. Friedrich Nietzsche led the Romantic revolt against reason and logically-planned social organization by stressing natural instinct, self-assertion and passion. Charles Sanders Peirce (1839-1914) formulated a pragmatic theory of knowledge by which the test of the truth of any proposition was its practical utility. John Dewey (1859-1952) developed Peircean pragmatism into a comprehensive system of thought that emphasized the biological and social basis of knowledge, as well as the instrumental character of ideas. Edmund Husserl (1859-1938) went further than any of his predecessors in stressing the phenomenological basis of all cognition. For Husserl, only that which was present to consciousness was real. *Phenomenology* has, since Husserl, come to be a very powerful movement dedicated to describing the structures of experience as they present themselves to consciousness, without recourse to any theoretical or explanatory framework. Alfred North Whitehead (1861-1947) revived the Platonic theory of forms to show the failure of mechanistic science as a way of fully interpreting reality. Bertrand Russell (1872-1970) applied the methods of logic, mathematics and physics to the investigation of mentality. Finally, Martin Heidegger (1889-1976) combined the phenomenological approach of Husserl with an emphasis on emotional experience into a modern form of Nietzschean nihilism.

It was only toward the end of the previous century that the "scientific" study of the mind severed its connection with Aristotelian philosophy, declaring its autonomy through the development and institutionalization of a rigorous empirical method. This led to the birth of modern psychology as an experimental science. The precise observation and measurement of mental behavior gave the fledgling enterprise its brand-new scientific personality. It was Wilhelm Wundt (1832-1920) who founded the first "laboratory" of experimental psychology in 1879 in Leipzig. Since then, psychologists have shaped their discipline into one that has become almost exclusively reliant on statistical observation and inference. Wundt's laboratory became the model for conducting research on the mind. It is somewhat humorous to reflect, in hindsight, on the practice of the early psychologists of wearing white lab coats, thus bestowing upon their craft the symbolic connotations associated with laboratory experimentation in the physical sciences.

In this century mainstream psychology has undergone two revolutions—"behaviorism" and "cognitivism." Based on Pavlov's discovery that an animal's hunger could be conditioned to respond to a ringing bell—by simply associating the bell with a piece of meat and by eventually removing the meat stimulus (see Chapter 14)—behaviorism became the main school of psychology from the 1920s to the 1960s. The movement was initiated by John B. Watson (e.g. 1929) and developed by B. F. Skinner (e.g. 1938). Watson maintained that all complex forms of behavior could be observed, measured, and explained by simple motor and glandular processes. These constituted the organism's response patterns to specific input stimuli. Skinner took stimulus-response theory further by adding the individual's interactions with the environment as crucial determinants of behavior.

Since the 1960s cognitivism has come forward to replace behaviorism as mainstream psychology. The term *cognition*, rather than "mind" or "behavior," was employed widely in that decade in order to eliminate the artificial distinction maintained by behaviorists between inner (mental) and observable (behavioral) processes. Indeed, this word has now come to designate all mental processes, from perception to language. Adopting insights and terms from the new science of artificial intelligence, cognitivists aim to study the mind by seeking parallels between the functions of the human brain and computer concepts such as the "coding," "storing," "retrieving" and "buffering" of information.

The entrenchment of cognitivism in psychology ultimately led to the *cognitive science* movement in the early 1970s. As Howard Gardner (1985: 5-6) points out, this crystallized from the realization that the time had come to amalgamate the scientific approaches, located within separate disciplinary domains, into a single interdisciplinary focus. The term *cognitive science* thus refers to an approach that extracts from linguistics, anthropology, psychology, and other sciences information and theories in order to formulate its own theories about the mind. There are now autonomous university departments and research centers of cognitive science. In my view, this new enterprise has taken a wrong turn by basing its investigation of the mind on the simulation and modeling of human thought on computers. Cognitive science has, in effect, adopted the notions and methods of communications engineers and artificial intelligence researchers, viewing the mind as essentially a computing device crunching and churning out strings of symbols. While this seems to be a modern premise, it really is no more than a contemporary version of what can be called the *computational fallacy*—the belief that the human mind is a machine programmed to receive and produce information in biologically-determined ways. The new impetus and momentum that this fallacy has gained has rekindled the mind-body problem. As Gardner (1985: 6) himself has put it, the guiding assumption of mainstream cognitive science is that there exists "a level of analysis wholly separate from the biological or neurological, on the one hand, and the sociological or cultural, on the other," and that "central to any understanding of the human mind is the electronic computer."

Needless to say, not all cognitive scientists think in the way just described. But "computationism" is, as Gardner (1985: 6) correctly phrases it, "symptomatic" of the entire cognitive science enterprise. Computationism is based on the metaphorical formula: *the mind is a machine*. Cognitive scientists are quick to emphasize that their idea of a "machine" is not at all anti-human. They point out that it is simply an abstract, technical concept developed by the mathematician Alan Turing (e.g. 1936). By "picking" an operation and loading a program—a specific Turing machine—for doing it into the computer's memory, the computer—a general Turing machine—can then simulate what would happen if one actually had that specific machine. But cognitive scientists do not stop there. In leaping to the conclusion that the human mind is such a "machine," they have fallen into a metaphorical trap. Since the computer is itself a product of the mind, models of cognition based on computation are no more than artifacts, and certainly no more "real" than were the speculations of philosophers or the experiments of behaviorist psychologists. The fundamental assumption is that the mind's functions can be thought of as attendant to neurological states (e.g. synaptic configurations) and that these, in turn, can be thought of as operations akin to those that a computer is capable of carrying out. That this was a viable approach to "intelligent systems" was demonstrated indeed by Turing (1936) over five decades ago. He showed that four simple operations on a tape—*move to the right, move to the left, erase the slash, print the slash*—allowed a machine to execute any kind of program that could be expressed in a binary code (as for example a code of blanks and slashes). So long as one could specify the steps involved in carrying out a task and translating them into the binary code, the Turing machine would be able to scan the tape containing the code and carry out the instructions.

It was not long thereafter that "Turing machines," and similar notions derived from computer science, became analogues for the study of human cognition. The heuristic employment of machines—the use of computers to test notions about mentality—is the "weak" version of computationism, and, as such, it has helped to shed some light on how logical processes such as ratiocination might unfold in the human mind. But it defies all sense to suggest that machines can actually be built to think and feel like human beings. This "strong" version, as espoused for example by Minsky (e.g. 1986) or Konner (e.g. 1987, 1991), claims that all human activities, including emotions and social behavior, are not only representable in the form of computer programs, but that machines themselves can be built to think, feel and socialize. This extremist movement depicts human beings as no more than protoplasmic robots in the service of their genes.

Not all cognitive scientists have adopted the strong version of computationism. Indeed, it has been the source of much acrimonious and, ultimately, futile debate in the field. But even in weaker forms, it is a fact that computationism is still the principle that guides most of the research within the field. The view that the contents of mental states are encodable in the same general way as computer representations are encoded has now become an entrenched one. My aim is not to criticize the use of the computer to conduct research. On the contrary, I see the computer as a versatile human artifact that can help the researcher come up with, and formulate, meaningful questions about mental functioning. But there are fundamental differences between biological and mechanical systems that cannot be studied within the framework of the computationist methodology set up by cognitive science.

Computationism traces its roots to the philosophy of Plato and Aristotle which laid the foundations for the experimental investigation of matter, by claiming that the laws of nature were determinable objectively by observation and human reason. The discoveries of Copernicus and Galileo led, by the late Renaissance, to the entrenchment of Aristotle's idea that a meaningful understanding of reality could be gained only by exact observation and ordered thinking. By the seventeenth century this very same idea was extended to the study of mind. The origin of computationism can, in fact, be traced to the emerging view in that century that the mind's activities could be understood objectively if they were to be simulated, modeled, and recreated in mechanical ways. That was the century that saw Leibniz build a device which could perform elementary arithmetical operations by means of interconnected rotating cylinders which, he maintained, modeled human thought processes in their essence . And that was the century in which the ideas of Thomas Hobbes and René Descartes came to the forefront to give birth to, and eventually ensconce, the computationist view of mental functioning.

It was Thomas Hobbes who defined ratiocination bluntly as arithmetical computation: i.e. as a process akin to the addition and subtraction of numbers. Hobbes claimed that thinking was essentially a rule-governed mechanical process and that, in principle, machines capable of thought could be built. His solution to the mind-body problem was a blunt reduction of mental operations, including value and judgment, to the internal activities of the body. Like Plato before them, Hobbes and Descartes took their models of knowledge from mathematicians. Modern computationists also lean heavily on mathematical principles to draw their conclusions about mentality. They encode these principles in computer programs and then draw their conclusions from how these operate in the hardware of the computer.

In 1747, a century after Hobbes and Descartes, Jacques de la Mettrie published a highly influential book with the title *L'homme machine* (see Vartanian 1960). This influential text came to constitute the crowning eighteenth-century expression of both the human body and the human mind as machines. The nineteenth century consequently witnessed a growing spread and refinement of computationist tendencies. The Cambridge mathematician Charles Babbage designed an *analytical engine* which was capable of elementary logical operations. Its principles of construction foreshadowed those of the modern computer. George Boole (1854) drafted a logico-symbolic system which he claimed would be capable of representing the main laws of thought. In so doing, he laid the foundations for the development of modern formal logic and contemporary mathematical theory. Gottlob Frege (1879) then combined Boolean algebra with Aristotelian logic, thus completing the edifice of modern mathematical logic initiated by Boole. In the present century, Frege's work greatly influenced Bertrand Russell, who together with Alfred North Whitehead, axiomatized the Boolean-Fregean system into a series of propositions (Russell and Whitehead 1913).

The efforts of Russell and others to develop a formal, propositional system for representing thought that could be "verified" simply by experience, and thus to "purify" language—i.e. to eliminate from it all its metaphorical richness, playfulness and ambiguity—led directly in the thirties and forties to the first serious attempts to take the study of mind "out of the body," so as to be able to study it more objectively "in a computer." As mentioned, Alan Turing (1936), Claude Shannon (1948), Norbert Wiener (1949) and John von Neumann (1958) provided the conceptual frameworks and the technical systems for representing information, independently of its specific content and of the devices that carried it.

The Turing Test

Turing's work constitutes the cornerstone notion in the contemporary cognitive science edifice. As discussed in chapter 13, he suggested that one could program a computer in such a way that it would be virtually impossible to discriminate between its answers and those contrived by a human being. Let us recall the Turing test here for the sake of convenience. Imagine being an observer in a room which hides a programmed computer on one side and a human being on the other. The computer and the human being respond to questions that you formulate in writing by passing pieces of paper on to you through slits in the wall. If you cannot differentiate, on the basis of the written responses, the computer from the human being, then you must conclude that the machine is "intelligent." It has passed the "Turing test."

For Turing, every intelligent response could be described in computational terms; i.e. in terms of basic building blocks that can be carried out mechanically. The Turing test has become a persuasive argument in favor of computationism, convincing many that we are no more than "biological machines" programmed by nature to carry out computational tasks. When Claude Shannon demonstrated in 1948 that information of any kind could be described in terms of binary choices between equally probable alternatives, and when von Neumann built a rudimentary computer a decade later which allowed him to point out the remarkable similarities between mechanical and neural processes, Turing's perspective appeared to have been correct all along. By the 1950s, enthusiasm was growing over the possibility that machines could carry out rational thinking processes and that the brain could finally be studied as an information-processing device. By the 1960s, phenomenal advances in computer technology further entrenched the emerging computationist mindset. Computer terms to refer to mental processes started to proliferate, shaping the technical lexicon and discourse of psychologists, as they talked about "memory storage and retrieval," "processing information," "mental states" and so on. The idea of trying to discover how a computer has been programmed in order to extrapolate how the mind works was fast becoming the guiding assumption in cognitive psychology. Even though some have become openly hostile to the strong computationist perspective, arguing that it is incapable of taking world knowledge into account, in at least its weaker forms it still remains the *modus pensandi* of the mainstream.

The Chinese Room

Aware of the inherent absurdity of the Turing test as a template for judging human intelligence and mentality, the American philosopher John Searle came up with a brilliant counter-argument to the test in 1984. Known as the "Chinese Room" analogy, John Searle attacked the Turing test as follows. He argued that a machine does not "know" what it is doing when it processes symbols, because it lacks intentionality. Just like a human being who translates Chinese symbols in the form of little pieces of paper by using a set of rules for matching them with other symbols, or little pieces of paper, knows nothing about the "story" contained in the Chinese pieces of paper, so too a computer does not have access to the "story" inherent in human symbols. Searle's is a profound semiotic argument. The human mind can process symbols at a rational surface level in the same way that a computer does. But only at a deep level of consciousness does it put them together into a narrative whole. This is beyond the capacities of a machine whose operations are defined completely by formal syntactic structure.

Searle's critique has led many to reassess the goals and methods of cognitive science. A radical restructuring of this scientific enterprise would most certainly not study the nature of human thought in the algorithms of computer programs. It would start looking for it in the form and contents of our myths, stories, works of art and other products of the Vichian *fantasia*. All cultures seem to be more protective of products of the *fantasia* than of those of the rational mind. We are more likely to safeguard in its original form, say, a piece of music or a poem from a previous epoch than a scientific theory from that same era. We may find all these creations to be anachronistic, but we are willing only to modify the scientific theory to meet modern standards.

Computationist cognitive science cannot explain, for example, why metaphor constitutes such a vital mental function at all levels of cognitive behavior (Chapter 6). When the mind cannot find the conceptual means for understanding a new phenomenon, it invariably resorts to its innate capacity to scan its internal space metaphorically. There is no innovation in science or art without this capacity. Indeed, there is no coherent discourse without it . The computational approach has provided a highly technical theoretical apparatus for explaining how the surface level of cognition can be reproduced in computer software. But it has completely ignored the possibility that the formation of any new cognitive activity is anchored in a metaphorical transformation of imagistic models of lived bodily experiences.

The essence of the human mind is its capacity to transform sense impressions into memorable models of reality through the formation of iconic signs, and then to "extend" their cognitive utilization. The world of abstraction is a kind of evolutionary "outgrowth" of this ability. As an example, consider the formation of the concept *drop* in its full semantic range. This word was probably formed originally as an onomatopoeic word-model of the sound associated with an object falling to the ground. It was forged, more specifically, as an audio-oral iconic sign. Once it entered the language system at the surface level, it was connected to a range of actions resembling the original model. These are its so-called connotative extensions: *I dropped out of school, Drop the argument,* etc. Connotation is, clearly, an extension of the iconic sign's function by association. It is, therefore, a product of metaphor doing its work at the surface level.

The transformation of iconic units into conceptual ones by metaphor is the essence of how the mind works. A word like *person* is now conceived as a word *symbol* because it stands arbitrarily for a "two-legged animal of the genus *Homo sapiens.*" Any other word, or indeed sign, could have been used to designate this referential domain. However, the original construction of the symbol reveals a different story. The word *persona*, as discussed in Chapter 1, originally meant "mask" in Greek. It was only when the metaphorical capacity connected the "mask" worn by actors on stage to the "behavioral characteristics of the mask-wearer" that the word *person* took on symbolic value. In this case the connectivity process was metonymic.

Sociobiology

The ideas of the sociobiologist Richard Dawkins, with whom I started off this chapter, form a kind of complementary biological counterpart to the computationist study of mentality: rather than reducing human cognition to mechanical processes like cognitive science does, Dawkins reduces it to purely genetic tendencies and proclivities. In both cases, the central idea is that human cognitive processes are determined or "hard-wired" in the brain.

The perspective adopted by sociobiologists and philosophers who are sympathetic to it (e.g. Wilson 1975, 1979, 1984, Lumsden and Wilson 1983, Dennett 1991) sees the origins of consciousness in a coevolutionary partnership between genes and culture. Culture is viewed by sociobiologists as furnishing the original context for the generation of consciousness and, subsequently, as providing the channel for its continuity and development. Social behavior, like physical evolution, is considered to be an adaptive survival strategy. As part of social behavior, therefore, sociobiologists include the human mind and human culture. Moreover, for sociobiology, there is an evolutionary kinship among all organisms. And in arguing that all life is connected and related, sociobiology has indeed done humanity a great service.

In the sociobiological scenario, the mind was spawned by genes in response to new cultural demands. As cultures became more complex, so did the human mind. The conscious choices that humans were capable of making, so the story goes, conferred upon them greater survival and reproductive abilities. Gene evolution gradually gave way to cultural evolution. The body's survival mechanisms were eventually replaced by those of the mind. As Lumsden and Wilson (1983: 118) summarily put it, "culture is created and shaped by biological processes while the biological processes are simultaneously altered in response to cultural change." Certain revulsions, such as incest, are seen as belonging to humanity's organic heredity. These revulsions, as Freud (1913) also claimed, have generated the moral behavior patterns that have ensured the survival of our species. They are built into our genetic structure.

The notion of the *selfish gene*, made popular by Richard Dawkins, is a concrete example of how sociobiologists think. According to Dawkins, if reproductive success is the measure of fitness, then evolution boils down to which genes have the ability to prosper and multiply in a population's gene pool. Genes are sealed off from the outside world. But they manipulate it by "remote control." They created us, literally, body and mind; and their preservation is the ultimate rationale for our existence. Human beings are their "survival machines."

But the case against selfish genes is just as persuasive. Why would our selfish genes also lead us to invent such superfluous things as law systems to protect ourselves against the persistence of such "aberrations" as incest? And why would our selfish genes have impelled us to have invented religions, marriage rites and burial rites? Language and culture have certainly enhanced survivability in some ways, but in others they have actually made humans much more susceptible to environmental dangers. The domination of behavior by the mind has concomitantly attenuated our inbuilt instinctual survival system. Sociobiologists have clearly missed a crucial point made by Vico—language and culture are artifacts of the human mind. To use these artifacts to understand how the mind originated is a *post hoc, ergo propter hoc* argument. Sociobiologists have simply replaced the word *soul* with the term *selfish gene*. In so doing, they have invented an eloquent and persuasive story of human origin with their own imaginations.

Apparently captivated by sociobiological logic, the philosopher Dennett (1991) has even explained the Self from a purely biological perspective. For Dennett the proclivity to distinguish the Self from the rest of the world is a distinction that all living organisms must make, from the lowly amoeba to the rational human being. The Self is thus reduced to a principle of genetic organization and response to the world.

Sociobiology and computationism are products of what Immanuel Kant

(1790) called theoretical reason. As Nadeau (1991: 194) has recently put it, such exercises in theoretical reasoning can be dangerous: "If consciousness is to evolve on this planet in the service of the ultimate value, we must, I think, quickly come to the realization that reality for human beings is a human product with a human history, and thereby dispel the tendency to view any 'product' of our world-constructing minds as anything more, or other, than a human artifact."

Concluding Remarks

My aim in this chapter has not been merely to criticize, or to antagonize, cognitive scientists and sociobiologists. As a matter of fact, I am strongly attracted by the very idea of a *cognitive science* and a *sociobiology*. And, like everyone else in our technological society, I cannot but admire and delight in the staggering achievements made possible by the computer revolution. This is why my critique has been a narrowly-focused one: i.e. it has been directed at the computationist orientation that cognitive science has taken, which, as I have attempted to argue, is grounded on a 400-year-old fallacy. If I have been at times perhaps too critical, my reason is, I think, understandable. I feel that modern-day computationism is reflective of a generalized cultural malaise whose major symptom is a naive faith in machines.

The computer is one of our greatest intellectual achievements. It is an extension of our rational intellect. We have finally come up with a machine that will eventually take over most of the arduous work of ratiocination. This could then leave the *fantasia* much more time to roam the mental universe of the deep level and search out new associations in poetry, art and music which we still find to be much more fundamental to our nature, and to our origins, than solving a problem in logic. Arnheim's (1969: 73) two-decade old *caveat* is still valid today: "There is no need to stress the immense practical usefulness of computers. But to credit the machine with intelligence is to defeat it in a competition it need not pretend to enter."

It is no coincidence, in my view, that cognitive science has surfaced at a time when a belief in the *soul*, which in the "age of the gods" was motivated by a universal instinctive religious feeling, has been replaced by materialistic and mechanistic notions such as the *selfish gene*. Sociobiology and cognitive science are "postmodern" sciences. They constitute a kind of critical response to the disenchantment with the traditional narratives of our culture. But underlying their vision is rational thought, which is itself logocentric.

The concern I have expressed in this chapter is not new. In Sumerian and

Babylonian myths there were accounts of the creation of life through the animation of clay. The ancient Romans were fascinated by automata. By the time of Mary Shelley's *Frankenstein* in 1818, the idea that robots could be brought to life both fascinated and horrified the modern imagination. Since the first decades of the present century the quest to animate machines has been relentless. It has captured the imagination of a large segment of our image-makers. Movie robots and humanoid machines like *Hal* (in *2001*), *Robocop Terminator*, have all the attributes of gods. But I tend to think along the lines of someone like William Barrett (1986: 160) when he says that if a machine will ever be built with the features of the human mind it would have "a curiously disembodied kind of consciousness, for it would be without the sensitivity, intuitions and pathos of our human flesh and blood. And without those qualities we are less than wise, certainly less than human."

The perspective adopted in this book has been that semiosis interconnects the body, the mind and culture. As a science of signs, including bodily symptoms, semiotics grew out of attempts by the first medical doctors to understand how the body and the mind influenced each other within specific cultural domains. The underlying theme of this book has been that human beings are meaning-makers. The outer world of nature and culture and the inner world experience have no meaning in the sense that they want to "say something" about themselves. Only reflective humans feel the need to make meaning. Hopefully, this book has shed some light on why and how we do it.

SUGGESTIONS FOR FURTHER READING

Arnheim, R. (1969). *Visual Thinking*. Berkeley: University of California Press.

Barrett, W. (1986). *The Death of the Soul: From Descartes to the Computer*. New York: Anchor.

Bechtel, W. (1988). *Philosophy of Mind: An Overview for Cognitive Science*. Hillsdale, N. J.: Lawrence Erlbaum Associates.

Boole, G. (1854). *An Investigation of the Laws of Thought*. New York: Dover.

Dawkins, R. (1976). *The Selfish Gene*. Oxford: Oxford University Press.

Dawkins, R. (1987). *The Blind Watchmaker*. London: Longmans.

Dennett, D. C. (1991). *Consciousness Explained*. Boston: Little, Brown.

Descartes, R. (1637). *Essaies philosophiques*. Leyden: L'imprimerie de Ian Maire.

Eccles, J. C. (1992). *The Human Psyche*. London: Routledge.

Frege, G. (1879). *Begiffsschrift eine der Aritmetischen nachgebildete Formelsprache des reinen Denkens*. Halle: Nebert.

Gardner, H. (1985). *The Mind's New Science: A History of the Cognitive Revolution*. New York: Basic Books.

Gaylin, W. (1990). *On Being and Becoming Human*. London: Penguin.

Hobbes, T. (1656). *Elements of Philosophy*. London: Molesworth.

Johnson-Laird, P. N. (1983). *Mental Models*. Cambridge, Mass.: Harvard University Press.

Johnson-Laird, P. N. (1988). *The Computer and the Mind*. Cambridge, MA: Harvard University Press.

Kant, I. (1790). *Critique of Judgment*. New York: Hafner Press.

Konner, M. (1987). On Human Nature: Love among the Robots. *The Sciences* 27: 14-23.

Konner, M. (1991). Human Nature and Culture: Biology and the Residue of Uniqueness. In: J.J. Sheehan and M. Sosna (eds.), pp. 103-124, *The Boundaries of Humanity*. Berkeley: University of California Press.

Lumsden, C. J. and Wilson, E. O. (1983). *Promethean Fire: Reflections on the Origin of Mind*. Cambridge, Mass.: Harvard University Press.

Minsky, M. (1986). *Society of Mind*. New York: Simon and Schuster.

Nadeau, R. L. (1991). *Mind, Machines, and Human Consciousness*. Chicago: Contemporary Books.

Neumann, J. von (1958). *The Computer and the Brain*. New Haven: Yale University Press.

Russell, B. and Whitehead, A. N. (1913). *Principia mathematica*. Cambridge: Cambridge University Press.

Schank, R. C. (1991). *The Connoisseur's Guide to the Mind*. New York: Summit.

Searle, J. R. (1984). *Minds, Brain, and Science*. Cambridge, Mass.: Harvard University Press.

Shannon, C. E. (1948). A Mathematical Theory of Communication. *Bell Systems Technical Journal* 27: 379-423.

Skinner, B. F. (1938). *The Behavior of Organisms*. New York: Appleton-Century-Crofts.

Turing, A. (1936). On Computable Numbers with an Application to the Entscheidungs Problem. *Proceedings of the London Mathematical Society* 41: 230-265.

Turing, A. (1963). Computing Machinery and Intelligence. In E. A. Feigenbaum and J. Feldman (eds.), *Computers and Thought*, pp. 123-134. New York: McGraw-Hill.

Varela, F. J., Thompson, E. and Rosch, E. (1991). *The Embodied Mind: Cognitive Science and Human Experience*. Cambridge, Mass.: MIT Press.

Vartanian, A. (1960). *La Mettrie's "L'homme machine": A Study in the Origins of an Idea*. Princeton: Princeton University Press.

Watson, J. B. (1929). *Psychology from the Standpoint of a Behaviorist*. Philadelphia: Lippincott.

Wiener, N. (1949). *Cybernetics, or Control and Communication in the Animal and the Machine*. Cambridge, Mass.: MIT Press.

Wilson, E. O. (1975). *Sociobiology: The New Synthesis*. Cambridge, Mass.: Harvard University Press.

Wilson, E. O. (1979). *On Human Nature*. New York: Bantam.

Wilson, E. O. (1984). *Biophilia*. Cambridge, Mass.: Harvard University Press.

Wittgenstein, L. (1921). *Tractatus Logico-Philosophicus*. London: Routledge and Kegan Paul.

Wittgenstein, L. (1953). *Philosophical Investigations*. New York: Macmillan.

Glossary of Technical Terms

A

addressee the receiver of a message

addresser the sender of a message

aesthesia the ability to experience sensation; in art appreciation it refers to the fact that our senses and feelings are evoked by the art form

artifactuality the term used in this book to refer to the process of converting **factual** states (unconditioned responses to the world) in the human organism into representational and culture-specific codes

C

channel the physical means by which a signal or message is transmitted

code the system in which signs are organized and which determines how they relate to each other and make meaningful texts

cognitive science an approach that extracts from linguistics, anthropology, psychology and other human sciences information and theories in order to formulate its own theories about the mind

common sense meanings shared by everyone in a "meta-cultural" way (i.e. meanings that transcend cultures)

communal sense	meanings shared by members of a culture
communication	social interaction through **messages**; the production and exchange of messages and meanings; the use of specific modes and **media** of sign-making to transmit feeling-states and messages
computationism	the view that the mind's activities are reducible to the computations that characterize, for example, the elementary arithmetical operations; the view of some cognitive scientists that the computer can reproduce human mental operations
conative	a communicative function that describes the effect of the message on the **addressee**
concept	a connection made by the human mind (within cultural contexts)
connotation	the extended or secondary meaning of a **sign**
contact	Jakobson's term for the physical **channel** and the psychological connections between **addresser** and **addressee**
context	the environment (physical and social) in which **signs** are produced and messages generated

decoding	the process of deciphering the message inherent in a **code**
deixis	the process of locating beings, objects, and events in space through **signs**
denotation	the primary meaning of a **sign**

diachrony	the study of change in **signs** and **codes** over time

E

emotive	a communicative function that describes the relation of the message to the **addresser**
encoding	the process of constructing a **code** or of putting a message together in terms of a specific code.
entropy	that which is unpredictable in a message
ethology	the study of animals in their natural habitats
etymology	the study of the origin and evolution of **signs**

F

factuality	the term used in this book to refer to basic biological and psychic tendencies, urges, feelings, etc. in the human organism (unconditioned responses to the world) which are acultural and ahistorical
feedback	the information detected by the sender of a message that allows him or her to adjust his or her message **text** in order to make it more effective

G

gesticulation	the use of **gestures** accompanying speech
gesture	**signification** and **communication** by means of the hand, arms and, to a lesser extent, the head
ground	the part of a **metaphor** that creates its meaning

haptics   the study of touching patterns during social interaction

icon   a **sign** which has a direct (nonarbitrary) connection with a **referent**

Id   Freud's term for the unconscious part of the psyche which is actuated by fundamental impulses toward fulfilling instinctual needs

image schema   the term used by Lakoff and Johnson to refer to the recurring structures of, or in, our perceptual interactions, bodily experiences and cognitive operations that portray locations, movements, shapes, etc. in the mind

index   a **sign** that has an existential connection with a **referent** (i.e. it indicates that it is located somewhere)

interpretant   the process of adapting a **sign's** meaning in terms of personal and social experience

intertextuality   the allusion of a **text** to some other text

kinesics   the study of bodily **semiosis**

lexical field   a set of lexical items (words) related to each other by some characteristic (weather vocabulary, geometrical terms, etc.)

medium	the technical or physical means by which a message is transmitted
meme	sociobiologist Richard Dawkins' term for replicating patterns of information (tunes, ideas, clothes fashions, etc.)
message	any meaningful **text** produced with **signs**
metalingual	the communicative function by which the **code** being used is identified
metaphor	the signifying process by which two signifying domains are connected
metonymy	the signifying process by which an entity is used to refer to another that is related to it
mimesis	the conscious acquisition and use (imitation, emulation, etc.) of signifying structures
model	the result of the process of taking in and *re*-forming the *in*-formation emanating from our sensorial and affective responses to the world
morphology	the study of formal structure of **signs** in **codes**
myth	any story or **narrative** that aims to explain the origin of something
mythology	the study of **myths**, or the creation of mythic **connotations** associated with some person or event

N

narrative mode	the use of **narrativity** as the cognitive means by which something is conceptualized and then expressed—"narrated"—in verbal or nonverbal ways
narrative	something narrated, told or written, such as an account, story, tale and even scientific theory
narrativity	the innate human capacity to produce and comprehend **narratives**
narratology	the branch of **semiotics** that studies **narrativity**
noise	anything that is added to the message/signal between **sender** and **receiver** that is not intended by the sender

object	a synonym for **referent**; what is referred to in **signification**
onomatopoeia	the **semiosic** feature of words by which they represent a **referent** by imitating some audio-oral feature of the referent (*drip, boom,* etc.)
ontogenesis	the development of all **semiosic** abilities (iconicity, symbolism, language, etc.) during childhood
opposition	the process by which **signs** are differentiated through a minimal change in their form (signifier)
osmosis	the unconscious acquisition of signifying structures in relation to environmental input

paradigmatic	a structural relation between **signs** that keeps them distinct and therefore recognizable
percept	a unit of perception (a stimulus that has been received and recognized); immediate units of knowing derived from sensation or feeling
phatic	the communicative function by which contact between **sender** and **receiver** is established
phoneme	the minimal unit of sound in a language that allows its users to differentiate meanings
phonology	the study of sound systems in language
phylogenesis	the development of all **semiosic** abilities (iconicity, symbolism, language, etc.) in the human species
poetic	the communicative function by which contact between **sender** and **receiver** is established
postmodernism	the term used to refer to the view of **postmodernity** that nothing exists outside of the human-made world
postmodernity	the contemporary state of mind which believes that all knowledge is relative and human-made
proxemics	the branch of **semiotics** that studies the symbolic structure of the physical space maintained between bodies in social contexts and of the physical space associated with buildings and places

receiver	the one who **decodes** a message (the **addressee**)

redundancy	that which is predictable or conventional in a message, thus helping to counteract the effects of **noise**
referent	what is referred to (any object, being, idea or event in the world)
referential	the communicative function by which a straightforward transmission is intended
representamen	Peirce's term for **sign**
representation	the process by which **referents** are designated by **signs**
rhetoric	the study of the techniques used in all kinds of discourses, from common conversation to poetry

S

semantics	the study of meaning in language
semiology	Saussure's term for the study of **signs**, now restricted to the study of verbal signs
semiosis	the comprehension and production of **signs**
semiotics	the science or doctrine that studies **signs**
sender	the transmitter (the **addresser**) of a message
sign	something that stands for something else
signal	any transmission of biological-based responses to stimuli; in communication systems it refers to the physical form of a message
signification	the process of generating meaning through the use of **signs**

signified	that part of a **sign** that is referred to (the **referent**; the **object**)
signifier	that part of a **sign** that does the referring/the physical part of a sign
sociobiology	the study of biological evolution in terms of its codependence with social and cultural evolution in all species
structure	any repeatable or predictable aspect of **signs**, **codes**, and messages
subtext	a text (message) hidden within a **text**
symbol	a **sign** that has an arbitrary (conventional) connection with a **referent**
synchrony	the study of **signs** and **codes** at a specific point in time (usually the present)
synecdoche	the signifying process by which a part stands for the whole
synesthesia	the evocation of one sense modality (e.g. vision) by some other (e.g. hearing); the juxtaposition of sense modalities ("loud colors")
syntagmatic	the structural relation that combines **signs** in code-dependent ways
syntax	the study of **syntagmatic** structure in language

T

tenor	the subject of a **metaphor** (a synonym for **topic**)
text	the actual message with its particular form and contents

topic	the subject of a **metaphor** (a synonym for **tenor**)
transmission	the sending and reception of messages
trope	figure of speech, figurative language generally

vehicle	the part of a **metaphor** to which a **tenor** is connected

zoosemiotics	the study of **semiosis** in and across species

Index